THE
ROMAN CONQUEST
OF SCOTLAND

ABOUT THE AUTHOR

James E. Fraser is lecturer in Celtic and Early Scottish History and Culture at the University of Edinburgh. His other books include *From Caledonia to Pictland: Scotland to 795* and *The Battle of Dunnichen 685*, also published by Tempus. He lives in Edinburgh.

THE
ROMAN CONQUEST
OF SCOTLAND

THE BATTLE OF
MONS GRAUPIUS AD 84

JAMES E. FRASER

TEMPUS

en amwyn breithell bu edrywant
Defending the land there was slaughter

ket rylade hwy wy ladassant
Although they were being slain, they slew

a hyt orfen byt etmyc vydant
And until the world's end, they'll be honoured.

– *E Gododin*, B text, ll. 1127-29

First published 2005

Tempus Publishing Limited
The Mill, Brimscombe Port,
Stroud, Gloucestershire, GL5 2QG
www.tempus-publishing.com

British Library Cataloguing in Publication Data.
A catalogue record for this book is available from the British Library.

ISBN 0 7524 3325 3

Typesetting and origination by Tempus Publishing Limited
Printed in Great Britain

Contents

Acknowledgements   7
A Chronological Note   9

I   An Expression of Filial Piety
       Cornelius Tacitus and Iulius Agricola   11
2   A Man Keen on Advancement
       The Rise of Agricola   19
3   Another Island
       The Background to Calgacos   33
4   When Shall We Have an Enemy?
       War in Caledonia   47
5   *Ad Montem Graupium*
       Where is Mons Graupius?   67
6   Striking Terror
       Prelude to Battle   79
7   Bringing Matters to a Decision
       The Battle of Mons Graupius, AD 84   97
8   Devastation and Silence
       Aftermath of Battle   113
9   Thoroughly Tamed
       Roman Conquest in Northern Britain?   117
10   Final Thoughts   127

Maps   130
Notes   134
Bibliography   150
List of Illustrations and Maps   153
Index   155

North–west Europe in the time of Agricola and Calgacos: some places mentioned in the text.

Acknowledgements

This is the first major piece of writing I have completed since losing my wife Morgyn to the scourge of breast cancer in November 2003, at the age of twenty-nine. Agricola's Caledonian war was 'one means he used to distract his mind from its sorrow' after profound personal loss. Nineteen centuries later this same war provided something of a similar distraction for the present writer.

I am grateful to Jonathan Reeve and Tempus Publishing for the invitation to undertake this fascinating project, and for allowing extensions of submission deadlines. The end product, I hope, will have been worth the wait. I am particularly indebted to Jim McMillan, Ewen Cameron, Donald Meek, and the rest of my colleagues at the University of Edinburgh for the exemplary and compassionate institutional and personal support I have received during the difficult period during which this book has been written. My most profound thanks are owed to my family and to Morgyn's. I should like additionally to thank in particular Shawn and Tammy Corrigan, William and Valerie Gillies, Courtney Harris, Karen Hartnup and Roy Spiers, Peter Switzer, Leslie Reid and Simon Taylor, Melanie Thorpe, and Alex Woolf for all that they have done and endured on my behalf.

I must also register my warmest appreciation of and admiration for Dr Angela Bowman, Mr Mike Dixon, Tessa Ogden, Rachel Dunbar Rees, Fiona Lightfoot, Dr Judith Richardson, Sheila Cowe, and the other healthcare professionals at the Western General Hospital and the Edinburgh chapters of Maggie's Centre and St Columba's Hospice, upon whom Morgyn relied so much in the course of her illness. Not all of today's warriors fight with swords.

Morgyn was subjected to many of the following arguments in their early stages of development. She endured them, as she did everything, with her characteristic good humour. A story of violence and 'human tragedy on a massive scale', as Gordon Maxwell has described it, may seem an odd tribute to the memory of such a gentle and kindly soul. Yet it is also a story of human courage and resolve to fight in the face of long odds, and of human resilience in the wake of adversity and disappointing setbacks. Above all else, perhaps, it is a story of a special person whose character and example inspired in one appreciative historiographer feelings of devotion, admiration and affection that death could not lessen.

Being far removed from Cornelius Tacitus in every possible sense, this writer has relied at many points upon the generous assistance of colleagues on many points of detail. My archaeological understanding in particular has been enhanced by the gentle and helpful criticisms of my colleagues Fraser Hunter, Ian Ralston and Eberhard Sauer. Dr Hunter and the National Museum of Scotland have provided additional valuable assistance in securing photographs. Professor Ralston and Dr Sauer, as well as Alex Woolf, have kindly joined me on productive trips to Perthshire. Shawn Corrigan has put up with many lengthy transatlantic correspondences on Flavian matters. Alex Woolf, Simon Taylor, and William Gillies have offered insightful and clear assistance on matters toponymic, demographic and linguistic. Mark Hall has offered guidance to the archaeological remains of southern Perthshire. None of these bears responsibility for the heresies herein espoused, or any incompetent handling of their advice. I am most grateful to them all.

DUM VIVIMUS, VIVAMUS

A Chronological Note

The chronology of Agricola's legateship has long been a matter of dispute, turning upon whether he arrived in Britannia in the summer of AD 78 or in the previous summer.[1] The year of his suffect consulship is not attested (as yet); we know only that it was busy with personal business. The implication of Tacitus is that these events belong to 77, and Richmond's anxieties that they do not allow time for an appointment and journey to Britannia – with all the necessary preparations involved – seem to be borne out by other evidence, such that one may regard it as very unlikely that Agricola arrived in Britannia in the same year as his consulate.[2] Numismatic evidence shows that Domitian assumed the title *Germanicus* late in 83. Tacitus informs us that the victorious imperial campaign against the German Chatti thus commemorated preceded Agricola's victory at Mons Graupius, which may itself have been commemorated on coins issued in the autumn of 84.[3] In addition, Tacitus tells us of the mutiny of a cohort of German Usipian auxiliaries in Britain in the summer prior to the battle of Mons Graupius. Although it would appear that the Usipian homeland on the Rhine did not begin to be occupied by the Romans until the summer of 83, the mere presence of these men in Agricola's army is not much chronological help, since there is every likelihood that they had been recruited years before this occupation.[4] It seems to have escaped notice, however, that, if the battle of Mons Graupius took place in 84, this mutiny will have taken place in the same summer as the conquest of the Usipian homeland was begun. This would seem to offer a satisfying context for what would otherwise have been a random event. If the tendency of the circumstantial evidence available to us at present, then, is to favour both the view that the battle of Mons Graupius took place in 84 and the complementary view that the mutiny of the Usipi took place in 83, it is reasonable to place Agricola's arrival in Britannia in the summer of 78. This is the chronology that shall be observed throughout this work, and we shall encounter further support for this decision in due course.

CHAPTER ONE

An Expression of Filial Piety

Cornelius Tacitus and Iulius Agricola

In what seems to have been the year 98, the prominent Roman senator Cornelius Tacitus wrote what he called a *laudatio* – a short eulogy modelled upon earlier examples – celebrating the life of his wife's late father, Iulius Agricola, who had passed away on 23 August 93.[1] A recent recipient of the consular *fasces* himself, Tacitus attained this most prestigious of the city of Rome's annual public magistracies as a suffect (or supplementary) consul in 97,[2] exactly twenty years after Agricola's own suffect consulate. Destined to be a consular legate governing an overseas province of the city's great empire, Tacitus was already regarded as a skilful orator, and it is not for his accomplished political career that he is remembered 1,900 years after he lived. The student of the writings of Tacitus must always remain mindful, all the same, of how he was shaped and influenced by his public life.

It is of course from these writings, tracing the history of Rome and its empire in the first century, that the renown of Tacitus has stemmed, since they came to be regarded in antiquity as the standard account of this age of Roman history. His *laudatio* in praise of his departed father-in-law, now generally known to scholarship as the *Agricola*, was the very first of these written works. It contains very little history as compared with his *Annals* and *Histories*. It seems fair to surmise that, had it not been for the fame these later compositions brought to their author, the little eulogy would not have survived into the middle decades of the ninth century, when it was copied afresh into a manuscript now contained in the *Codex Aesinas* in a library at Jesi in Italy.[3] This now incomplete copy of the *Agricola* would subsequently serve as the ultimate source of all three surviving later medieval copies, and represents the whisker by which this work was saved.

The *Agricola* outlines an impressive political and military career that climaxed in a great victory in battle over the barbarous tribal peoples of northern Britain on the slopes of a hill called Mons Graupius. We would know nothing whatsoever about this battle had the Jesi text of the work not avoided oblivion. Not surprisingly, an examination of this critical first-century account must lie at the heart of this and every study of the battle of Mons Graupius. Much depends upon how each individual student goes about interpreting the famously concise prose of Tacitus, whose testimony cannot for the most part be corroborated. Scholarly views of the battle since 1960 have been shaped by the efforts of three major studies in particular: that of Sir Ian Richmond, which formed the backdrop to Richard Ogilvie's 1967 edition of Tacitus's text;[4] that of Bill Hanson published in 1987, who, twenty years after the fact, and relying largely upon a growing body of archaeological evidence, criticised and revised many of Richmond's views and models;[5] and that of Gordon Maxwell, a more focused study of the battle itself published in 1990, which included a fascinating consideration of the long history of the modern search for the battlefield.[6] Each of these studies, the most recent of which is now some fifteen years old, was the work of an accomplished archaeologist. The present work is offered in the expectation that both the passage of years and the disciplinary background of the present author will conspire to render worthwhile both the effort and the contribution to the subject.

CAN WE TRUST TACITUS?

Coming to terms with the *Agricola* as a source of information requires us to come to terms with Cornelius Tacitus as an observer in 98. The eulogy was written some fifteen years after the battle, in the year in which Ulpius Traianus ('Trajan') became sole emperor of the Romans, having succeeded the caretaker emperor Cocceius Nerva, who died in January 98 after a stroke. It had been a short principate for the 'safe and quiet' Nerva,[7] who had assumed the imperial purple only sixteen months before, in the aftermath of the assassination of Flavius Domitianus in September 96. In the opening chapters of the *Agricola*, Tacitus expresses the heartfelt elation and sense of liberation he and others were feeling as a result of the murder of 'Domitian', giving voice to frustrations he had felt compelled to keep quiet while that emperor had reigned.

> We have certainly established a magnificent record of forbearance: as the former age explored ultimate freedom, so have we witnessed ultimate servitude, robbed by the informer even of exchange of words heard and spoken. We should have lost memory as well as voice, had it been as easy to forget as to stay silent.
>
> Now at last our spirit returns.
>
> But even so, although, in the first dawn of a most blessed age, Nerva Caesar combined the principate and freedom (things once irreconcilable) and Nerva Trajan

now daily enhances the prosperity of the times… still, because of the necessary condition of human frailty, the remedy works less quickly than the disease… [I]t is easier to crush than to revive genius and its pursuits: a fascination with idleness steals over us, and the indolence that we loathed at first we afterwards love.

What does it matter that in those fifteen years, a large portion of a life, although many were cut down by ordinary fortune, the most able fell by the cruelty of an emperor? Or that those many years, which brought the young quietly to old age (and the old almost to the very verge and end of existence), have been taken from the few of us that survive, from the midst of our lives? At any rate we shall not regret that we have borne witness (if in language unskilled and rude) to the memory of our former servitude and to our present happiness. In the meanwhile this book, intending to honour my father-in-law Agricola, will be commended (or at least pardoned) as an expression of filial piety.[8]

Already in 98, then, Tacitus was a man on a literary mission, having it in mind to compose the substantial historical narrative that was to fill the pages of his *Histories*. His words here suggest that he had already begun the latter work in 98,[9] inspired by 'our present happiness' and a desire to record for posterity 'the memory of our former servitude', about which he remained both defensive and bitterly resentful. Being an historian of his times, and not of our own, his researches were never intended to produce sober and objective interpretations of historical evidence. They were instead part of an exercise in reflecting upon past events as a vehicle for moralistic social commentary in a Rome officially 'reborn' (*Roma renascens*) after the murder of Domitian.[10]

However much it may pale in comparison to these later works, the *Agricola* was an important text at the time of its composition. It announced its author's literary plans to the reading public, affording him an opportunity to gauge intellectual and political reaction to certain ideas and moral positions upon which he would expand in his later and greater works. The reader is provided with glimpses of Tacitus's impulsive and unjust Gaius Caesar ('Caligula'),[11] his covetous and fearsome Nero Claudius Caesar,[12] his successful and admirable Flavius Vespasianus ('Vespasian'),[13] and, of course, his frivolous, suspicious and tyrannical Domitian.[14] Also placed before the reader of the *Agricola* is an idealised vision of Rome's republican past, in which Roman citizens 'explored ultimate freedom', along with a number of wary fears about the principate of the emperors, by then more than a century old.[15] The way had been paved for this aspect of Tacitus's works by the Latin historiographical genre itself. Roman readers of history were commonly invited to contrast the present times against 'the grave and worthy standards of the virtuous past'.[16] Tacitus had read historical inquiries made by the first men to take up the challenge of such moralising in the Rome of the dictator Iulius ('Julius') Caesar and his heir Caesar Octavianus ('Augustus'), the architect and first *princeps* of the principate, both of whom he mentions briefly in the

Agricola.[17] Like many social commentators of this and later ages, there can be little doubt of Tacitus's patriotism even, or indeed particularly, as he heaps scorn upon what he regarded as 'the seduction of such vices as arcades, baths and sumptuous banquets',[18] and suggests that the city's empire, a republican legacy, had, under the principate, become a powerful corrupting influence upon the Roman citizenry. He summarises such anxieties in one of the best known passages in the *Agricola*, in which he imagines that an outsider might criticise the Romans as follows:

> Escape from their arrogance is vainly sought through either obedience or sub-mission. Pillagers of the world, they ransack the sea, having exhausted the land by complete devastation. They are greedy if the enemy is wealthy, hungry for power if he is poor: neither the east nor the west will satisfy them, for they alone among all peoples covet poverty as much as riches. To robbery, slaughter and rape they give the false name of *imperium*, and where they wreak desolation they call it peace.[19]

Quite apart from giving such thinking a dry run in anticipation of exploring it further in future works (thus testing the attitudes of 'Rome reborn'), Tacitus also, of course, explicitly set himself the task in the *Agricola* of honouring his father-in-law 'as an expression of filial piety'.

Tacitus prepared his audience for the kind of subjective treatment of Agricola's life and career that the first-century reader expected from any *laudatio*, and the modern listener, for that matter, expects from any eulogy. This one, unsurprisingly, contains nothing but praise for its subject. This fact, no less than an apprecia-tion for Tacitus's motives for writing history, presents the scholar of the battle of Mons Graupius with difficulties in determining the reliability of the *Agricola* as a source for the study of Iulius Agricola and his most famous victory. One is justi-fied to begin from a position of great optimism. Tacitus does not seem to have been present at the battle in person, but he was nevertheless clearly in a position to be uniquely well informed about this and other aspects of his father-in-law's political and military career. It has been suggested that Tacitus served his military tribunate in Britain under his father-in-law, and it is not beyond the realm of possibility that he was himself posted to Britannia after his praetorship in 88.[20] Even so, 'to postulate his presence' wherever Tacitus narrates events was regarded by Ronald Syme as 'a cheap device, neglecting the quality of Tacitus' main source for those events – and denying his imaginative powers'.[21] He may or may not have been posted to Britannia during his early career; in any event he became sufficiently well connected generally as a senator to acquire interesting informa-tion from good sources and eyewitnesses, including participants in battles. All indications are that, when possible, Tacitus had recourse 'to a plurality of sources' in composing his historical narratives.[22]

He had also been particularly close personally to Iulius Agricola himself, who was obviously a key eyewitness of the battle of Mons Graupius. The ambitious

Tacitus, probably a native of Gallia Narbonensis like Agricola,[23] had it in mind to emulate his father-in-law's successful political career and reach the consulate. His own first legateship seems to have taken place from about 89 to 93, during which period he probably corresponded with his countryman, from whose mentorship he might learn a great deal for the furtherance of his success.[24] It is beyond dispute that Tacitus spoke with his wife's father about his time in Britain on many occasions, for the *Agricola* creates the impression that the older man was often to be heard speaking on that subject.[25] Quite apart from such reminiscences, Tacitus can have had access to the portfolio of assorted correspondence and other papers that Agricola will have retained from his time as governing legate of Britannia, to his father-in-law's official contemporary reports, and to the archives of the Senate, where, as we shall see, aspects of Agricola's activities in northern Britain were debated. Agricola may even have kept something of a war diary on the famous model of Caesar's commentaries on his campaigns in Gaul. It is notable that his military mentor, Suetonius Paulinus, had done so.[26]

On the matter of Mons Graupius, then, Cornelius Tacitus can hardly have been better placed to know the facts, even if he never set foot in Britain himself. The choices he made in presenting what he had learned is another matter. If Tacitus was no journalist, neither was he writing in a vacuum. The public career of Iulius Agricola was a matter of public record. We shall see that at many points throughout the *Agricola* Tacitus is to be found interacting with that record, selecting certain aspects for emphasis, and others for contradiction. Literally thousands of Roman citizens had been eyewitnesses to the military operations conducted into northern Britain as legionary soldiers, officers and functionaries in the British legions. Some at least of these will have gone on to have senatorial careers of their own as Tacitus's contemporaries, including among their credentials their own achievements as participants in the campaigns of Agricola. By way of example, we know, because he happened subsequently to go on to teach Plutarch, of one such Agricolan campaigner called Demetrios, who served in the *classis Britannica*, the fleet of ships based in Britannia, and encountered British holy men on an offshore island while on 'a voyage for inquiry and observation'.[27] Similarly, as a result of the *ornamenta triumphalia* Agricola received in Rome, Tacitus's wider Roman readership must have had a general sense, years before he set about writing on the subject, of what had been reported to have happened in northern Britain during the legateship of Agricola, and publicised at the time in Rome. There can be no doubt that his narrative is open to questions of interpretation at many points. It is nevertheless important that the *Agricola* was the literary debut of a man who was already planning (and may already have begun) a career as an historian and social commentator for what he regarded to be the betterment of his people. It would have been fatally counter-productive for such a man to earn a reputation as a liar or a mishandler of well-known facts as his first work circulated from salon to salon.[28]

On the whole it is reasonable to conclude that, as regards the comparatively narrow subject of the battle of Mons Graupius, probably the most discussed
episode of Agricola's career among Tacitus's contemporaries, it cannot have served
the author's interests or satisfied his *pietas* that other Roman eyewitnesses to this
engagement (and to Agricola's career generally) should have found his presentation of it wholly and patently unrecognisable.[29] To a certain extent he could expect
to be pardoned where his sense of 'filial piety' resulted in particular interpretations
with which others might disagree. In the event it is a matter of general agreement
among scholars that Tacitus opted for a somewhat vague and generalised approach
rather than a detailed one which might have invited more quibbling. It is also true
that, in keeping with the expectations of the reading public of his times, Tacitus,
by that time an accomplished but increasingly disillusioned orator, put his narrative forward artfully in a rhetorical literary style that influenced even his choice of
language, sometimes modelled upon other learned works.[30] That he decided upon
such a stylised and artificial presentation is no guarantee that he was any less careful
about the content of his narrative. Oratory and historiography were regarded as
two quite distinct literary genres by Roman writers and readers. With the *Agricola*,
a work that lies 'half-way between oratory and history', Tacitus announced that it
was no longer as an orator, but as an historian – akin to the poet – that he would
be expressing himself thereafter, pausing after a few years to explain his disillusion-
ment with oratory in his *Dialogue on Orators*.[31]

The strength of the archaeological evidence that some British peoples adopted
accommodationist tendencies in the face of the expansion of Roman interests
into the island has suggested to some commentators that Tacitus was inclined
to exaggerate the level of native hostility to Rome in the first century. The
mounting of such worthy challenges against prior models seeking to understand
the nature of the Roman 'conquest' of the tribes of southern Britain, a subject
beyond the scope of this study, is to be welcomed. The accompanying thesis that
Tacitus fraudulently invented the battle of Mons Graupius, however, is scarcely
deserving of credit, not least for the reasons outlined above. In suggesting that 'in
building up the importance of Agricola he downplayed that of Rome's powerful
British allies', the evidence of whose might is derived almost entirely through
a particular interpretation of a range of archaeological evidence, Martin Henig
raises a possibility that cannot be dismissed lightly. In contrast, his 'contention that
no such battle [i.e. Mons Graupius] ever took place' pushes his innovative model
too far, and is palpably suspect in arguing from archaeological silence and precon-
ceived notions regarding how British leaders ought to have responded to Roman
invasion.[32] It must be obvious that Tacitus's freedom simply to invent fictional
Agricolan campaigns was constrained by a number of factors. We shall see more
over that there is too much about his description of the battle that fits alongside
other evidence for there to be any serious possibility that his account of the battle
of Mons Graupius is no more than a farrago of lies and clever wordsmithing.[33]

If there can be no serious doubt that the battle of Mons Graupius took place, and if we may rest assured that Tacitus knew a great deal about it, we must nevertheless temper our initial optimism by recognising Henig's essential point, even if we reject his *reductio ad absurdum*. Tacitus's doubly one-sided presentation is certainly biased. It is (naturally) pro-Roman, in keeping with the author's particular ideas about what was (and was not) praiseworthy about Rome. It is also (just as naturally) highly partisan in favour of Agricola personally. Without much in the way of other written evidence to provide alternative perspectives on Tacitus's narrative, it is a challenging prospect to separate the author's rhetoric from the facts, or his exaggerated claims from the fairer and more reliable ones that Agricola is entitled to stake. Attempts at this will be made below. Attempts will also be made to keep Agricola's own potential contributions to his son-in-law's narrative in sight, in particular as regards what John Keegan termed 'the Bullfrog Effect', warning military historians about:

> the danger of reconstructing events solely or largely on the evidence of those whose reputations may gain or lose by the account they give: even if it is only a warrior's self-esteem which he feels to be at stake, he is liable to inflate his achievements… and *old* warriors, particularly if surrounded by Old Comrades who will endorse his yarn while waiting the chance to spin their own on a reciprocal basis, are notoriously prone to do so.[34]

Archaeologists in particular have zeroed in upon the perceived flaws and faults of the *Agricola*, some of which may reflect such a 'Bullfrog Effect' on the part of Tacitus's main informant, as they continue to unearth detailed material evidence, enabling them to formulate models that are at odds with Tacitus's overview of the history of Roman Britain before Agricola, and his presentation of the overall achievement of Agricola in Britain. It hardly needs emphasising that his testimony must continue to be tested in this way, but one jettisons Cornelius Tacitus wholesale to one's cost. It is no less perilous to trust him implicitly down to the minutiae of his testimony. Between the two extremes lie the fertile fields of interpretation and the harvest of which great historical debates are made.

CHAPTER TWO

A Man Keen on Advancement

The Rise of Agricola

Iulius Agricola was born on 13 June 40 during the third consulate of the infamous emperor Caligula,[1] the first of the Roman emperors seriously to contemplate the invasion of Britain. That island would dominate Agricola's own destiny. *Agricola*, a *cognomen* meaning 'farmer', would seem to have been chosen for him because his father, the senator Iulius Graecinus, had written a well-received tract on viticulture. The *nomen* or family-name *Iulius*, inherited from both his father and his mother Iulia Procilla, has been taken as an indication that both his paternal and maternal grandfathers had belonged to families that had been extended Roman citizenship and voting rights either by Iulius Caesar, the founder of his hometown, or by his nephew Augustus, who elevated it to the status of a Roman colony (*colonia*).[2] Both grandfathers had been prominent gentlemen who distinguished themselves in the service of the emperors. His father in turn served as a praetor, or judicial magistrate, under Caligula until a disagreement with the emperor led to his execution.[3] Agricola cannot have been more than about a year old. We may suspect, but cannot know, that this intimate experience of arbitrary tyranny at a tender age contributed both to Agricola's survival instincts as a Roman politician during the principates of Nero and Domitian, and to the balanced view of the exercise of authority he is alleged by his son-in-law to have developed by adulthood.

As a boy, as was typical among the male children of senatorial families, Agricola, now fatherless, was sent from his hometown of Forum Iulii on the Mediterranean coast of the province of Gallia Narbonensis (modern Fréjus, at the mouth of the river Argens in Provence) to be schooled in the liberal arts. His school was in Massilia (modern Marseilles),[4] an old city, formerly a Greek colony, that had long been highly regarded as a centre of education. Massiliot schools were known latterly in particular for having taught the children of Gallic tribes to the north of the province in the days before the Gallic conquest, and they continued to serve this function thereafter.[5] As all indications are that Agricola's maternal forebears – and perhaps his paternal ones as well – had been local Narbonensian Gauls who had become romanised and enfranchised,[6] it may be postulated that his Massiliot education came as something of a family tradition. Tacitus, as might be expected, gives no impression that there was anything particularly Gallic or even provincial about Agricola or his family. It would seem at least possible that these Narbonensian Iulii had a degree of conversance with Gallic culture and tradition. In any event, as a schoolboy in Massilia the young Agricola is very likely to have had among his fellow pupils natives of other parts of Gaul, not all of whom will have come from families as thoroughly romanised as his own. We cannot know how much, if anything, he may have known or learned of traditional Gallic ways as a result of his childhood and background, but the possibility that they were not utterly alien to him is worth keeping in mind.

Iulius Graecinus had been a writer, a senator and a praetor, and a man 'notable for his study of eloquence and philosophy'. His son Agricola, though apparently fascinated by these same subjects as a pupil, was discouraged by his mother from what in senatorial circles was considered an unseemly interest in philosophy.[7] It may be that Procilla blamed his study of philosophy for the execution of her husband, which has all the hallmarks of stemming from a refusal to budge on a matter of principle.[8] It would be unwise to dismiss out of hand the impression created by Tacitus that his father-in-law was a man of principle in his own right.

AGRICOLA, CERIALIS AND THE BOUDICAN UPRISING

Agricola's public career began in the usual way. In about the year 60, having recently attained the usual age of twenty, Agricola took an apprenticeship as a military tribune (*tribunus laticlavius*), one of the twenty-seven legionary deputy commands filled by the government each year.[9] It was the consular legate of the Roman province of Britannia, Suetonius Paulinus, who now selected him to serve his tribunate in one of the four British legions.[10] Tacitus's opinion of Paulinus as having been 'a diligent and sensible general' may well reflect Agricola's own.[11] It had then been almost twenty years since the governing legate of the province of Pannonia, Aulus Plautius, had organised and overseen the Roman military and other interventions, under the authority of the emperor Claudius, which in 43 had led to the establishment of this province among the British allies and enemies of Rome in the south-east of the island. Now, four legates later, the authority of the Romans extended as far north as the rivers Humber and Mersey, along which frontier they faced the Brigantes, a native tribe with whose queen, Cartimandua, Rome had established a number of treaties of peace. The most recent of these agreements had been hammered out in the early 50s, after she had captured and handed over to the Romans their intractable enemy, the Catuuellaunian overlord Caratacos, bringing to an end his decade-long personal war with Rome.[12] Cartimandua's reward for this act of conspicuous dutifulness towards her powerful Mediterranean ally was to come in the form of Roman troops, deployed to support her against her domestic enemies.[13] To the west, Paulinus's legatine authority extended into what are now the Welsh mountains, where the Romans were faced by two British tribes, the Silures in the south and the Ordouices in the north. Both of these mountain peoples had been to war against the Romans in the 50s under the direction of the ubiquitous Caratacos, and were left vulnerable to reprisals after he had been captured and removed to Rome.[14]

Within this perimeter, arcing from the Humber to the Severn, at least six large British peoples and countless smaller ones had been persuaded into making treaties of peace and friendship with Rome under varying degrees and sorts of coercion. The eagerness with which some of these may have given up key aspects of their self-determination in return for the rights and privileges of Roman provincials can clash with anachronistic modern expectations. Modern liberal distaste for imperialism can lead us cynically to scoff at the notion that Rome can have offered free peoples something that they considered to be worth the surrender of their sovereignty, but we cannot expect ancient peoples to have behaved like modern liberals. There can be no doubt that the Romans applied various forms of pressure, including threats and overt military action, to secure the necessary agreements, but we ought not to underestimate the unwitting effectiveness of careers like that of Caratacos in engendering fondness for Rome among those who feared or resented him. Twenty years later, six British peoples maintained something of their tribal identity as *civitates*, the basic political units into which the Roman empire had become organised. Beyond the frontier when Agricola first arrived in Britannia, the Silures of southern Wales in particular were, as Tacitus puts it, 'exceptionally stubborn', not least, it was said, because of one Roman commander's pronouncement that 'the name of the Silures ought once and for all to be extinguished'.[15] Although such details are contained in the later works of Tacitus rather than in the *Agricola*, one can hardly ignore the likelihood that his father-in-law was one of Tacitus's main sources of information about the history of Roman activity in Britain. It was in the west, and against the Silures, that Paulinus (58–61) was engaged in campaigning as governing legate when Agricola took up his tribunate. He arrived just in time to bear witness personally to the province's most famous native uprising against Roman authority.

The unrest was inspired and led by the Iceni, a tribe based in what is now East Anglia, who had initially passed into the Roman sphere of influence by treaty rather than by conquest.[16] In the 50s, however, the disenchanted tribe had risen up under their king Prasutagos after Ostorius Scapula (47–52), the second governing legate of Britannia, had ordered their disarmament along with the other *civitates* within the provincial perimeter.[17] The bearing of arms was deeply ingrained in native British elite culture as one of the more important symbols of social status, not to mention for the prosecution of war and feuding. The warriors of the Iceni were not yet prepared to abandon their weapons. Ostorius had suppressed this unrest at the time, but bad blood clearly lingered, particularly at the local level, between both the incoming Romans of the *civitas* and the Icenian natives. A concerned Prasutagos named the emperor one of his co-heirs in what proved to be a vain hope that, as a matter of imperial interest, his extensive wealth and property would be inherited in the main by his daughters when he died.[18] Instead, local Romans, perhaps in the emperor's name, seized what they liked of the king's legacy, savagely defiled his daughters, and humiliated the king's widow Boudica with physical abuse.

The affronted princes of the Iceni now rose up in a second rebellion in 60, this time while the unsuspecting legate was campaigning in Wales.[19] It is important not to lose sight of the particular and strictly local grudges that became the powder-keg of this very famous 'Boudican' uprising. This was no general rebellion, but a very specific dispute that was allowed to get out of hand. The Trinouantes of modern Essex, a neighbouring tribe with a tradition of hostility towards Rome, were aggrieved at the appropriation of their lands for the establishment of the Roman colonial settlement (*colonia*) of Camulodunum (modern Colchester). They now joined the uprising of the vengeful Iceni, and together the two tribes sacked this new colony of Roman ex-soldiers.[20] Upon hearing the distressing news, Suetonius Paulinus hurried eastwards. He was eventually able to crush the insurrection with all of the brutality of the destruction of Camulodunum, but not before the triumphant insurgents had humiliated a relief force led against them out of the north by the legionary legate (*legatus legionis*) of *legio* IX *Hispana*, Petillius Cerialis, who within ten years would himself become the ninth governing legate of Britannia.

The decisiveness exhibited by Agricola at the end of the decade in taking up the cause of Vespasian, to whom Cerialis was linked by marriage, not to mention the latter's selection of Agricola to receive the honour of campaigning with him in Britain during his subsequent legateship, suggest that the two men had forged a prior relationship. It may therefore be suspected that Agricola served out his tribunate in Britannia under Cerialis in IX *Hispana*, and thereby acquired his first practical experience of combat, military life and the native peoples of Britain both within and beyond the frontier.[21] There is reason to believe, in other words, that the young Narbonensian was present when the Boudican insurgents bested Cerialis 'as he was coming to the rescue' of Camulodunum, probably from Lindum (modern Lincoln), with what would seem to have been a vexillation of his legion, 'routed his troops, and destroyed all his infantry'.[22] In his *Histories* Tacitus records in another and later context the implication that Suetonius Paulinus took excessive pains as a general, being 'naturally inclined to delay, and a man who preferred cautious and well-reasoned plans to chance success'.[23] Now, before the legate had gathered what seemed to him sufficient strength to intervene decisively, he was forced to abandon the cities of Londinium (modern London) and Verulamium (modern St Albans) to Camulodunum's grim fate. The result was that, according to Tacitus, something like 70,000 Romans and provincials, mostly civilian inhabitants of the three cities, were massacred by Boudica and her allies, who were in vengeful mood and seem to have seen little point in taking and providing for prisoners.[24] The modern observer, and in particular the modern partisan, often feels compelled to explain or defend such horrors in terms of the anachronistic morals of the present. Here and elsewhere in this study it is enough to observe that neither the British nor the Roman perpetrators of what appear to us as atrocities and war crimes may be regarded as sharing our view of such things. Neither Paulinus nor Boudica, and later, neither Agricola nor Calgacos, will have imagined for a moment that the murderous rampages their followers unleashed upon their enemies and the bloodbaths that followed required a single word of justification, as if they were anything but glorious.

Richmond was not unreasonable in forming the impression from his son-in-law's prose that Agricola experienced first-hand the catastrophic consequences of this combined mistreatment of the natives and misreading of their mood.[25] Tacitus's handling of the episode in his *Annals* may therefore be read as a fair reflection of the views espoused by his father-in-law in hindsight. Here, no less than in the brief glimpse of the uprising earlier included in the *Agricola*, Tacitus remained consistently favourable in his appraisal of Paulinus, the man responsible for first bringing Agricola to Britannia. He sympathised with, rather than criticised, his decision to allow Londinium and Verulamium to be sacked and pillaged, describing Paulinus as a man of 'wonderful resolution',[26] and rationalising his replacement in that same difficult year by Petronius Turpilianus (61–63) as being necessitated by Paulinus's vindictiveness, which had compromised a legate who was otherwise 'outstanding'.[27] Tacitus reserved his scorn on the matter of the uprising for the Romans whose despicable behaviour had provoked the Iceni and Trinouantes to rise up as a matter of tribal and personal honour, and whose short-sightedness had exacerbated the scope for British brutality at Camulodunum. He also blamed Catus Decianus, the procurator upon whom the legate had initially relied to suppress the uprising, for having failed to prevent such local disputes as these from becoming such a severe threat.[28]

All indications are that, as the eleventh consular legate of Britannia, Agricola (78–84) dealt firmly with unscrupulous behaviour if it arose within his administration, while treading cautiously in his dealings with the British population. His circumspect approach was self-consciously shaped in no small degree by hard lessons learned during his first short but highly eventful posting to Britannia. As Tacitus puts it, he had 'a deep understanding of the feelings of the province, having learned as well from the experience of others that little is gained by arms if oppression follows', and he regarded harsh rule and corruption as 'the causes of wars'.[29] According to Tacitus, who probably heard it from his father-in-law in the packaging of general advice, Agricola believed it to be important that a governing legate make a genuine effort, whether he was dealing with civilian or military matters, to be fair and balanced in his approach to taxation, in his judgements and his recommendations, and, when filling vacancies, to try to privilege men who could be trusted not to abuse their authority.[30] In a cynical age it is tempting to regard these as the empty words of a hypocrite, but there are no grounds beyond our own cynicism for disbelieving the evidence that Agricola was a thoughtful and principled man of moderate temperament, unlike those fiercely single-minded extremists among the senators whom Tacitus loathed.[31]

Moreover, it would seem to have been Agricola's experience that British tribal princes, once they had acquired an appreciation for the amenities and honours it could afford, were easily won over to the settled lifestyle of the Roman equestrian. As Tacitus put it, they would 'bear with pleasure conscription, taxation and the other obligations imposed by government, provided that there is no oppression, which they tolerate only with difficulty'.[32] That Britannia and the Britons had made such an impression upon Agricola, and so demanded the appointment of such a consular legate, was the legacy of Boudica and her fellow insurgents to the province, though we cannot know how many legates remained as mindful of that uprising as Agricola, for whom it was a matter of personal experience. If he had indeed been one of the mounted officers who escaped death in the rout of IX *Hispana* in the fateful summer of 60, fleeing with Cerialis to cower behind their fortifications,[33] one wonders whether at that moment he can have imagined that both his commander and himself would one day govern in Britannia. Yet in those later years he harboured little of Paulinus's alleged vindictiveness towards the native peoples of Britain. Unlike some modern commentators, he did not believe them to be intractably or patriotically hostile to pacification and romanisation, and he admired the acumen of those who were given the opportunity of a Roman education, which he was inclined to compare favourably with that exhibited by Gauls,[34] alongside some of whom he had probably studied himself as a pupil in Massilia.

All of this was yet to come when Agricola was still a mere *tribunus laticlavius* in his early twenties, albeit one who had learned a great deal in his short time in Britannia. The province and the native peoples of the island made a significant impression upon the young man. Tacitus is clear about his father-in-law's intense political ambition and 'passion for military glory' in these years. They would seem to have been made manifest during his tribunate in a no-nonsense attention to duty in an age when such tribunes, appointed for political reasons, could be more given to the leisure that a privileged senatorial background could afford them.[35] Tacitus portrays Agricola as having been a serious and attentive young officer with a curious mind focused upon his future career, and a measured approach to the self-promotion required of all men who sought to make names for themselves in the Roman political arena.[36] We must always allow for the likelihood that Tacitus exaggerates such qualities in his father-in-law. He criticises the hated emperor Domitian for having allegedly been one such frivolous and negligent youth whose father's status 'meant nothing but licence to enjoy himself',[37] and in general he tends to depict Agricola as the antithesis of everything Domitian's recent career called to mind. Indeed, Agricola is made to be a man very much in the different mould of Trajan, newly possessed of the principate in 98.[38] As ought to be expected of a eulogy, it seems unlikely that Agricola was as two-dimensional as emerges from his son-in-law's *laudatio*, and likelier that he was a multi-faceted and complex man. Yet we must also acknowledge that Agricola, the son of a praetor put to death for failing to appease his emperor, not only managed to survive, but also prospered, during the principate of Nero, in reference to whose reign Tacitus speaks of 'an age which put sinister construction upon distinctive merit, and made fame as dangerous as infamy'.[39] There seems little reason to doubt that Agricola, who had dabbled in philosophy at school, was indeed a shrewd, careful and calculating thinker, whose gifts as a self-promoter included the necessary subtlety to avoid the less desirable consequences of catching the imperial eye.

AGRICOLA, CERIALIS AND VESPASIAN

When his tribunate in Britannia had run its course, Agricola returned to Rome. He was ready, as was entirely typical of men of standing in his age, for a marriage that could 'give distinction and support to a man keen on advancement'.[40] He was fortunate, or perhaps discriminating, to choose a wife in Domitia, the daughter of the distinguished Narbonensian senator Domitius Decidius,[41] with whom he could live 'in rare harmony, maintained by their mutual affection and unselfishness'.[42] Their first child, a son, died as a boy in the province of Asia while his father was posted there c.63–64.[43] Their second child, Iulia their daughter, grew to adulthood and was given in marriage in 77 to the ambitious Cornelius Tacitus, probably another Narbonensian who was then about twenty.[44] In the decade following his tribunate and marriage, Agricola was able to secure public office three times. As quaestor in c.63–64, one of twenty fiscal magistrates, he was posted to Asia and served under an allegedly unscrupulous legate. As 'tribune of the people' he gave himself over to 'inaction and retirement', for, as Tacitus alleges, 'he understood those times of Nero, when inactivity stood for wisdom'. As one of the city's eighteen praetors in 68–69, the judicial magistracy that his father had held when he was executed, Agricola seems to have distinguished himself.[45]

At the age of about twenty-eight, Agricola had already equalled the success of his father's political career. He had, moreover, risen through the Roman social hierarchy about as quickly as his age would allow, suggesting that, his merits apart, Agricola had become fairly well connected in Rome since his tribunate in Britannia.[46] Tacitus composed the *Agricola* thirty years later in the time of the accession of Trajan to the principate, whose appointment as the successor of Nerva had been presented as a matter of merit and the good of the Roman people winning out over dynastic and political connections. It is probably no coincidence that Tacitus presented his father-in-law as a man ahead of his time, who would have done well for himself in the 'reborn' Rome of Nerva and Trajan had an early death not prevented it. Yet there are indications that the presentation is overdone. Agricola was a man of his own time who successfully cultivated the kind of dynastic and political connections, and *obsequium* to imperial authority, that paved the way for a successful career. With a praetorship to his name, Agricola could now expect to be appointed to a praetorian legateship in the provinces, a distinction that brought with it either the governorship of a minor province, the vice-governorship of a major province, or the command of a legion.

Civil war had however been brewing in Rome in the wake of the suicide of Nero in a military *coup d'état* during Agricola's praetorship in 68. Like the other senators of the city, Iulius Agricola was now confronted with a host of crucial and risky decisions that promised either to assure or ruin his political future. His old mentor Suetonius Paulinus became a leading general in the service of Salvius Otho, who had seized the principate in January 69. Agricola's home province, on the other hand, supported Otho's powerful rival, the rebel Aulus Vitellius, as did the province of Britannia. We do not know if Agricola, like his fellow Narbonensians, was initially a supporter of Vitellius, or whether, like Paulinus, he backed Otho, in the service of whose brother, Salvius Titianus, Agricola had been quaestor in Asia.[47] We know only that, in a raid upon Gallia Narbonensis in the spring of 69, a gang of Otho's men sacked Agricola's familial estate near Forum Iulii and murdered his mother Procilla.[48] Small wonder, with both his parents having fallen victim to the excesses of imperial violence, that Agricola seems to have developed a strong distaste for political machinations. In the event he sided against Vitellius when the rebel captured the principate from Otho in April 69, declaring his support for a new competitor for the purple, the esteemed general Flavius Vespasianus, consular legate of the province of Judaea.

Vespasian was a veteran of the war of conquest in Britain, and had distinguished himself in Plautius's army. There are indications that Agricola was already closely connected with the Flavii and their most avid supporters, including Petillius Cerialis,[49] and it has been suggested above that Agricola had fought alongside the latter in Britannia. Vespasian's bid for the principate proved successful. By July 69, Agricola, still not yet thirty years old, suddenly found himself high in the imperial favour. By accident or design he had played his cards exactly right, and for his efforts had secured a winning hand. The next year, after a brief commission recruiting volunteers and conscripts in Italy for military service, and before the new emperor had even reached Rome from the east, Agricola was posted back to Britannia for a second tour of duty and his first legionary command.[50]

He was charged with the legionary legateship of *legio* XX *Valeria Victrix*, a legion which to that point, along with *legio* XIV *Gemina*, had borne the brunt of the tough fighting in the rugged country of Wales. It is thought that in 67 XX *Valeria Victrix* had taken over the legionary fortress of Viroconium (modern Wroxeter) when XIV *Gemina* had been redeployed to the Continent by Nero.[51] When Agricola arrived there to take command of the legion, there can have been no men more battle-hardened in the province, nor more experienced in upland campaigning. Like any legion in this period, XX *Valeria Victrix* notionally consisted of ten cohorts (*cohortes*) of citizen soldiers, mainly volunteers, the first of which was further divided into five 160-man centuries (*centuriae*). The remaining nine cohorts were sub-divided into six eighty-man centuries, but in practice, as a result of such things as sickness, injuries and the need to devote detachments of men to various essential duties, no legion could call upon its full notional complement of 5,120 legionaries at any given moment in time.[52] Constant drilling taught the soldiers of each unit obedience, bolstered their prowess and confidence, and implanted in them a sense of corporate identity and *ésprit de corps*. Typically, each legion had attached to it a number of additional cohorts of auxiliary soldiers. These were not Roman citizens, but had been recruited instead from among the allies of Rome and were led and drilled by Roman officers. Senatorial officers of a Roman legion like Iulius Agricola came and went every few years. It was in its centurions, each of whom was an experienced soldier posted to the legion for a full term of service (probably twenty-five years) and in direct command of a century, that a legion like XX *Valeria Victrix* found stability in its command structure, and from its handful of senior centurions in particular that it derived its character. The legions of Britannia, in many ways societies unto themselves, had supported (but had not fought in) the rebellion of Vitellius against Otho, and XX *Valeria Victrix* 'had been slow to take the new oath of allegiance' to Vespasian after his successful overthrow of Vitellius.[53] Unsettled political times like these tended to ignite the *ésprit de corps* and petulance of a Roman legion. The centurions knew that their men stood to gain considerably from a display of ambiguous allegiance, asserting their right as a body of citizens to be wooed and won.[54]

It is a mark of the new emperor's faith both in Agricola's fidelity and in his potential as a commanding officer that he was given the legateship of this potentially hostile body of tough veteran soldiers. The legionary ranks seem to have been something of a haven for vagrants and ne'er-do-wells whose lives prior to volunteering are unlikely to have been characterised by great self-discipline. A legate relied upon his centurions in particular to maintain disciplined units with robust morale.[55] Although in his *Histories* Tacitus would exhibit a certain fascination with the qualities that made Roman generals effective and ineffective disciplinarians, he makes less of this point in Agricola's career than he might have done. In observing that 'of course, even for legates of consular status it was too much, and terrifying',[56] he was perhaps thinking about better known contemporary examples from elsewhere in the empire, in which men like Agricola had proven unequal to such a challenge. Perhaps there is a hint here that Tacitus himself had found discipline to be a particular challenge during his own career. The man described by Tacitus, characterised above all by a moderate tempera-ment and a veteran himself, if in a limited sense, of fighting British tribal forces, ought to have been well suited for the task at hand, and unwilling to exhibit or tolerate excesses of either generosity or coercion as he sought to cultivate the loyalty of XX *Valeria Victrix* without overindulging his centurions or breaking the spirit of the men. It was not an easy job. We ought not to lose sight of the fact that all indications are that Agricola succeeded at it.

The province was now being overseen by its eighth consular legate, Vettius Bolanus (69–71). Vespasian's rival Vitellius had only recently appointed him, and the new emperor may have wished Agricola to monitor Bolanus's loyalty.[57] It is unclear whether the legate became compelled to march upon the Brigantes beyond the northern provincial frontier before or after Agricola's arrival to assume com-mand of XX *Valeria Victrix*. Inspired, according to Tacitus, by the distracting power struggles of Rome, the Brigantian prince Uenutios now made a second bid for dominion over that people. Having once been Cartimandua's husband and friendly to the Romans, Uenutios had first turned violently against both, apparently with considerable grass-roots support, in the time of Britannia's third consular legate, Didius Gallus (52–57), having been spurned by the queen in favour of his follower Uellocatos.[58] Just as Gallus had done twenty years before, Bolanus now sent Roman troops north of the frontier into 'Brigantia' to support Cartimandua at her request. This time she and her supporters had been overcome by Uenutios, and were forced into exile in Britannia, having been extricated from danger, as Tacitus reports the matter, by the Romans.[59] Vespasian's response to such treatment of a valued ally of Rome was entirely predictable, and can have come as no surprise to Uenutios. The responsibility of executing the emperor's will would not, however, be given to Bolanus – or so Tacitus would have us believe. Instead, it was given to a man who, like Agricola, was a member of Vespasian's inner circle of *amici* or 'friends'.

A year after his arrival at Viroconium to take charge of XX *Valeria Victrix*, Agricola was joined by this new governing legate, Petillius Cerialis (71–73/4), probably Vespasian's son-in-law. Ten years before, Cerialis had been legate in com-mand of IX *Hispana* when it had suffered defeat during the Boudican uprising. More recently, he had enjoyed an upturn in his military and political fortunes, fighting for Vespasian in the civil war of 69 and earning glory in suppressing native unrest on the Rhine, though not, it would seem, without errors in judge-ment that had cost Rome many lives.[60] Now it was being left to him by Vespasian to administer the *coup de grâce* to the triumphant Uenutios, something that had probably been made very difficult for his predecessor by the unsettled political times.[61] There is every possibility, however, that Bolanus achieved far more in the north than Tacitus reveals, and that the latter marginalised his initial successes in order to magnify the glory of Cerialis and Agricola in finishing the task at hand. It may perhaps be pointed out, given Cerialis's chequered military record and Agricola's youth and inexperience, that it is difficult to believe that Vespasian expected the conquest of Brigantia to be much of a trial.

At Viroconium, Agricola was evidently proving himself an able legionary legate and effective disciplinarian at the head of XX *Valeria Victrix*, thus earning the confidence of both his emperor and his centurions as war loomed in the north. If Cerialis and Agricola were bolstered in their personal relationship by their common commitment to the cause of Vespasian, it may be suspected, as we have seen, they could also reminisce about serving together in IX *Hispana* during the legateship of Paulinus, and facing the Boudican insurgents. Their first campaign against the Brigantes in 71 was spearheaded by this legion, based at the legionary fortress of Lindum, and supported from Viroconium by Agricola and XX *Valeria Victrix*. IX *Hispana* campaigned extensively on the eastern side of the Pennines, establishing for itself at least the beginnings of a new legionary fortress on the river Ouse at Eboracum (modern York). For Agricola in the west, in the characteristically vague words of Tacitus, which seem as often as not in his writing to hint at known details glossed over for narrative or stylistic reasons, 'merits had room for display'.[62] Just as war against the Icenian and Trinouantian insurgents had probably afforded Agricola his first taste of military experience, so did he acquire his first command experience on these difficult Brigantian campaigns into the mountainous country of Lancashire and Cumbria. Everything he knew about generalship and warcraft, in terms at least of practical experience, he had learned on British soil. By the end of his legionary legateship there must have been few men of senatorial rank in the empire who could rival his expertise on the subject of fighting in Britannia.

There followed 'many battles' after the initial push into Brigantia. We may suspect that it is again in large part with the voice of Agricola himself that Tacitus speaks of Cerialis's competence as a general, striking terror into the hearts of the tribe 'said to be the most populous in the whole province', though not without setbacks or the shedding of blood on the Roman side.[63] Such casualties seem indeed to have been a particular feature of the campaigns of Petillius Cerialis wherever he led men into battle. If Tacitus seems to exhibit more restraint here than elsewhere on the subject, this may again be an act of deference to his father-in-law, whose inclination may have been to think the best of a commander with whom he shared many experiences and much common political ground. Proving himself deserving of the confidence Cerialis was allegedly inclined to place in him, Agricola also managed to earn a share of the credit as the Romans took the upper hand in this taxing Brigantian war. about which we have few details save what the archaeologist can uncover.[64] Tacitus ascribes Agricola's buoyant reputation to his humility and characteristic caution about upstaging his superiors.[65] One suspects nevertheless that Cerialis, the emperor's son-in-law, was in fact grooming the young Agricola, in reputation as much as in skill, for an eventual appointment of his own to a consular legateship in Britannia. There are hints in the *Agricola* that point in this direction. The new emperor had rewarded Agricola's willing allegiance by sending him to Viroconium on the eve of the Brigantian war, thus intentionally providing him with an opportunity for military prestige. Tacitus notes in addition that, by the later 70s, 'there was a general belief that the province of Britannia was to be his [i.e. Agricola's], not because he had himself suggested it, but because he appeared worthy of it'.[66] We are here asked by Tacitus, famous for his disdain for arbitrary imperial behaviour, to believe that Agricola's political successes under Vespasian stemmed not from imperial favouritism but from his merits. We may be forgiven if we remain unconvinced that his future had not already been mapped out for him by his emperor, perhaps because he had indeed requested an eventual appointment to the legateship of Britannia. One wonders, then, whether Tacitus's somewhat ambiguous presentation of Cerialis as a man prone to jealousy, and at first reluctant to give Agricola the opportunity for glory,[67] was a literary strategy intended to make Agricola's success under him seem less orchestrated and dependant upon Cerialis's goodwill than had actually been the case. Although it would seem that he and Agricola managed to strike a decisive blow against Uenutios, we have no indication that Cartimandua was ever restored to her dominions by Cerialis or anyone else. Instead, Tacitus makes the queen culpable for her own downfall, moralising about her unseemly passions and no doubt reflecting the rhetoric upon which the Romans had relied in suppressing her principate.[68] The conquest of the rugged territory of the Brigantes would prove a formidable task. The ninth governing legate had not yet completed it when he was reassigned in 73 or early 74.[69] Indeed, it remained an issue that, a few years later, would also concern Agricola.

The good sense (or good fortune) of Tacitus's father-in-law in having backed Vespasian 'at once' (*statim*) earned him the necessary imperial favour, when his own second tour of duty in Britannia had come to an end, to attain Rome's most prestigious public offices during that emperor's ten-year principate. His next appointment, following honorary elevation by Vespasian and his son and heir-presumptive Titus to patrician status, the highest social stratum in Rome, was to the praetorian legateship of the minor province of Aquitania in Gaul.[70] Agricola held this post for some three years in the middle of the 70s. It was a homecoming of sorts, affording him renewed experience of Gaul and the Gauls in the province adjoining his native Gallia Narbonensis. From this first gubernatorial post he proceeded directly to the consulate as a suffect, receiving the *fasces* in 77 at the age of thirty-seven.[71] He was some six years younger than the usual consular age in this period, indicating, as suggested above, that the emperor did indeed have this valued supporter on a 'fast track' to proconsular governorship, likely with Britannia as his intended destination.[72]

The son of a disgraced provincial expert in viticulture, Iulius Agricola had become a 'new man' (*novus homo*) at Rome. Ennobled by the magistracy at the very pinnacle of the Roman political and social system, he was now entitled to pass on that nobility to his descendants as a birthright. In a career now peppered with honours and accolades, here was the greatest of all. It was probably more than Agricola had dared to hope as a fatherless boy in Gallia Narbonensis, in the knowledge that perhaps one senator in three ever became consul. Yet in political terms he was a young man still. He now had every reason to expect to benefit from a lengthy proconsular career under Vespasian and, when the time came, under Titus. Already in this period the emperor's son, who was Agricola's own age, was being marked out as his father's heir, and, if he was not co-ruler, Titus was steadfast in his willingness to help the emperor to work his will.[73] This included the appointment of Agricola to the Roman priesthood as a *pontifex*, as well as a major provincial governorship.[74] Despite Tacitus's protestations to the contrary, we are permitted to suspect that his father-in-law was not passive about his future, and seeded the ground regarding that next appointment. In Britannia, the province he knew best of all after two tours of duty as a legionary officer, Agricola must have seen much scope for furthering his ambitions still more.

CHAPTER THREE

Another Island

The Background to Calgacos

I n the year 80, for the first time, a Roman army crossed northwards over the Ochil Hills of central Scotland into Strathearn, ravaging that fertile country as far as the river Tay, which the local population probably called *Tauia*, the Flow.[1] Encountering little resistance of note from the 'new peoples' (*novae gentes*) inhabiting the central lowlands, the Roman general, the legate Iulius Agricola, gathered his troops and marched them back across the Ochils.[2] The decision to turn back may have been predicated upon news from Rome that the emperor, Titus, had fallen gravely ill in Italy. In any event, there was work to be done cultivating new relationships with the peoples of the territories through which Agricola and his army had moved with relative ease that year.

CALEDONIA

So ended Rome's first promising taste of war in Caledonia. In the *Agricola*, one of our two detailed sources relating to this point, Tacitus implies that this name is to be applied to the whole land mass of northern Britain north of the Forth-Clyde isthmus.[3] Our other detailed source reveals this to be an exaggeration. Roman observers at work in this Flavian period, and so at an earlier date than Tacitus and with a far greater knowledge of the place itself, produced a survey of northern Britain that was transformed into a map by Marinus of Tyre. That map is lost, but came to be described in two surviving texts, the more accurate of which being the second-century *Geography* composed by Claudius Ptolemaeus ('Ptolemy'), and the less accurate an anonymous eighth-century *Cosmography* composed at Ravenna. The Flavian survey placed the territory of the Caledonii – in British the name was probably *Calidonii* – between the Moray Firth in the north of Scotland and the

Firth of Clyde west of Glasgow [see Map 1].[4] The implausibility of a single tribal territory extending along a straight line between these two estuaries, thus straddling the highland massif, has been duly observed.[5] It is much more likely, as Hind has suggested, that the Flavian surveyors envisioned a territory that ran instead in a great crescent, from the Lennox on the Firth of Clyde to Buchan in the Moray firthlands, encapsulating the coastal lowlands of north-east Scotland from the 'central belt' to Kinnaird Head.[6] They also placed the Calidonii to the east of 'wooded hills' named after them, almost certainly correctly identified as Drumalban, the mountain range (literally 'Spine of Alba') dividing the west highlands of Scotland from this eastern lowland crescent.[7] The modern place-names of Dunkeld (in the ninth century *Dún Chaillden*, almost certainly signifying the impressive King's Seat hillfort to the west of the modern village), Rohallion and Schiehallion (*sìdh Chaillean*, 'sacred hill of the Calidonii') in Atholl,[8] the highland region of Perthshire to the south of the Grampian highlands and east of Drumalban, are suggestive of a frontier region between Caledonian and non-Caledonian territory, thus providing additional support to the Flavian data. The swathe of fertile country thus defined, whatever the exaggerated generalisations of Tacitus and other commentators, may therefore be regarded as Caledonia, as those Romans who were most familiar with northern Britain saw it. We shall refer to it as 'the Caledonian zone' throughout the rest of this study, in order to avoid confusion with the more generalised vision of Caledonia current in popular usage.

There were sound enough geographical reasons, of course, for describing northern Britain as being 'as if it were another island' (*velut alia insula*).[9] Such a description was also useful, however, to the panegyric purposes of Tacitus. Along with the application of the single name *Caledonia* to encapsulate this 'island', the idea encouraged the reader to regard the Caledonian conquest as being no mere mopping-up operation within an island already largely subdued, but rather as the acquisition for Rome of what was effectively a new island unto itself, captured in its entirety. The Flavian survey demonstrates that we must treat Tacitus's presentation of these issues with caution, but it is an important point that both sources are clear that *Caledonii* is to be understood as a general name applied to several peoples. The British form *Calidonii* is a Celtic ethnonym that may denote 'shriekers' and refer to fearsome or distinctive war-whooping, which would suggest coinage by outside observers or enemies. The name has also been related to that of the Ancalites, the 'very hard' tribe in south-east Britain, and to other related names in Gaul denoting 'hardness', but the fact that *Calidonii* contains a -*d*- instead of a -*t*-, and so developed into Welsh *Celyddon* while 'hard' is *caled* in Welsh, is a significant problem undermining the suggestion that these two words share the same root.[10] It seems unnecessary to postulate the existence of a single first-century tribe known as *Calidonii* when all indications are that it was an inclusive name, perhaps borrowed from more southerly tribes, for the peoples of the Caledonian zone that we have defined above. It would also seem that it was these peoples in the main who, in the wake of this first Roman raid into Strathearn in 80, formed the tribal coalition that would be defeated by the Romans four years later at Mons Graupius.[11] In other words, the Caledonian zone as outlined in the Flavian survey may be thought to indicate the extent of that conspiracy, on a par in Roman eyes, perhaps, with any of the three *gentes* of pre-conquest Gallia Transalpina, each of which had consisted of a number of tribes (*civitates*).

THE DUMNONII

The Flavian survey named several Caledonian peoples whose names are preserved in our surviving texts. The place-names of the most southerly of these, the Dumnonii, include the common British toponym *Alauna*, which may confidently be assigned to the Roman fort of Ardoch in Strathallan, the impressive remains of which over-look the Allan Water (*Alauna* > Allan).[12] As a group, these Dumnonian toponyms have been taken as denoting a territory 'stretching from Ayrshire and Renfrewshire across the Forth-Clyde isthmus into Stirlingshire and southern Perthshire',[13] at least as far as Strathearn. At the heart of this territory lay the plain of the river Forth, termed *Manau* by its British-speaking inhabitants in the early Christian period. This toponym is preserved in the modern gaelicised place-names of Slamanann and Clackmannan, and there is reason to suspect the latter (denoting 'stone of Manau'), or more particularly its hill of Craigie, of having been an important tribal centre.[14]

Clackmannanshire is drained principally by the river Devon, which proba-bly preserves in its name the memory of an Iron Age riverine divinity (perhaps *Dubona*, 'black one').[15] Another early medieval ethnonym *Dumnonii*, interpreted as a Celtic ethnonym signifying 'people of *Dumnonos*' (linguists use an asterisk to indicate a hypothetical form that, on analogy, probably existed, but is not actually attested), the latter being the name of a divinity, underlies the modern county-name of Devon in south-west England.[16] It may therefore be proposed that the names of the Clackmannanshire Devon and the Dumnonii of central Scotland are related, both containing the name of the same divinity. It is possible that the ethnonym *Dumnonii* endured, after a fashion, into the early Christian period, when, according to what appears to be a sixth-century funerary inscription, two sons of an individual named or described as DVMNOGENOS, '*Dumno*-born', were buried near Yarrow west of Selkirk.[17]

THE UEPOGENI

DVMNOGENOS is reminiscent of UEPOGENOS, '*Uepo*-born', an ascrip-tion attested in a third-century inscription by an explicitly Caledonian dedicant on a bronze tablet from Colchester.[18] The latter ethnonym is taken to contain the element, *Uepo*-, that would develop into the more familiar and gaelicised early medieval place-name *Fíb*; Fife (modern *Fìobh*), like Strathearn, was one of the principal regions of lowland Scotland in the early Middle Ages.[19] If DUMNOGENOS derives from or relates to *Dumnonii*, one may postulate an ethnonym something like *Ueponii*.

The Flavian survey does not seem to have made any mention of any such people. This is no guarantee that they did not exist in the first century, given that the survey also did not mention the only northern people named by Tacitus. That being said, it is also possible that these Ueponii (or whatever they were called) arose in a subsequent period. It would nevertheless seem prudent to allow for Fife to have been the domain of this people of the first century, whose name we shall render as *Uepogeni* for convenience's sake, and which the region would one day assume.

THE UENICONES AND THE UACOMAGI

In the early Middle Ages, the lowlands of the Caledonian zone consisted of four principal regions, of which we have already encountered two, Strathearn (with Menteith) and Fife (with Fothrif), and assigned them to the Dumnonii and, potentially, the Uepogeni respectively. It may be helpful for argument's sake to keep these territorial divisions in mind in assigning rough locations to our other first-century peoples, with the proviso that we cannot assume that the rough tribal boundaries so implied must have matched exactly the early medieval ones. The Flavian survey placed a people called Uacomagi, whose Celtic ethnonym seems to denote something like 'irregular plains', to the north of the Uenicones, whose Celtic ethnonym may mean 'hounds of the kindred' and is thought to have survived into the early Christian period to be recorded in one of the *Gododdin* elegies.[20] With the early medieval political landscape of the Caledonian zone in mind, it may therefore be suggested that, as Richmond argued, the Uacomagi be assigned to Angus and the Mearns,[21] and the Uenicones to Gowrie, as Rivet and Smith have suggested,[22] and also perhaps to Atholl. *Uacomagi* would seem not to have survived into the early Christian period. At that time, Angus and the Mearns appear to have included a region that bore the name gaelicised as *Círech*, denoting something characterised by 'crests' or, with reference to land, by ridges.[23] There is no etymological connection between *Uacomagi* and *Círech*, but the concepts of 'irregular plains' on the one hand, and 'ridges' on the other, would seem to bear a compelling similarity that may be thought unlikely to be wholly coincidental.[24]

THE TAIXALI AND THE DECANTAE

The peoples of Moray and Aberdeenshire, presumably the Decantae and (more certainly) Taixali, respectively,[25] lived to the north of the Grampian highlands (the Mounth), which in early medieval times stood as a significant boundary between the northern and southern zones of Pictland. It is perhaps unsurprising, therefore, that the Flavian survey seems to have provided less detail about these more northerly peoples of Britain than it did about those to the south of the Mounth, noting only the names of the rivers Dee (*Devona*), Deveron (*Caelis?*), Spey (*Tuesis*) and Lossie (*Loxa*).[26] Thus the evidence of the Flavian survey conspires with archaeological evidence, as we shall see, that the Spey marked the effective northward limit of Agricola's significant military activities in northern Britain during the Caledonian war. We have seen that the Flavian survey defines a Caledonian zone with its northern boundary at the Moray Firth. There would therefore seem to be grounds for suspecting that the Taixali, whose ethnonym is famously obscure, and the Decantae, whose ethnonym, denoting 'goodness' or 'nobility', also occurred in Wales at *Dygant*, modern Degannwy, participated to some extent in the tribal coalition that fought for Calgacos at Mons Graupius.[27]

CALGACOS

Tacitus makes no explicit suggestion in the *Agricola* that Calgacos, the leader of the British host at Mons Graupius, was the driving force behind the totality of the native war effort against the Romans during Agricola's Caledonian war – a Caledonian Caratacos.[28] He portrays him instead as 'one of the many leaders (*duces*)' of the natives on that day, a man 'outstanding in valour and birth' who 'addressed the close-packed multitude clamouring for battle'.[29] Besides his name, which meant 'swordsman' in the Gallo-Brittonic Celtic language spoken by the peoples of northern Britain in this period,[30] we know next to nothing about Calgacos. We do know, or rather we may expect, something about what sort of man he ought to have been. It is to be expected that he cut a rather spectacular figure. Almost certainly he was, by the standards of that time and place, tall, well fed and imposing, for the Celtic-speaking tribal peoples of north-west Europe (hardly uniquely) did not entrust the security of their territories to men or women who did not look the part. The culture within which Calgacos had come to prominence in the Caledonian zone probably required him to be showy in his attire, typically favouring armlets in the wonderful 'massive' metalwork style, finger rings, and a bronze torc, to judge from the Scottish archaeological record. His accoutrements will have been elaborately and artfully constructed and decorated with skill. His hair may have been shoulder-length and combed back from the forehead in a particular and distinctive style, as is attested not only in pre-conquest Gaul,[31] but also in the Caledonian zone, if centuries later, in the idealised image of the warrior encapsulated in Pictish sculpture. It would be a mistake, all the same, to assume that fashions in such matters were not changeable. His hair may also have been artificially coloured: Roman commentators speak of the Gauls artificially lightening their already blond hair with a lime wash,[32] but the Caledonian peoples apparently sported red hair (*rutila coma*).[33] Possibly some other technique was used in northern Britain to redden hair that may already have been commonly auburn. Among Gallic nobles it appears to have been the fashion to go beardless with a long and bushy moustache[34] – almost the classic image of the Celtic tribesman in modern iconography – but in northern Britain, if Pictish sculpture is anything to go by, the fashion is as likely to have been a short beard coming to a point below the chin, or indeed something else entirely. Caesar famously reported that 'all the Britons dye their bodies with woad, which produces a blue colour',[35] but he saw very little of Britain in his time there. It is generally agreed that the ethnonym *Picti*, applied to the fourth-century and later descendants of the first-century northern Britons, referred to this practice among some element, at least, of Pictish society in the provincial period. It is perhaps likely, though not certain, that Calgacos and his people engaged in it. It will be evident from this brief discussion that, while instructive parallels may be drawn between first-century northern Britain and aspects of the social behaviour of contemporaneous Continental peoples and later Pictish ones, such parallels can not be treated as decisive evidence of the customs and practices of Calgacos and his contemporaries among the Caledonian peoples. In all of this there was a significant cultural gulf between Calgacos and his Roman opposite number, for such ostentation in one's appearance was regarded as distasteful among Roman gentlemen. It is not surprising that, as a result, Roman elites generally regarded their tribal counterparts as gauche, vain and 'particularly covetous'.[36]

The matter of social organisation in Iron Age northern Britain is relevant to this study in that it will have informed how its societies fought. Unfortunately, it is a daunting proposition to draw firm conclusions from the archaeological record. Calgacos is far more likely to have been a leader than a ruler, having earned the recognition of his kinsmen to be the best suited of them to assume the headship of their kindred. Like many prominent Roman politicians of his age and the tribal elites of pre-conquest Gaul, he was surely a man of 'martial skill, family nobility [and relative] wealth'.[37] The possession of such qualities brought such a man particular prestige within the network of relationships, based upon mutual obligations, that will have defined his kindred and governed its relationship with other kindreds. As head of his kindred, Calgacos ought to have been entitled to an extra degree of respect, which might have meant, for example, that when feasting with his kin he was given the first pick of the food, or that he chose first from the spoils of hunting or war.[38] A fundamental question, which remains uncertain, is whether his society was one in which men like himself tended on the whole to co-operate as co-equal leaders of kindreds linked by various 'cross-cutting ties', thus providing the tribe with joint leadership, or whether they strove instead to establish unequal competitive relationships, such that one of them could establish himself as a 'big man' with a degree of chiefly authority over the others.[39] Joint leadership on the part of co-equals is more in keeping with dispersed hunter-gatherer and pastoral societies than the settled agrarian societies of Iron Age northern Britain. On the other hand, the settlement record in the later centuries of the pre-Roman Iron Age in lowland Scotland shows 'a clear trend in favour of the erection of smaller structures' than the substantial, even monumental roundhouses of the earlier part of that epoch.[40] To some extent this trend towards smaller dwellings seems inconsistent with societies dominated by local 'big men', like Gaulish societies in the Iron Age, where above all else the measure of such a man's importance in society was the size and composition of his personal retinue of warriors, free clients, servants and other hangers-on, of which, Caesar observed, 'each noble has a greater or smaller number according to his birth and fortune'.[41]

If Calgacos and his fellow headmen were potentates of this kind, rather than co-equal leaders, it will have made a significant difference to the character of the British host faced by Agricola at Mons Graupius. They will have been attended by a force of household warriors which, in other contexts, Tacitus called a *comitatus*. The corresponding term in medieval Welsh, where a conceptual distinction was maintained between such a force and more extended armies, was *teulu*. These *teuluoedd* were essentially bands of professional warriors from different social backgrounds whose motivation, cultivated by their lord's largesse and the establishment of genuine personal affection, was expected to be sufficient to elicit extreme acts of self-sacrifice on his behalf, even to the point of giving their very lives.[42] The size of such a force will have varied from household to household, depending upon a number of factors, including the power and character of each individual potentate. At most it will have tended to number in the tens of men, princes perhaps being able to maintain in the region of fifty such henchmen, some of whom may have been his kinsmen and others of very high social background.[43] Household retinues will have sustained themselves on the resources of their potentate, and probably generated their own sub-culture, rituals and codes of conduct that revolved around training, exercise, forging mutual bonds and making the most of the relationship with the potentate. More than any other of his clients, a potentate will have relied upon and carefully managed the support of his armed henchmen. He fed, entertained and equipped them, and will have entrusted them, whether severally or individually, with any number and manner of important roles, tasks and assignments to be carried out on his behalf.[44] Membership of such a company will, in other words, have involved many household warriors in elite affairs at the highest level. This will have provided some of them with an importance well above what would otherwise have been possible based upon their social station. In addition to his household warriors, some of whom may have been mercenaries or men from other tribes, a potentate preparing for war in this kind of society will have been able to augment his military strength by summoning to arms a posse of his other, less intimate, clients. In the main these will have been freeholding farmers whose primary activities and skills were agricultural, but who must nevertheless have built up a certain amount of military experience of different kinds during the course of their lives. In medieval Welsh, such an expanded military force of household warriors supplemented by a posse of skirmishers may generally have been known as a *gosgordd*.[45]

The observed trend in the later Iron Age towards smaller domestic dwellings does not disprove the existence in northern Britain of a society dominated by potentates attended by personal retinues. It suggests only that, if such local 'big men' did exist, they did not regard large and elaborate domestic buildings as necessary for the maintenance of their status.[46] There is anthropological precedent for this, allowing for a loose model that takes a moderate position between the two alternative social models already discussed. Agrarian tribal societies are known in which one headman might enjoy higher than co-equal status among his fellow headmen, and yet remain very difficult to detect archaeologically. With reference to the Anuak of north-east Africa, for example, one could envision such a potentate signifying his elevated position through a degree of superficial domestic decoration, including the display of hunting and military trophies, yet otherwise living in a settlement no greater than those of the other nobles of his community. Such a potentate might hold – but not possess - communally owned emblems of his position, but would strive to remain materially indistinguishable from his fellow nobles, since he risked ostracism and removal if he seemed to be keeping his wealth to himself rather than distributing it among his kinsmen, supporters and community. Where he successfully managed his resources, and was perceived to be both generous and an effective defender of the prestige and order of the community, he could expect to maintain his position, to have his fields and flocks tended for him at least some of the time, and to attract energetic young henchmen.[47]

It does seem unlikely, if mainly on analogical evidence, that Caledonian leaders like Calgacos dominated their societies as an elite military class of 'big men' like those known in late-Iron Age southern Britain and Gaul. It cannot be shown, however, that there were no Caledonian potentates of greater than co-equal local influence and prestige, and that instead they were all co-equal leaders. Indeed, it is to be remembered that archaeological investigation of Iron Age settlement in eastern Scotland has focused on visible remains in upland areas; aside from the study of the uneven and selective evidence of cropmark aerial photography, archaeology has been rare in the lowland regions.[48] This means that we have comparatively little evidence pertaining to settlement and social patterns in those areas that must have been home to the majority of the Iron Age inhabitants of Scotland. It is also the case that the nature and social roles of the hillforts of lowland Scotland remain controversial.[49] Although the scale of domestic architecture cannot therefore be regarded a priori as decisive evidence against potentates with retinues of armed henchmen, both the evidence and analogy suggest that, while local potentates can have existed in lowland northern Britain in the later Iron Age, they are likely to have been able to maintain only comparatively small retinues deserving of the name. The precise kinds and degrees of martial, moral and political support owed between potentates and their henchmen in early northern Britain lie beyond our reach, as nothing survives of early medieval Pictish customary law that might have shed light upon the intricate workings of Pictish and earlier societies. We may feel confident, however, that at the very least, and where they existed, Caledonian potentates, like any Gallic potentate, earned favour by giving generous gifts shrewdly, and occasionally hosting feasts.[50] Such feasts, held perhaps at hillforts or other gathering-places rather than at a potentate's dwelling, will not have been so very far removed from the senatorial dinner parties of Roman high society, nor indeed from the 'bread-and-circuses' approach by which Roman politicians, including the emperors themselves, sought to influence public opinion. We would like to know, but cannot, whether Calgacos was himself a chiefly potentate of this general kind, or whether he was a headman of less day-to-day status who became entrusted by his people with their leadership in war, possessing renown for bravado in combat, personal prowess as a warrior, and canniness in securing military success.

THE CALEDONIAN PEOPLES AT WAR

It is to be expected that war and bloodfeud, and the acquisition thereby of surplus livestock, slaves and other booty, were important aspects of first-century headmanship in the Caledonian zone. It is also to be expected, however, that Caledonian peoples devised various efficacious strategies for minimising such violence as much as possible. In early Ireland the attainment of manhood and its associated social status, including legal protection, came with inheritance or marriage (which itself involved a degree of inheritance before-the-fact). The sons of freemen, having reached the end of their fosterage in their mid-teens, expected to wait several years before reaching full manhood in this way. Until then, as Kim McCone has argued, young freemen existed in a kind of limbo state in which, being without property, they ceased to some extent to be the legal responsibility of their kin. It seems to have been expected that these youths, having become notionally outlawed in this way, would join a band of other similar young men, known in Old Gaelic as a *fian*. It is not surprising that these *fianna* of early medieval Ireland, gangs of outlawed young men predominantly between the ages of about fourteen and twenty, were notoriously prone to engage in sexual licence, as well as 'theft, plunder, slaughter of people and brigandage' (*gat 7 brat 7 guin daíne 7 díberg*).[51] There are sufficient parallel examples of *fian*-like social institutions in tribal and militaristic cultures the world over to suggest that something similar may have existed in northern Britain in the late Iron Age. It served a number of very useful functions of relevance to the present study. For example, in addition to being a constant threat to settled communities, such bands could be marshalled to face threats to those communities wherein lay the future hopes of such young men as heirs-in-waiting. Membership of such a band will, moreover, have furnished most of the men of the tribe with fighting experience, a basic level of renown (or infamy) based upon their deeds and accomplishments during this phase of their lives, and also bonds of friendship and shared experience that could continue to influence their relationships once they had inherited property, married and become invested with the social obligations of settled adults.

It seems likely that an adult Caledonian free farmsteader could, nevertheless, still expect to be called upon formally to take up arms by the head of his kindred, in order to protect or advance its honour and interests in times of war or bloodfeud with other kindreds. Where chiefly potentates existed, they too could probably send out such a call to arms, unless that right was reserved for a specially constituted tribal war leader. The early Christian poetry addressed to Urbgen m. Cinmarch describes a Pictish host advancing into battle as a composite force consisting of a number of large companies (*lluyd*),[52] and the Gaelic text *Míniugud Senchasa Fher nAlban* suggests that a tribal hosting in seventh- or eighth-century Argyll was expected to raise in the region of 700 men. Perhaps first-century tribal hostings were of a size with such early medieval examples: if so, the levy will have been constituted somewhat differently. In any case, it is to be expected that tribal hostings consisted in the main of kindreds-in-arms roused by their headmen, and that the majority of the men who went on the war-path were adult farmsteaders who had accrued a certain amount of military experience in previous conflicts and, in their youth, perhaps as members of *fian*-like bands. It is likely that such kindreds-in-arms formed the basic fighting units of such a host. It is also to be expected that, where they existed, *fian*-like bands will themselves have responded to a tribal hosting and fought as units unto themselves within the host, whether in the first or in the seventh century. In the latter period, individual potentates within a kindred-in-arms will have been attended in battle by their personal war-band of professional warriors attached to their household, which may have numbered as many as 100 in some exceptional cases.[53] The example of the mustering described in the early Christian *Gododdin* elegies shows that potentates of this period need not have bothered with a tribal hosting in certain circumstances, being happy enough to rely entirely upon their own war-bands in making war.[54] We have seen that it is unlikely that first-century potentates in lowland Scotland, where they existed, maintained large numbers of henchmen of this kind who, whether in Calgacos's time or in early Christian times, will have formed the core of the fighting strength of such levies.

Given the degree of admiration he was once afforded by scholars, it is worth emphasising that it is most unlikely that Iulius Agricola, with some eight seasons of legionary command experience under his belt at the outset of his Caledonian war, can have been a more seasoned military commander than Calgacos, for whom war and bloodfeud must, since his youth, have been central to his way of life. Only in its most senior centurions will a Roman legion have contained men whose courage, toughness and leadership experience in combat situations will have rivalled or surpassed that of the British potentates and their henchmen who were the centres of gravity, if small ones in northern Britain, around which revolved the native forces faced by the Romans in Britain. It was in the transient nature of the military service provided by the rest of his warriors, and more particularly in his composite host's inability to match the level of organisation characteristic of Roman legions, that Calgacos faced grave disadvantages in facing Agricola. Although they are likely to have had considerable combat experience, especially in their younger days, the bulk of the men in any British force of the period were skirmishers who for some years are unlikely to have received much beyond the rudiments of drilling or training, and so could not be relied upon to exhibit great discipline or high morale under duress, nor the capacity to perform successfully tactical manoeuvres of even moderate complexity.[55] A *fian*-like band or the small household force of a potentate, acting alone, may well have been impressively drilled and disciplined by a captain corresponding roughly to the medieval Welsh *penteulu* or 'head of the *teulu*', and so a body of versatile warriors even by Roman standards.[56] Large British levies, however, were limited in what they could be expected to achieve on campaign, and on the battlefield.

It would be unfair to expect more from the Caledonian peoples in their war against Agricola than northern British society was capable of producing in military terms. Similarly, it would do a great disservice to the native peoples of northern Britain to presume that their leaders were unassuming yokels incapable of measured and intelligent responses to Roman activity, or prone in their rustic innocence to be hoodwinked and victimised by cold-hearted Roman imperialists. As regards modern liberal morality, too often and inappropriately trotted out in a post-imperialist age to pass judgement upon the Romans, the tribal leaders of Britain, like those in Ireland and elsewhere within, and indeed beyond, the Celtic linguistic zone, have no better claim to the moral 'high ground' than their Roman counterparts. The average British tribe was probably intimately familiar with the threat of *imperium* from within its own region. In what is now south-east England, for example, the Catuuellaunian overlord Cassiuellaunos 'had been continually at war with the other tribes' before the arrival of Caesar in the 50s BC.[57] Similarly, a century later, Caratacos, by 'many successes, partial and total, had raised himself to predominance over the other leaders (*imperatores*) of the Britons',[58] first among the Catuuellauni and, latterly, among the Ordouices. No less than the Romans, such strong and prosperous men and their henchmen were – to judge them according to our own standards – neighbourhood bullies who intimidated neighbouring peoples into paying them tribute in return for peace, and lived luxuriously off the proceeds, surrounded by fickle sycophants and ingratiating clients trapped in what was for most of them a permanent state of indebtedness. The potentate sought to maximise his own position and prestige through a complex range of interpersonal relationships with his fellow potentates, among whom each was sometimes forced to acknowledge some neighbours as his betters, while forcing others into recognising his own superiority. The same games were being played, of course, if not always according to precisely the same rules, in villas, military headquarters and curial-houses all across the Roman empire. We

ought not to assume for a moment that, when Roman and Celt came into contact, the Roman politician was consistently more accomplished, more calculating,
more dishonest, or more worthy of our contempt in conducting his affairs than
the Celtic tribal prince. These were men – and, in some British cases, women
– who probably understood one another well, and whose principal ambitions
differed but little.

CALGACOS AND TACITUS

Cornelius Tacitus was a survivor, but an embittered one. He was defensive about
having behaved as had been necessary in order to flourish as a man of senatorial
rank and ambition in Domitian's Rome. His resulting disdain for the 'slavery' of
autocracy became an axe that he felt compelled to grind in his different writings,
shaping his appraisal of barbarian peoples like those of the Caledonian zone as
much as it shaped the way in which he presented Domitian and his predecessors. Thus he can be found speaking of the natives of northern Britain as 'the
last of the free',[59] who, if they could but overcome the Romans in arms and
'be not scared by the loss of one or two battles',[60] might serve as an inspiration
to others to choose liberty over 'the demoralising temptations of arcades, baths
and sumptuous banquets'.[61] Having had access to Agricola's extensive first-hand
experience of both romanised and unromanised Britons, Tacitus believed that he
had something to contribute on the matter of the British natives. He observed in
this regard that 'matters shall be related as fact which, as being still not accurately
known, earlier writers embellished with eloquence'.[62] The end result, however, is
disappointing in this respect. With regard to his treatment of the British peoples
in the *Agricola*, Tacitus is fairly typical for a Roman writer, characterising them
as 'warlike' (*ferox*) and providing few particular details,[63] while using them as a
vehicle to complain about his own society.

   No doubt it was because he had already distinguished himself in the war that
Calgacos, like Cassiuellaunos and Caratacos before him, found himself compelled
to organise and lead his free clients, kinsmen, fellow tribesmen and allies in their
joint war effort against the Romans in the summer of 84. In rising to this formidable challenge, Calgacos was assuming an unenviable position, to which the
prior unpleasant fates of these earlier British potentates stood in grim testimony.
It seems inconceivable that Calgacos did not know something, at least, of the past
history of the Romans in Britain. In Caesar's time, Cassiuellaunos had watched
the Trinouantes and several other British tribes choose subjugation under Rome
over subjugation by their erstwhile Catuuellaunian overlord. Similarly, and
earlier, the Gallic Aedui, chafing under the dominion of their rivals the Sequani,
had also invited and profited under Roman protection.[64] The choice presented
by the Romans to the tribal princes of Britain was a consistent one throughout
the first century, and had not changed from the time of Iulius Caesar, who had

instructed his erstwhile Atrebatian ally Commios 'to visit as many tribes as possible to urge them to entrust themselves to the protection of Rome'.[65] We must therefore remain open to the possibility that such tribes as the Uepogeni of Fife (if they existed at this date) and the Dumnonian peoples of Strathearn and Manau similarly embraced this kind of offer after 80 out of fear and loathing of more aggressive neighbours.

In other words, we must avoid the temptation to assume that British tribes must always have regarded resistance to the presence of the Romans in southern and central Scotland as being in their best interests. In addition to the protection of her legions from the likes, in Caesar's case, of Cassiuellaunos and the Catuuellauni, Rome offered its allies access to the collective cultural package that the Romans had pulled together from across the Mediterranean basin. Whatever the strengths of Rome's military machine, the expansion of her empire was owed in no small part to the attractiveness of that package. If it was not attractive to Calgacos and his own tribe – whichever tribe that was – this marks them as typical of those other dominant peoples who chose to fight the Romans rather than to embrace them, and whose aggressions were probably important in providing their neighbours with the motives to seek alliance with the Romans. 'I had horses and men, arms and riches,' says Caratacos to the Roman emperor Claudius in a speech placed in his mouth by Tacitus in his *Annals*, 'is it any wonder it pains me to lose them?'[66] In dealing with Calgacos in the *Agricola*, Tacitus takes a very different approach. When presenting the British leader's motives, he transforms Calgacos into a mouthpiece for the author's own social criticisms. Yet it is probably Tacitus's Caratacos, with his list of motives for resisting Roman expansion, who more accurately encapsulates the chief worries of the Caledonian leader in the 80s. It will always be tempting to perceive in him something of the patriotic hero whose struggle with his Roman enemy in some way foreshadows later events in Scotland's history. It is more likely, however, that Calgacos, like his predecessors in opposition to the expansion of Roman authority in Britain, was driven by rather different motives.

CHAPTER FOUR

When Shall We Have an Enemy?

War in Caledonia

The least problematic reading of the chronological evidence indicates that Iulius Agricola took up his consular legateship in Britannia in the heart of the summer of 78. He had married his daughter Iulia to Cornelius Tacitus in the previous year, and had recently turned thirty-eight years of age.[1] As Dobson has pointed out, 'only Agricola among all the senators whose detailed careers are known served as tribune, legionary legate and governor in the same province'.[2] It is therefore difficult to escape the conclusion that Tacitus's father-in-law was drawn to Britannia. As consular legateships went, the province was perhaps no great prize. Even so, Agricola must have derived greater honour from the appointment than either of his two predecessors, who had been men of much higher social distinction by birth than himself. By placing four experienced legions under the command of such a young legate, Vespasian was surely affirming his continuing confidence in Agricola's loyalty and trustworthiness. The emperor was also, of course, signalling his acquiescence – and indeed his expectation – that the legateship would be characterised by warfare.[3] There would also be a substantial civil element to his legatine responsibilities, but as we are interested here in the battle of Mons Graupius, and not in the wider achievement of Agricola as such, the details of the latter, which have been extensively discussed by Hanson, will not concern us.[4]

The eleventh consular legate of the province was a man who had acquired extensive experience of the place, its legions and its populace – and in particular in its upland areas – during two prior tours of duty on the island over the previous twenty years. He had also amassed his share of experience leading men into battle against hostile British tribes, having participated in the suppression of the Boudican uprising as a tribune in his twenties, and, a decade later, having led XX *Valeria Victrix* on extensive difficult campaigns against the western Brigantes. It has been fairly said of him that 'few governors could have brought with them better qualifications for the job in hand'.[5] He had shed a great deal of British blood, itself not an inconsiderable aspect of his personal history. The central philosophy that appears to have crystallised in his mind and guided his policy towards such antagonistic tribes was doggedness. 'At all times he would give the enemy no rest,' says Tacitus, 'laying waste their territory with sudden strikes', so that, 'having sufficiently alarmed them, he would then offer clemency and demonstrate the attractions of peace'.[6] Steady aggression, designed to force decisive confrontations as soon as possible, was in fact textbook Roman military thinking.[7] As already mentioned, it is not impossible that Tacitus, newly Agricola's son-in-law in 77, here writes from personal memory. It was common practice in this period for military tribunes to take positions in the command of a relative, and Agricola, who certainly brought his wife Domitia along with him to Britannia, may also have brought his daughter and son-in-law.[8]

At any rate, the new legate's experience extended as well, of course, to the vagaries of the British climate and terrain, though these were in any case already quite familiar to his centurions and soldiers. Both he and they had seen much in the way of the strategies and combat tactics employed by British war parties in both open and rough country, whether in the south or in the rugged terrain of the Pennines. Though still a young man for the job by Roman standards, Agricola had already developed into an accomplished commander and astute political observer who knew the value of leading by example and a well-chosen word of praise.[9] He may not have been as outstanding in his talents as his son-in-law would have the audience of his *laudatio* believe, but if Richmond was too inclined to trust Tacitus on such matters, Hanson has probably been too sceptical.[10] Agricola seems to have been cut from much the same cloth as his emperor, whom Syme described as 'the subtle Vespasian', who 'had never been tempted by splendour or risks'.[11] The younger man may indeed have modelled himself to some extent after the old emperor's example (or may have been following his august advice), in addition to contemplating what he had learned from his own experience.

The legate's old legion, XX *Valeria Victrix*, was still based at Viroconium where he had left it. IX *Hispana*, of which he also had some knowledge (and perhaps intimately so) had its base at the fortress it had erected at Eboracum, from which it had operated during the Brigantian war. Further south, tracing the dispositions of the other British legions in this period is not without its problems and controversies. It seems that, in order to prosecute his Silurian war in the rugged country that is now Wales, Agricola's predecessor Iulius Frontinus (73/4–78), another Flavian favourite, had relocated *legio* II *Augusta* from its old base at Isca Dumnoniorum (modern Exeter) to establish a new legionary fortress at Isca [Silurum?]

(modern Caerleon).The legion had once been commanded byVespasian himself,and no doubt made much of the fact. Meanwhile *legio* II *Adiutrix*, brought to the province by Cerialis in 71, had perhaps been relocated from Lindum to Deva (modern Chester). Across the western frontier, Frontinus had subdued the Silures in the south and latterly had been making inroads into the territory of the Ordouices in the north.[12] His probing of the frontiers of his province may well have been more extensive, including expeditions into the north; if so they attracted little comment from Tacitus.

The transfer of legatine power to Agricola would seem to have presented the Ordouices with an opportunity to avenge recent setbacks. Despite the fact that the campaigning season was over and Frontinus had already withdrawn the legions to winter quarters, Agricola leapt at the chance to punish the Ordouices for an attack upon a Roman garrison. He mustered an assault force, launched an invasion of northern Wales and 'cut to pieces almost the whole tribe', a claim that no doubt overstates (to some extent) the success of this operation.[13] Reaching the Menai Strait, the new legate cast his eyes across to Anglesey (*Mona insula*) as Suetonius Paulinus had done twenty years before. On that occasion the Romans had assailed the island in pursuit of refugees from their recent wars with the intransigent Caratacos.They had been faced by a native force that, according to Tacitus, included 'black-robed women with dishevelled hair like Furies, brandishing torches' and 'druids raising their hands to heaven and screaming dreadful curses'.[14] Not without some trepidation at this 'weird spectacle', which the Romans, no less than the natives themselves, expected would be efficacious in bringing about a measure of divine protection, Paulinus and his army, who no doubt had called upon their own divine defenders for help, had stormed and occupied the island.[15] That legate's victory was thus no less a victory of the Roman divinities over those invoked by the defeated Britons of Anglesey. It was in keeping with the intimidating tactics of the latter, then, that Paulinus had ordered the demolition of 'the groves devoted to Mona's barbarous superstitions' that had proved so unequal to the task of defending their observants from the Romans.[16]

Paulinus had been forced by Boudica to leave off this conquest of Anglesey. It is not difficult to appreciate Agricola's determination to take the island now that the Romans had returned to northern Wales under Frontinus, nor his dismissive belief in later years that, in crossing the Menai Strait to victory, 'he had merely kept a defeated tribe under control'.[17] Such a claim paid due respect to the achievement of the old legate who had first brought him to Britannia. At the same time, as Tacitus puts it, Agricola 'realised that he must continue to live up to his reputation, and that the outcome of his first enterprises would determine how much fear his subsequent operations would inspire'.[18] The daring decision to cross to Anglesey by swimming, shocking the population into surrendering the island and earning a share of the scorn of those modern observers who have lamented the fall of Anglesey as the fall of the druid, was therefore inspired by more than a desire to finish what Paulinus had begun. It was also inspired by a desire to pave the way for future glory in 'subsequent operations' sanctioned by Vespasian. That kind of glory was never going to be forthcoming from 'merely keeping a defeated tribe under control' like the Ordouices or even the Brigantes, in whose territory Agricola seems to have undertaken some similar mopping-up in 79, 'occupying terrain,' as Hanson reminds us, 'already overrun by Cerialis or even Frontinus'.[19] Tacitus has been accused of having churlishly sidelined these two predecessors in his narrative in the interests of promoting his father-in-law's achievement. Syme reminded us some time ago, however, that he will have perceived little need to comment at length upon these men if, as is entirely possible, they had already been the subjects (or indeed were prospective subjects) of *laudationes* in their own rights.[20] It is a rare eulogy that devotes much time in praising others than its subject.

THE CALEDONIAN CONTROVERSY

As presented by Tacitus, the battle of Mons Graupius was the culmination of a two-year war waged by Agricola north of the river Forth. There are two telling phrases in the *Agricola* that shed crucial light upon this war, providing us with a measure of understanding as regards its cause, Agricola's approach to its prosecution, Rome's attitude towards it, and its effect upon Agricola's subsequent career. The first of these phrases is contained in the speech that Tacitus puts in Agricola's mouth at Mons Graupius. Here the legate encourages his men to 'prove to your country that her armies could never have been fairly charged with protracting war or with inciting rebellion'.[21] The words were never spoken save in the imagination of Cornelius Tacitus, which was inclined to furnish his historiography with orations of this kind. This does not mean that they are wholly useless for understanding the writer's appraisal of the scene as it unfolded.[22] Rather, they indicate that, to Tacitus's dismay, such criticisms as these were levelled at Agricola in Rome during the Caledonian war. His Welsh and Brigantian campaigns had been mopping-up exercises occasioned by the activities of Frontinus, who by the time of the composition of the *Agricola* had become one of the most prominent and ubiquitous men of consular rank in Rome.[23] It can only have been in reference to Agricola's campaigning in northern Britain that these complaints were raised. Neither are the details of the case that was brought against the legate wholly lost to us. In attempting to undermine it, Tacitus enables us to glimpse it in a further important phrase. 'A limit to our intervention (*inventus*) might have been found in Britannia itself', he observes, in reference to the fortification of the Forth-Clyde isthmus in Agricola's fourth summer in Britain, 'had the valour of the army and the Glory of the name of Rome permitted it' (*ac si virtus exercituum et Romani nominis Gloria pateretur*).[24] It is worth noting that Roman military intelligence can have become aware of this isthmus and its strategic potential many years earlier.

Taken together, these two important passages imply that Agricola had, at some point, come under strict – presumably imperial – orders to make no further inroads into the island than the Forth-Clyde isthmus, and that the campaigns of his Caledonian war in the summers of 83 and 84 were vulnerable to criticism for seeming to violate such a directive.[25] In June or July 79, within weeks, probably, of the first anniversary of his arrival in Britannia, Agricola learned, no doubt with some sorrow, of the death of Vespasian, his great imperial benefactor. We may rest assured that it had not been this emperor who sought to curtail Agricola's military exploits in the indicated manner. In addition to factors already discussed, the old emperor had arranged that the consular legate, who would normally have been responsible for overseeing the workings of Roman justice within his province, should be furnished with a judicial legate (*legatus iuridicus*), a special deputy to shoulder this judicial burden and free Agricola's hand to concentrate upon war.[26] It has been suggested that the judicial legateship was an innovation occasioned by Agricola's particular case, and that his *legatus iuridicus*, Gaius Salvius Liberalis Nonius Bassus, was the first man ever to hold this office in the Roman empire.[27] If it had been Vespasian's intention that Agricola should confine his military activities to the lacklustre Ordouician and Brigantian campaigns, he surely would not have thought it necessary (or indeed desirable) to provide the governing legate with such a deputy.

It is probable, moreover, that the emperor's son Titus was satisfied both with Agricola's position and in his mandate as it had been outlined by Vespasian. Titus, who succeeded Vespasian in the principate upon his death in the summer of 79, enjoyed a buoyant reputation among the Roman people and the legionaries, built upon his strenuous suppression of rebellion in Judaea and the now infamous sack of Jerusalem in 70. Like his father, Titus was also a veteran of British wars. He proved to be an emperor in whom 'it is difficult to detect any divergence from his father's provincial and foreign policies'.[28] We may therefore take it that the first Agricolan campaign into the Caledonian zone in the summer of 80, which has already been mentioned, and the underlying expansionism it entailed, were undertaken with the support of this new emperor in Rome. At any rate, the latter was apparently happy enough to bask in the reflected glory that it brought. It is therefore no surprise that the news of the sudden death of Vespasian and installation of Titus in the principate seems to have occasioned no particular abatement in Agricola's avowed usual aggressive approach to the management of his frontiers. This may be contrasted against the fact that, after two seasons and a half of relentless military activity, the legate set down his sword and spent the summer of 81 'in securing what he had overrun', particularly through the building of new forts.[29] At first glance this unprecedented pause in the legate's doggedness has the look of nothing more than conscientious prudence, reflecting perhaps the remarkable ease with which the neighbours of the Brigantes had capitulated.[30] Yet we have now noted that a limit came to be set upon Agricola's northward campaigning.

It is therefore to be suspected that this limit was imposed not by Titus, but by his brother Domitian, who was acclaimed in the principate upon the former's death in September 81.[31] The cause of the young emperor's passing is not known. There are conflicting indications that it occurred after a lengthy illness,[32] the news of which may well have stayed Agricola's normally aggressive hand in Britannia that summer. Men whom Titus was inclined to regard with favour could expect cold comfort from his younger brother (and *vice versa*).[33] It is not difficult to empathise with the uncharacteristically hesitant Agricola as uncertainty descended upon Rome in the summer of 81, and the partisans of Titus grew nervous. As more than one commentator has suggested, the legate may well have been preparing for the real possibility that he might now be recalled from Britannia before the real task set for him by Vespasian had been accomplished.[34] After all, he had governed the province now for a span of time comparable to those given to his predecessors. The fact that Agricola's next campaign, undertaken in the summer of 82, took him into what is now south-west Scotland rather than north of the Forth would seem, considered in the light of the foregoing evidence, to confirm our initial suspicions.[35] It may be suggested that before the beginning of the campaigning season in perhaps May of that year the legate had received word from Rome that Domitian wished him to stay on as governing legate in Britannia, but to make no further inroads into the north. Perhaps the emperor had included these instructions in his reply to the inevitable salutation he will have received from Agricola after the death of Titus, expressing the legate's condolences and assurances that the British legions had acclaimed his succession with enthusiasm, and had sworn the necessary oaths of allegiance.

That Tacitus, some fifteen years after the fact, still regarded Agricola's eventual failure to be satisfied with a frontier on the Forth as a matter requiring justification is strong additional evidence that the directive in question was not one of Titus's that Domitian subsequently revoked. In that event there would have been nothing to justify. It is more reasonable to conclude that it was orders received from Domitian that Tacitus felt still needed to be addressed in the *Agricola*, because their violation by his father-in-law continued to cast a shadow across Agricola's career in these later years.[36] Once this background to the campaigns of Agricola is appreciated, it must strongly incline one to accept, as we have done here, the later chronology of Agricola's British legateship.[37] By the time of the installation of Domitian in the principate, the Senate was becoming increasingly uneasy about the security of their provinces along the Danube frontier. More and more men were being deployed to Pannonia and Moesia. British wars were perhaps becoming an extravagance – even a dalliance – and the suggested directive received by Agricola from Domitian may have reflected a general view among Roman senators that 'the Forth-Clyde line [was] too good a frontier not to use', and that affairs in Britannia 'might be expected to wait upon events'.[38] There are indications that about this time various detachments from all four legions based in Britannia were reassigned to positions on the Continent.[39] For the first time since the Claudian invasion of the island forty years earlier, 'a policy other than complete conquest was being seriously considered for Britain', just as we know that Domitian established a shortened frontier in Germany.[40] This was not by any means the only change in the air as Domitian assumed the principate.

His ambitions and thirst for glory having been curtailed by a new imperial mandate outlined by an emperor who would soon make a personal visit to the Continental frontiers, Agricola changed tack with admirable, if suggestive, flexibility. It is thought that, two years before, his northward thrust through Dumnonian territory had been launched from Coriosopitum, modern Corbridge on the Tyne, and had brought him to the Forth via Redesdale, Lauderdale and Lothian.[41] Such a line of advance would have carried the Romans through the territory of the Uotadini, a people who, like others mentioned above, would endure after a fashion into the early Christian period, and whose ethnonym would eventually develop into Welsh *Gododdin*. On his westerly campaign of 82, the legate and his army drove through the territories of the two peoples to the west of the Uotadini, the Selgovae of the dale country of the central uplands, including Tweeddale, in whose territory at Newstead near Melrose the fort of Trimontium would be established, and the Nouantae beyond them on the north shore of the Solway Firth.[42] The vagaries of Tacitus's language here suggest that, in what was to be a harbinger of things to come for the more northerly peoples, a measure of sea-borne raiding was also undertaken along the Nouantian coast by the war-galleys of the *classis Britannica*.[43]

Reaching these shores of modern Galloway, Agricola began seriously to contemplate the logistics of an invasion of Ireland, and almost certainly secured substantial reconnaissance reports of that island from some of the same surveyors who would produce the survey of northern Britain.[44] The legate's restlessness is perhaps palpable here, and underlines the point that the decision to call a halt to northward expansion at the Forth-Clyde isthmus was not his own. If he was now feeling constrained by imperial frontier policy, and if northern Britain had indeed been closed off to him by that policy, an invasion of Ireland was nothing like as 'distinctly inopportune' as it first appears.[45] Having been based formerly at Viroconium in the early 70s as legionary legate in command of XX *Valeria Victrix*, and having campaigned extensively in northern Wales and Cumbria, Agricola must already have become aware of Ireland. He may even have had some prior contact with some of its inhabitants. Now, a decade later, with the Caledonian zone closed off to him, he had returned to the Irish Sea. He had even received 'a minor king (*regulus*) of that people' who had come to him as an exile, driven from his lands,[46] thus providing Agricola with all the pretext he required for armed intervention in Ireland. It may overstate the case to some extent, but it nevertheless seems to have been something of a crucial moment for the future of

Ireland that, upon his return to winter quarters in 82, Agricola found his attentions drawn beyond the Forth once more. All thought of an invasion across the
North Channel now apparently abandoned, in the following summer, Agricola
was once again at war in the Caledonian zone.

Tacitus shows us that this return to the north in the summer of 83, and the
resulting Caledonian war, involved a controversial decision laden with great risk.
He complains that his father-in-law 'was accused frequently before Domitian in
his absence, and in his absence was absolved', and claims that 'the cause of the
danger was not any crime or any complaint of injury, but rather in a *princeps*
who was a foe of virtue and his own glory, and in flatterers, that worst order
of enemy'.[47] In these first generations of the Roman principate, it had become
fashionable among senatorial orators, no longer safe to debate public policy for
fear of angering the emperor, to publicly harangue one another instead. As Syme
put it, 'to win a name and a career by prosecution tempted the ambitious ener-
gies of the young, the impoverished, and the obscure'.[48] The grounds for such
prosecutions tended to be that a particular senator's activities were a danger either
to the security or to the dignity of Rome. What Tacitus appears to be telling us
is that Agricola became the subject of exactly this kind of public mud-slinging,
but was never formally indicted to stand trial before his fellow senators in Rome.
It is apparent from the evidence we have already considered that the substance
of the accusations levelled at Agricola in his absence were that his operations in
Caledonia, beyond limits set by imperial instructions, were needlessly 'protracting
war'. As Hanson has noted, 'expansion of the empire was emphatically the emper-
or's business',[49] but it does not follow that the Caledonian war must therefore
have received prior imperial sanction. Agricola could not have been attacked as a
warmonger had Domitian been behind the legate's incursion into the Caledonian
zone in the summer of 83. On the contrary, Tacitus alleges, the emperor 'was a foe
of his own glory'. We may take this as a reference to opposition to the idea of
a war of conquest across the Forth, that arbitrary frontier which, according to
Tacitus, Agricola was unable to maintain because of both 'the valour of the army
and the Glory of the name of Rome'. Before the year was out, news would reach
Rome of legionary casualties suffered in the fighting of that summer. No doubt
opportunistic protestations and accusations now began in earnest in the Senate,
before the eyes and ears of Tacitus himself, whose military tribunate, whether or
not it was served in Britannia, was completed perhaps in 80 and followed immediately by a quaestorship in the service of Titus.[50]

In appreciating the context of this criticism, alongside Tacitus's great and
explicit loathing for Domitian, we cannot incautiously accept without question
our author's allegations that Agricola suffered unjustly from imperial ill will, due
to nothing more than the jealousy and anxiety of Domitian 'that the name of a
private man might be raised above that of the *princeps*' by the Roman people.[51]
This is a theme to which we shall return. It would seem instead that, from the

beginning of the Caledonian war, Domitian, guided by the voices of some of his counsellors and familiars, and influenced by pressure in some parts of the Senate, was inclined on the whole to trust his consular legate in Britannia. He seems to have allowed him the benefit of the doubt, despite his seemingly disobedient behaviour. Subsequent events have been taken as showing the extent to which the emperor displayed his displeasure towards Agricola, but it must be assumed that Tacitus is inclined to exaggerate this point at every opportunity. There is little reason not to interpret Domitian's reluctance to see formal proceedings brought against Agricola as evidence that the new emperor, however ill at ease, was more inclined to exhibit patience than hostility towards this man, whose loyalty to the Flavian dynasty had so far been beyond question. Indeed, and if Syme was correct in observing that *obsequium*, or 'rational deference to authority – the obedience which an officer owes his commander', was 'put on show in the exposition of Agricola's career',[52] it is difficult not to suspect that the legate's decision to contravene his new restrictive mandate was an agonising one for him. He cannot have taken it lightly, not least because he cannot have been particularly secure in his relationship with Domitian.

NORTHERN ALLIES?

In his defence, to judge from Tacitus, the beleaguered Agricola protested through his spokesmen – his son-in-law perhaps now among them – that 'the valour of the army and the glory of the name of Rome' had compelled him to act as he had done. This is a compelling hint that the campaign in question, and the larger Caledonian war which Tacitus calls an 'intervention' (*inventus*), was not a war of conquest intended to expand the frontiers of the province. After all, that would have required Domitian's express orders. Instead, it may be thought likely that Agricola returned to the Caledonian zone in fulfilment of alliances he had made with peoples whose protection now required him, as he saw it, to advance beyond the Forth to preserve 'the glory of the name of Rome'. By mentioning 'the valour of the army', Tacitus further hints that the legate sought and was granted the assent of his soldiers in pursuing this course of action. If we have correctly deduced that the imperial order to hold firm at the river Forth was not delivered until after the death of Titus in September 81, the legate would indeed have found himself in a difficult diplomatic and personal position, provided he had established treaties of alliance and friendship with the Dumnonii or, if they existed, the Uepogeni, upon his invasion of their territories in the summer of 80. Such alliances were taken seriously, not least by Domitian himself. In 89, the emperor, fresh from the defeat of a usurper, would lead punitive strikes across the Danube against the Suebi, the Marcomanni and the Quadi because they had failed to provide his legions in Dacia (modern Romania) with levels of support agreed by treaty.[53] It may therefore help to explain why Agricola's accusers failed to secure his condemnation, if the emperor had a degree of sympathy for the view that it ought not to be acceptable for the legate's altered mandate to render him unable to comply, should an ally call upon Rome for her support. At any rate, that Agricola should have risked personal condemnation and the real threat of indictment in order, as his advocates argued, to spare Rome and her emperor (and the legate himself) the ignominy of failing tribes that had become her allies may say something about his character. On the other hand, his protestations may have been the devious legal wranglings of a frustrated legate bent on the conquest of northern Britain from the outset of this war, and who perhaps had calculated that a great victory in the field would sufficiently offset ill will in Rome.

There are archaeological grounds for suspecting that the inhabitants of Fife did indeed avoid war with Rome in the Flavian period by entering into alliance with Agricola after his Dumnonian invasion in 80.[54] The Flavian fortification scheme begun by Agricola saw the building of forts on the Forth-Clyde isthmus and, it would seem, an additional curtain of strongholds in Strathearn as far as the fort at Inveralmond on the river Tay, where the river Almond empties into the Tay opposite Scone. These installations offered ready protection from more northerly tribes not just to Fife, but also to the Dumnonii, across whose territory these forts had been established, almost certainly with their agreement by treaty.[55] As has already been mentioned, the threat of inter-tribal strife beyond imperial frontiers was very real, and for Roman writers it was becoming axiomatic. 'If they cannot love the Romans', wrote Tacitus in his *Germania*, 'may tribes persist in hating one another', for 'fortune can offer no greater boon now than the disunion of our enemies'.[56] Evidently such work on behalf of the tribes of central Scotland was not pleasing to some of those who had Domitian's ear. To them, the whole business of extending Roman protection into the southern regions of the Caledonian zone, upon which Agricola's defence of his actions would seem to have been based, smacked of 'inciting rebellion' in order to prolong the fighting in northern Britain. In the event, such suspicions about the provocative effect of these Dumnonian forts would be borne out. Any corresponding suspicions about Agricola's motives may well have deepened as a result.

Tacitus makes little attempt to conceal his father-in-law's ambitious vision. He claims that he belittled his early military successes in Britannia, so that 'men gauged his splendid hopes for the future by his reticence about an exploit so remarkable'.[57] Despite such acknowledged ambitions perceived from afar by the imperial court, Agricola had not been rash so far. We have seen that he had borne witness personally to the consequences visited upon the province, and upon certain political careers, as a result of the great Boudican uprising of the Iceni and Trinouantes while Suetonius Paulinus had been far away on campaign. Perhaps it was for this reason that he spent his first years in the legateship assuring himself that the tribes of the Pennines and the Welsh mountains, subdued by his most recent predecessors, posed no similar threat to him in the northward thrust that he was planning. There can be little doubt that this conscientious domestic policy, assisted by his judicial legate Bassus, which according to Tacitus also involved gaining the confidence of legionaries, who were no strangers to mutiny,[58] was formulated and implemented with one eye ever focused upon the 'new peoples' beyond Brigantian territory, against whom Agricola must always have intended to try his hand. His first foray against them in the summer of 80, his third summer in Britannia, he could regard as something of a dry run, testing the mettle of the natives and giving his troops some experience of the terrain and the climate of northern Britain. It had also provided him with the opportunity to establish more northerly bases of operations and – should one wish to be cynical – the necessary pretext for further operations in the form of new allies and installations to protect in Fife and Strathearn.

THE LAST REFUGE OF THE VANQUISHED

If we follow the suggested model, the precise nature of the threat to the Dumnonii and their neighbours that emerged in the summer of 83 is obscure to us. It is nonetheless likely to have originated further north, beyond the Tay. Its result was that, for the second time under Agricola's command, the Romans again marched beyond the Forth, ostensibly in answer to the imprecations of these allies. If the invading army was roughly on a par with that which returned to the north in the following summer, which seems reasonable, it ought to have consisted of between 4,000 and 7,000 legionary troops and some 13,000 or 14,000 auxiliary infantry and cavalry, perhaps a little over half the total military strength of the Romans in Britannia.[59] On campaign against the Catuuellauni, Caesar had demanded both hostages and grain of the Trinouantian allies to whom he had offered his protection.[60] It may be that Agricola made similar demands of the Dumnonii and, if they existed, the Uepogeni, especially if this campaign was being envisioned as being in support and defence of these peoples. At the same time, or perhaps beforehand, the *classis Britannica* was sent on up the coast to monitor the movements of 'the more remote peoples' (*ultra gentium*) whom Agricola feared might imperil his army.[61] It is likely that the expeditionary force of 83 consisted of vexillations from three of the four legions stationed in Britannia.[62] It is certain that IX *Hispana* was one of these, and a good bet that Agricola extended to his old legion, XX *Valeria Victrix*, the honour of participating in this campaign, perhaps with pride of place. Of the other two legions, II *Augusta* had the greater experience in Britain and intimate Flavian connections, but II *Adiutrix* was perhaps based nearer the northern theatre. It is difficult to decide between them.

On this opening Roman campaign of the Caledonian war, according to Tacitus:

infantryman (*pedes*), cavalryman (*eques*) and marine (*nauticus miles*) often mingled in the same encampment and, joyfully sharing the same meals, would dwell on their own achievements and adventures, comparing at one time, with a soldier's boastfulness, the deep recesses of the forest and the mountain with the dangers of waves and storms, or at another time comparing battles by land with victories over the ocean.[63]

This passage is quite important for understanding the extent of the Roman incursion into northern Britain in 83, for Tacitus goes on to point out that the northern natives now became dismayed that 'the last refuge of the vanquished was closed off as their innermost seas were opened'.[64] It would seem that Tacitus's particular intention here was to focus upon the efficacy of Agricola's strategic use of the *classis Britannica*, hoping presumably that his readers would acknowledge his father-in-law as having been a gifted strategist. Taken as a whole, however, his description of the campaign of 83 implies that if the war-galleys of the fleet were threatening 'the last refuge of the vanquished', so too were Agricola's ground troops, with whom the marines often intermingled during the course of this campaign. The Roman operations of the summer prior to the battle of Mons Graupius look, in other words, like a very deep and extensive penetration indeed into the 'more remote' parts of northern Britain as far, probably, as the river Spey (*Tuesis*), ravaging and plundering all along the way. Hanson has noted that the most northerly of the Flavian temporary camps to be discovered, of which the camp at Kintore has received the most recent attention from archaeologists, fit logically into this context.[65]

The temporary marching-camp was a feature of Roman armies on campaign. It provided the men with a defensible enclosure, usually consisting of a ditch and rampart, within which they could pitch their tents and bed down after a day's march.[66] The precise level of advantage gained by an army so encamped, forced to defend itself, will have varied widely and depended upon factors ranging from the terrain and the weather to the relative competence of leadership on either side. If nothing else, the marching-camp gave soldiers a sense of normality and familiarity in an otherwise outlandish and intimidating environment, as if they were returning to the same home base at the end of each day. It also presented them with rigorously ordered surroundings to navigate should they be called to arms while half-asleep. As Adrian Goldsworthy has reminded us, it also made desertion more difficult.[67] Being temporary settlements constructed largely with prefabricated materials and subsequently dismantled, each such camp tends to provide archaeologists with precious little securely datable evidence. The camps that are agreed to have been established in northern Britain by Agricola's legions are so identified based largely upon style in size and layout – in particular the use of *claviculae* or gate defences – supported by dating evidence at some sites in a typological sequence. The extent to which these camps may be thought indicative of a superior military mind at work, as was once believed, is questionable.[68] At any rate, any of these camps north of the river Tay that have fascinated generations of archaeologists may be ascribed to these activities in 83. It may therefore be regarded as methodologically suspect to expect the elusive Mons Graupius to lie at the end of the line described by them – the approach first championed by General William Roy.[69]

Despite the panic implied by Tacitus, the British response to this devastating invasion appears to have been level-headed. Some unidentified group of them, probably Uenicones in the main, 'set about attacking the more remote forts (*ultra castella*) with great preparedness (*magno paratu*)'.[70] Tacitus's language here suggests that something of a sustained campaign was undertaken by the natives in question. Such an achievement ought to have been out of the question for a large composite host consisting of levied kindreds-in-arms, and it is therefore to be expected that these forts were assaulted by smaller companies of men, consisting mostly either of tribal potentates with the seasoned and disciplined warriors of their households, or else of *fían*-like bands of young warriors.[71] It is impossible to know whether or not Calgacos orchestrated these assaults, or had any part to play in them. The word *castellum* here is unlikely to refer to anything less substantial than a permanent base. This reference to 'more remote' forts has been recognised as a crucial piece of evidence demonstrating that Roman forts had been established in Perthshire before this campaign began. The most likely sites include Alauna, the fort at Ardoch on the Allan Water, and the forts of Strageath on the river Earn and Inveralmond on the river Tay. These ought to have lain within, or at the fringes of the Dumnonian territory through which Agricola had driven his forces in the summer of 80. It is notoriously difficult to prove that evidence of burning and destruction at a Roman fort site is to be ascribed to violence rather than to other causes, but Flavian Ardoch, as Ian Smith noted, has produced tantalising hints pointing in that direction.[72] It is thought possible that the fort at Cargill further up the Tay may also date to this period,[73] where it would have served as a forward position for the soldiers stationed at these Dumnonian installations. It may be noted that there was nothing that ought to have been particularly daunting to British attackers about the defensive earthworks of Roman outposts, which may be seen as having been roughly on a par with the ramparts that defended many native settlements.[74] Moreover, the foregoing evidence suggests the likelihood that these strikes were launched while Agricola and the main strength of his army were still operating well to the north, some distance beyond the Tay.

In other words, Agricola would seem to have made the surprising mistake of bypassing peoples with significant military potential in this campaign, and so to have overstretched himself somewhat, in his desire to overawe and pillage the 'more remote peoples' of northern Britain. In so doing, he left his return route into the safety of Dumnonian territory vulnerable to attack. It may be noted that attempts to anticipate and block an invader's line of withdrawal, such that he might be attacked and stripped of his plunder, have been regarded as particularly characteristic of medieval Welsh campaign strategy.[75] If this seems like a gross miscalculation on the legate's part, it is worth noting that bypassing difficult highland terrain in particular (and the peoples occupying it) in the interests of expeditious movement overland was not without precedent. Indeed, it was entirely in keeping not only with Agricola's personal practice – he having done so three summers before in pushing north into Dumnonian territory in the first place – but also with first-century Roman strategic thinking in Britain generally.[76] Although we cannot allow our wariness of Tacitus's desire to portray his father-in-law in the most positive of lights to blind us to the fact that Agricola was an experienced and, probably, entirely competent commander, neither are we compelled to believe that he was particularly visionary. In fact, insofar as it can be reconstructed, his strategic and tactical thinking appear, as on this occasion, to have been conservative and fairly predictable. It is therefore not beyond possibility that Caledonian leaders, Calgacos perhaps among them, anticipated that Atholl and Breadalbane, like Lanarkshire before them, would be bypassed by Agricola's advancing legions, and devised a plan to exploit the situation with some seasoned and energetic warriors. It is also possible that Agricola had thought to assure himself of a safe return to Dumnonia through an accommodation with the Ueniconian leaders, and that the latter now betrayed him by supporting or failing to hinder these attacks.

THE MAKING OF CALGACOS

In any event, the news of these events to the south, which may well have included attacks upon native strongholds in addition to strikes against Roman installations, seems to have come as something of a shock to Agricola and his officers. In vague language, Tacitus says that these installations were *oppugnati*, 'stormed'; they may well have been taken and destroyed. Both Ardoch and Strageath have produced evidence of multiple Flavian phases that could support such a suggestion.[77] The possibility may be raised that the lack of resistance he had encountered in the initial Dumnonian campaign three years before had led the legate to underestimate the scale of the response that Caledonian peoples within striking distance of the lower Tay could muster when roused. Some of his officers, according to Tacitus, recommended a withdrawal south of the Forth, particularly as news had reached the Romans that more than one British force was now on the move against them. This again suggests that the native forces in question were relatively small bands of accomplished and experienced warriors capable of extended and complex manoeuvres, rather than anything larger and less wieldy.

Instead, the legate divided his army into three (probably its three constituent legions) and went in search of the enemy, appreciating, according to Tacitus, the danger of becoming hemmed in by these aggressive Caledonian tactics.[78] The idea that Agricola chose to act boldly – even rashly – in the face of unnamed nay-sayers among his officers is something of a theme in this part of the *Agricola*. One suspects that it is employed by Tacitus for a two-fold purpose. On the one hand, it depicts Agricola as a brave and decisive commander, as ought to expected from a *laudatio*. On the other, it also creates the impression that he consistently preferred swiftness and decisiveness of action to dithering and delay, and so could not be said, as his accusers in Rome alleged, to have deliberately prolonged the conflict in the north. In this case in particular, Tacitus's narrative smacks of literary embroidery rather than of information derived from someone familiar with the geography of north-east Scotland. It must be obvious to us – as it ought to have been to Agricola and his officers – that no strategic withdrawal from beyond the Tay can have been advocated that did not require the Romans to march back into Perthshire, and so through the heart of what was now the war zone.

Being outmanoeuvred for the moment, at least insofar as he had left his Perthshire forts vulnerable to attack, and no doubt concerned by the situation that was now developing behind him, Agricola's response – a division of his forces into three – is an interesting response to the developing situation. Tacitus describes this as a defensive strategy, intended to prevent the encirclement of his entire army.[79] There is room for doubt on this point, given the relatively small numbers of warriors that are likely to have been on the move against Agricola. His decision suggests rather, as Goldsworthy has observed, that the legate had by now become convinced that there would not be any coalescence of these differ-ent native bands, and no concerted action taken against his army. *Quando dabitur hostis*, Tacitus has the soldiers ask: 'when shall we have an enemy?'[80] In that event the legate must have expected to be able to march his men back to the frontier without fear of significant attack from an enemy that refused – or rather feared with good reason – to give battle to such a concentration of Roman military might. Instead Agricola divided his forces. It would therefore seem that such a withdrawal, however possible, was the last thing on his mind at this stage. It has been remarked that 'when the Roman army abandoned the offensive… it was a sign that things had gone badly wrong'.[81] It is to be expected, in other words, that aggressive instincts and habits guided Agricola's reactions to the news from the south, and that is indeed what his actions suggest. The division of his army strikes one as a strategy that was both confident and aggressive, and devised to entice a reluctant and scattered enemy to fight on the legate's own terms. We may perhaps form a general impression of his thinking by noting that Strabo had observed of Agricola's Gallic forebears that, 'if roused, they come together all at once for a struggle, both openly and without circumspection, so that, for those who wish to defeat them by stratagem, they become easy to deal with'. This, that geographer had believed, was what had made the Gallic conquest so much easier for the Romans than the conquest of the Iberian peoples, for the latter, unlike the Gauls, 'would husband their resources and divide their struggles, carrying on war in the manner of brigands'.[82] The strategic lesson that Strabo drew from contrasting these two examples was this: provoke the enemy into collective effort and inflict upon him a massed defeat, lest one become embroiled in taxing piecemeal war-fare that might take generations to resolve.

Richmond appreciated that there is good reason to expect that Agricola's strategic thinking in the summer of 83 was along very similar lines, and that everything about this politically sensitive campaign was probably designed to provoke and rouse the peoples of the Caledonian zone.[83] By striking against as many tribes, and in as many places, as possible by land and sea, the legate was surely trying to goad these peoples into committing themselves to a massed effort and presenting him with the golden opportunity for a swift and decisive victory over several tribes at once. It seems to have been the more difficult kind of dale-by-dale piecemeal fighting that he had faced in Brigantian territory ten years before, where the fighting had gone on for the better part of the decade of the 70s. In the summer of 83, by dividing his forces in the wake of British counter-attacks in Perthshire, Agricola may have been intent upon avoiding a repeat of that situation in the Caledonian zone. Perhaps the native companies arranged against him, now given the impression that the odds were more favourable, could be enticed to give battle to smaller divisions of his army, thus enabling him to defeat them all severally in a single tripartite campaign if he could not compel them to mass their strength.[84] If this is indeed a fair reflection of what Agricola was plotting, it was a risky game to play in unfamiliar country, against an opponent with a predilection for ambush. That being said, we must not assume that he had not taken pains to add native informants to his staff as he planned and conducted this extensive northern campaign. It would have been a strategy that required the legate to place the utmost confidence in the morale and discipline of soldiers who, in effect, he was using to bait his enemy, in their resolve and combat skills, and above all in their mobility. In that event, one suspects that Agricola reminded his men of the faith he was now placing in them in executing his plans. In addition, he would have been relying upon the flexibility of a military command structure that, in this period, was ideally suited to cope with such *ad hoc* adjustments from large-scale to smaller-scale operations.[85] Although he chose to make the point through the literary device of nervous and doubtful officers, Tacitus was not wrong to regard his father-in-law's response to the developing situation as a bold one. It might have cost him dearly, for its consequences cannot have been according to plan from the legate's perspective.

We have seen that the division of his army indicates that Agricola had ascertained that the Caledonian leaders now moving against him were not going to mount a collective assault upon him. He was wrong. Perceiving that the Romans had divided their strength, the native war parties did indeed collect their dispersed forces, and together they mounted a night assault upon the men of IX *Hispana*, overrunning their marching-camp.[86] Possibly Agricola had been badly let down by his scouts.[87] At any rate, there can be little doubt that here again, for the second time in the same season, the natives had outmanoeuvred their adversary and caught him off his guard. Familiarity with the country must have been to their advantage, for among other things it will have enabled them to predict the movements of the Roman divisions moving against them through sometimes difficult terrain. A night attack like this may strike us as unseemly – even cowardly – but it ought to have been considered a bold manoeuvre among the Britons. After its initial phase, fighting in darkness became as risky for the attackers as for the defenders, and their decision to gamble in this way reveals that the British leaders who orchestrated this assault were under great pressure to strike directly against Agricola after all the devastation he and his men had wrought that year.[88] Here again we cannot be certain that this native operation was being led by Calgacos, but it seems inescapable that at the least he was involved either in this attack or else in those upon the Dumnonian forts. It is otherwise difficult to understand how he would have acquired the responsibility of leading the Caledonian peoples at Mons Graupius. The fact that both native enterprises involved the storming of fortified installations, however, suggests the strong possibility that the same strategic mind was behind them both. It is therefore difficult not to suspect that Calgacos was now leading the war effort against Rome in the Caledonian zone, which, as we have seen, is likely at this stage to have involved a relatively small number of particularly elite warriors, perhaps none of whom came from outside Calgacos's own tribe. If these war parties were proving to be rather more formidable opponents than Agricola had expected to encounter in the Caledonian zone, then, it would seem that much of the credit for this ought to be given to Calgacos himself.

The location of the temporary camp that weathered this ferocious ambush is not known.[89] Tacitus is particularly reticent about the details, but then, few of the participants will have been able to recount what had happened in the dark. There can be little doubt from his description that the defences of the camp were seriously compromised by squads of British warriors, filling the night air with the sound of the fearsome war-whoop from which the Calidonii seem to have taken their name, and that many legionaries were killed. It has already been suggested that the news of these deaths cannot have improved the mood of Agricola's detractors in the Senate when it reached Rome. The likelihood that the culprits were no farmers called up for military service, but rather bodies of the best and most highly organised warriors northern British society could produce, goes some way towards emphasising the danger they posed to IX *Hispana*, and explaining the general success they enjoyed as a result of this manoeuvre. No doubt they succeeded in carrying off considerable plunder from these Romans. The legate got wind of the attack and roused the rest of the army, the main strength of which arrived on the scene at daybreak. He may well have surprised the British leaders with the rapidity of his response. So complete was the Roman victory in the engagement that ensued, says Tacitus, that, 'had not their flight been sheltered by marshes and woods, this victory would have ended the war'.[90] The magnitude of the Roman achievement here is probably considerably exaggerated, perhaps as a result in the first instance of examples of 'the Bullfrog Effect' on Agricola's part. Certainly, it would seem that IX *Hispana* in particular managed to acquit itself admirably in very difficult circumstances in the defence of its encampment against very capable native warriors, but it may be suspected that it had been intended all along by their leaders that the attackers should melt away from the camp at daybreak. As Tacitus himself puts it, the result of this clash inspired the natives 'to give up nothing of their arrogance' (*nihil ex adrogantia remittere*). The news of it seems to have roused other tribes to rally in support of the men who had planned and executed it, with whom they now 'ratified a confederacy of tribes with assemblies and sacred rites'.[91] As Goldsworthy has noted, it is highly unlikely that tribes roused to war could regard pinpoint strikes against specific targets on the part of a few brave leaders and their henchmen as having the capacity to decide the outcome of that war: 'only the tribal army could do this'.[92] Tribal leaders across the Caledonian zone now seem to have placed their faith in Calgacos. Here was a man who had probably orchestrated the sacking of the *castella* that Tacitus describes as *oppugnati*, before turning northwards to engage the fearsome army that had built them, intending probably to employ a harrying strategy to wear away at that enemy's decisive strength and give heart to the Caledonian peoples. There must have been few Caledonian potentates who could now harbour doubts about a man whose warriors had spilled so much Roman blood.

A TENSE WINTER

Having relieved the men of IX *Hispana*, Agricola and his army had salvaged the situation. It was undoubtedly the closest-run engagement in which the legate had been involved in all his years in Britannia, save in that he may have been present when a vexillation of the same legion had been overcome by Boudica.[93] Now they disposed of their dead, presumably through cremation rites, and withdrew to winter quarters. All indications from the *Agricola* are that it had been a long and arduous campaign season, ending on rather a sour note, even if it had also resulted in extensive ravaging of the combined wealth of the Caledonian zone.[94] The talk at many native firesides that winter will have sounded distinctly optimistic, and far removed from the mutterings of disquiet among Agricola's critics in Rome. No territorial gains or treaties had been made beyond the territory of the Dumnonii, but this cannot be surprising, and is indeed to be expected of an *inventus* which seems not to have been supported by an imperial sanction of conquest. A more important measure of the consequences incurred by this first campaign beyond the Tay is the status of the Perthshire forts. The former presumption that the Roman army spent this winter at Inchtuthil is not supported by more recent archaeology.[95] Instead, the auxiliaries were probably quartered further south in forts like Trimontium, raised in the hiatus season of 81, while the legionaries will have withdrawn further south to their fortresses and associated bases in Brigantian territory.[96] It is open to question whether Agricola took the time, or indeed had the opportunity, to rebuild and staff the forts destroyed by Caledonian aggression. If he did not, it will have seemed to the northern peoples that Calgacos had succeeded in driving the Romans from Dumnonia, leaving the Dumnonii and the inhabitants of Fife vulnerable, and allowing for the possibility that some groups from among these now joined the Caledonian coalition.

As Tacitus describes it, both the Roman soldiers and their commander were eager to return to the Caledonian zone to continue the war, sensing that it was now going their way. This may reflect contemporaneous Agricolan spin rather than Tacitean hindsight. It is clear that neither a climate of pessimism, nor his legal difficulties back in Rome nor the constraints of his mandate from Domitian, could dissuade Agricola from taking up his unfinished business with Calgacos in the upcoming season. Certainly, if the legate's basic strategic approach to the war was in line with Strabo's discussion of the strategy that had got the better of the Gauls, reports of the establishment of a coalition of northern tribes can have been regarded as a strong indication that his provocative strategy of the summer had succeeded. He could focus upon this achievement, and encourage his men and his officers to do the same. It had come at greater cost than Agricola had wished or expected to pay. A decisive stroke could now be made in vengeance against the northern barbarians, if only the legate could keep his legions motivated. Adding to his difficulties was the sensational mutiny of a cohort of Usipian auxiliaries from Germania, who murdered their Roman centurion and other officers, seized ships and raided the coasts of northern Britain before heading off towards their homeland on the Rhine.[97] This was probably not as random an event as it appears in Tacitus's narrative. It was that same summer, on this chronological model, that the Romans had begun occupying the territory of the Usipi as part of a wider victorious German campaign. It is difficult not to suspect Agricola's mutineers of having been inspired by news of these events back home.

Despite such discouraging developments, the army remained resolute, according to Tacitus, in its determination to 'penetrate the recesses of Caledonia, and at last, by continuous battles, discover the end of Britain'.[98] Tacitus is careful here to speak of the army's motivation rather than of the intentions of Agricola, thus alluding back to his earlier point that 'the valour of the army and the Glory of the name of Rome' simply did not permit the consular legate any other course of action than further war, whatever his mandate might demand of him. We need not doubt the high spirits of the soldiers. Yet we must suppose that over the winter of 83–84 Agricola came to understand, through correspondents in Rome, how controversial had been the events of the preceding months. Perhaps to some degree he took heart from Domitian's failure so far to be persuaded of the need to indict him. He must nevertheless have come to suspect that his career, so carefully tended by Vespasian and Titus, was now entering a difficult phase. His days as governing legate in Britannia might now be numbered. Such a prospect can only have stiffened his resolve to secure the kind of victory that would help to diffuse the criticism and earn him the glory that his ambition had long sought. He could not now afford to let this opportunity slip through his fingers in the indefinite time that was left to him before his inevitable recall to Italy.

The summer of 84 began on a difficult personal note for Agricola with the death of his infant son.[99] The boy must have been born in Britannia. It was the second time that he and Domitia, who must clearly have accompanied her husband to his appointments in Asia and Britannia, had suffered this particular trauma. The legate was hardly a stranger to private tragedy: his father had been executed, and his mother murdered by marauders. Now he threw himself into his work, the Caledonian war serving, Tacitus reports, as 'one means he used to distract his mind from its sorrow'.[100] After several difficult months enduring the frustration of unfinished business in the Caledonian zone, personal attacks in the Senate, the mutiny of the Usipi, and, now, a father's grief at the death of his only son, Agricola may have taken some heart from the fact that there would seem to have been some sympathy in Rome for his arguments in justification of the Caledonian war. At any rate, the legate had decided over the winter, Tacitus tells us, to reinforce his army with auxiliaries from among 'the strongest Britons whose fidelity had been proven by the long peace'. These soldiers came from southern tribes, and like most Roman auxiliaries they probably consisted of certain noblemen with their household retinues, a more developed institution in southern Britain than in the north. Perhaps here and there they brought with them even larger bands that may have included paid troops.[101] It would be upon auxiliaries that Agricola would come to rely to fight the battle of Mons Graupius that summer. This was common Roman military practice in that period,[102] and the decision to reinforce his auxiliary ranks may have been intended to ensure that no more legionary lives should be lost in this sensitive war. It is not out of the question that, in organising his forces in this way in 84, Agricola was following advice from Rome – perhaps even from Domitian himself – that he should take particular care to protect Roman lives and his own future career. Yet it is difficult not to perceive a certain symbolism in the employment of British auxiliaries to help in securing what was intended to be the final conquest of the island of Britain.

CHAPTER FIVE

Ad Montem Graupium

Where is Mons Graupius?

I t has been fairly observed that, 'of all the questions concerning the Roman
conquest of Scotland, perhaps the most common is the location of Mons
Graupius'.[1] It is also arguably the case that, in this larger scheme of things,
it matters very little. Had Tacitus's *pietas* regarding Agricola been less, or
had the *laudatio* it inspired not survived the Middle Ages, we would now be
utterly ignorant of the fact that the battle of Mons Graupius ever took place. In
that event, the surviving material evidence of Roman occupation in northern
Britain in the Flavian period would not thereby be silenced in its testimony as
regards the nature and length of that occupation. For most scholars of Roman
activity in northern Britain, the long and lively historiographical debate surrounding the location of Mons Graupius can remain a curiosity without a great
deal of importance for the subject. It must be obvious, however, that students
of the battle itself are denied the luxury of indecision on this point. It may be
emphasised in addition that the search for Mons Graupius over the past few
centuries constitutes a fascinating history in its own right, and Maxwell has
shown it to be well worth the kind of detailed research that cannot be entered
into here.[2]

The Grampian mountains and administrative region have appeared on maps
of north-east Scotland in modern times, reflecting the first major retelling of
the events outlined in the *Agricola* by the sixteenth-century Aberdonian scholar
Hector Boece. In locating Mons Graupius among the mountains that became the
Grampians, Boece was not the last student of the battle to wish it to have taken
place close to home. The Lomond Hills in Fife and hills adjacent to Ardoch in
Strathallan, Fendoch in Strathalmond, and Dalginross at the head of Strathearn
are locations south of the river Tay that have each had their champion among

the antiquaries of Scotland. Further north than these, such locations as Stormont, Fortingall, Oathlaw in Strathmore, and various places in Kincardineshire were also advanced. In the twentieth century, the ongoing search for the battlefield saw the emergence of three main approaches to the evidence, each of which has tended to produce different rival candidates for consideration.

EVIDENCE FROM TACITUS

One such approach has been to privilege the evidence of Tacitus's narrative and the clues to the battle's location that are perceived to lie ensconced within the text of the *Agricola*. These are few and far between, however, and are open to a great deal of interpretation, such that the text is by no means capable of offering decisive evidence. 'Having sent on the *classis*', says Tacitus, 'that, by plunderings in many places, it might cause great and uncertain alarm, he [Agricola] advanced, the army marching light… as far as *Mons Graupius* (*ad montem Graupium*) which the enemy had already occupied'.[3] There is next to nothing here that is of much use in locating the battlefield. Moreover, the extent to which we may trust the narrative of Tacitus down to the minutiae of the invented speeches he placed in the mouths of his two protagonists, with their emphasis upon the notion that Agricola's victory brought nothing less than the final conquest of every last part of Britain, is open to question.

For any search for the battlefield, points worthy of note do emerge from Tacitus's prose, some of which we have already encountered and considered. It is important, for example, that the Britons had already occupied Mons Graupius, and that Agricola and his army approached them *expeditus* – marching light in the interests of haste. The impression is thus created that Agricola had received reports that the enemy was within striking distance of a quick advance – perhaps a forced march – and that the legate, sensing an unusual opportunity, rushed to take advantage of it. It has been presumed that Calgacos and his allies gathered at Mons Graupius for the express purpose of lying in wait there for the Romans – not unlike the Scottish army at Bannockburn. Tacitus's description does not require this to be so.[4] Indeed, the text may imply that Agricola and his army, by marching light and more quickly than usual, managed to catch the native host at or near a hosting place that may have been of less strategic importance and tactical advantage than is usually supposed. In the speech placed in his mouth by Tacitus in the moments before the battle of Mons Graupius commences, the legate suggests that he and his army had thus far been frustrated by the reluctance of the natives to meet them in a pitched battle. 'At last,' he proclaims, 'you have them, not because they have stood still, but because they have been caught out (*deprehensi sunt*)'.[5] These words are a good fit with the proposed scenario.

Tacitus was obviously given to know that native meetings were taking place in which Calgacos and his fellow conspirators against the Romans confirmed their solidarity with 'sacred rites'. It may be concluded that Agricola was particularly interested in keeping such gatherings of native strength under surveillance. Those who were expected to attend them are likely to have been much the same people – the kindreds of the tribe – who were expected to respond to a call to arms. It is to be expected that the process of assembling a number of tribal levies from across the Caledonian zone was a protracted one, affording Agricola considerable time to hear news of it from informants.[6] Neither the traditional concept of 'the folly of the native Caledonians' for having 'massed their forces for a pitched battle instead of dispersing their effort in guerrilla warfare',[7] nor the more recent and sympathetic idea that the Britons were driven to fight a pitched battle out of desperation and vengefulness occasioned by a summer of Roman terrorism,[8] would be safe if such an alternative interpretation of the evidence were accepted. It is possible instead that Agricola simply succeeded in turning the tables on his impressive adversary, and that this time it was the Caledonian leader, rather than the Roman legate, who found himself outmanoeuvred by his enemy. The likelihood has been questioned that a Roman commander can have managed to achieve such a triumph of manoeuvre against a native leader who ought to have known the country far better,[9] but if we may imagine that Agricola can have furnished himself with native guides, we have no particular reason to expect him to have been in any way disadvantaged on this point. This is particularly true, as we shall see if one accepts the general location of Mons Graupius put forward below.

In contemplating the various rival candidates for Mons Graupius, it has been regarded as the 'most important' point that 'the general arguments for a more northerly location for the battle still stand: Perthshire is much too far south'. Much has been made of 'the implication of Tacitus' narrative that a northern location is likely',[10] but it is by no means clear from what Tacitus says that Mons Graupius is not to be found in Perthshire. This is surely borne out by the fact that, without the benefit of the archaeological discoveries of later generations, several antiquaries relying in the main upon the *Agricola*, for all their other methodological flaws and foibles, had no difficulty in locating the battle south of the Tay. It is true that Tacitus, in a casual aside, maintains that, after the battle, 'summer being spent, war was not possible' (*exacta iam aestate spargi bellum nequibat*),[11] but the value of this statement as regards the location of the battle, and even when it was fought, is questionable. Its effect is to portray Agricola's great victory as the final culmination of his governorship, and to make it the climax of Tacitus's narrative. Weeks or months of relatively uneventful and anti-climactic subsequent campaigning and mopping-up is exactly the kind of thing that one would expect Tacitus to gloss over at this stage of the *Agricola*.[12] Indeed, it has been observed that 'several fairly time-consuming activities are fitted into this post-battle period' by Tacitus,[13] a matter to which we shall return. Such operations conducted in the wake of the decisive victory at Mons Graupius might easily smack of needlessly 'protracting war' in northern Britain to uncharitable ears, and we have already seen that Tacitus was particularly keen to undermine such a view of Agricola in his *laudatio*. Moreover, both Hanson and Maxwell have thought it not unlikely that additional Flavian campaigning and skirmishing took place in the wake of Agricola's return to Rome.[14] In that event Tacitus might also be regarded as offering an excuse here as to why, despite the alleged decisive success of the battle of Mons Graupius, northern Britain in later Flavian times had required ongoing attention.

In contrast to the idea that the battle of Mons Graupius took place late in the campaigning season, Tacitus tells us that Agricola's son died 'at the beginning of the summer' (*initio aestatis*), and so probably in May 84.[15] He then says that the legate subsequently threw himself into the business of making war, and that the army marched light and in haste (*expeditus*) to Mons Graupius, seemingly with no significant prior encounter.[16] On the basis of such information, as Hind has argued, 'we should conclude that the campaign of the seventh year [leading to the battle of Mons Graupius]... was a short one'.[17] In principle, when faced with the kind of challenge represented by the effective Caledonian counterstrikes of the previous summer, Roman generals 'seized the initiative and took the offensive as soon as possible', seeking to reassure nervous or wavering allies and 'to demonstrate that they were dictating the course of the war and would eventually win'.[18] Agricola had himself exhibited an appreciation of such standard practice when he struck out against the Ordouices immediately he had arrived in Britannia as legate. It would be surprising if he failed to adhere to it now and delayed his return to the Caledonian zone until late summer. Accordingly, as Hanson has put it, in the *Agricola*, the 'seventh and final campaign follows almost as though the winter had not intervened'.[19] The suggestion in the text that the battle of Mons Graupius arose from a disruption by Agricola of a native hosting further increases the likelihood that it was fought relatively early in the summer.

As regards the location of Mons Graupius, the implication of Tacitus is that it was no great distance from the Roman army's winter quarters: close enough for the legate to contemplate commiting men to action despite their being necessarily under-supplied. This is a typical problem taken on board by generals engaged in the kind of rapid response to a developing crisis that we have envisioned.[20] As Maxwell has observed, 'it is improbable that Agricola would have ventured into enemy territory in such conditions had it not been possible to extricate his army within a reasonably short period'.[21] Against these suggestions of a sudden and sharp strike launched soon after the death of his son, Tacitus observes that Agricola, 'leading the infantry and cavalry by a slow march (*lento itinere*) so as to overawe the new peoples by the deliberateness of his progress, brought them into winter quarters' at the end of the campaigning season, presumably in August.[22] The sense of urgency and haste that Tacitus creates at the beginning of his description gives us reason to believe that a great deal more time elapsed between the battle, which is likely to have been fought early in the summer, and this ostentatious withdrawal at the summer's end than Tacitus suggests at the end of his description.

EVIDENCE FROM TACITUS AND ARCHAEOLOGY

A second approach to locating Mons Graupius has been to privilege the physical evidence left behind by Agricola's forces in northern Britain, notably the *clavicular* temporary camps, in the expectation that archaeology will enable us to trace the legate's movements in the summer of 84. Richmond's was the first major study to be able to make use of the evidence furnished by aerial photography, which by then had located a number of previously unknown clavicular and other Roman temporary camps in north-east Scotland. Their distribution established, as we have already explored in the context of the summer of 83, 'the important fact that Agricola's operations extended not merely to Kincardineshire but to Banffshire'.[23] Richmond also regarded it as a matter of fact, extending from the idea of a battle fought late in the summer, 'that the culminating battle of *Mons Graupius* must have been fought much nearer Moray than was once thought possible',[24] for certainly few antiquarian students of the battle had contemplated the possibility that it was fought north of the 'Grampian' mountains. Work in this vein by several notable archaeologists ushered in the present situation in which a handful of rival candidates for the battlefield in the north or north-east of Scotland have been put forward, in each case in association with a nearby Roman marching-camp.

As the antiquarian students of the battle had been well aware, it is observed in the *Agricola* that the Roman legions kept in reserve at Mons Graupius were 'drawn up before the rampart' (*pro vallo*) of such a camp.[25] Of the different sites that have been identified as that camp, the 40 hectare example at Raedykes north-west of Stonehaven has attracted the sustained attention of generations of students since it was pronounced in the second half of the eighteenth century that 'there is not the least room to doubt of this place's being the spot whereon the battle was fought'.[26] The days of such certainty in the search for the battlefield are long past. The circumstantial case in favour of locating the battle here because of the size of the Raedykes camp and its obvious strategic significance at the 'bottleneck' of coastal routeways linking Angus with Aberdeenshire has recently been reviewed by Hanson and again by Maxwell, with the key point being that 'the surrounding hills lack distinction' as compared to that upon which the camp itself was made.[27] The visitor to the site forms the impression that it was chosen by its surveyors for its serviceable view down the Cowie Water to Stonehaven Bay, and there is little about the location to suggest its having been the staging point of an assault upon an assembled native force.

Such problems leave considerable room for doubt that the battle of Mons Graupius can have taken place at Raedykes, and it is not surprising how rapidly this site has become eclipsed since the late 1970s by the more northerly 58 hectare temporary camp at Logie Durno in Aberdeenshire. The camp was discovered through aerial reconnaissance in 1975 and put forward by that technique's most important pioneer, Kenneth St Joseph, to identify as Mons Graupius the picturesque hill of Bennachie to the south of the encampment.[28] Although this 'formidably persuasive' identification has enjoyed widespread acceptance and a measure of general currency besides,[29] Hanson has closely scrutinised the case and put forward strong arguments against it. On typological grounds, Durno and the series of large temporary camps north of the Mounth to which it belongs as the largest example, representing a 'unique concentration of military force' in relation to these other campsites,[30] have been thought to have the look of third-century, and not Flavian, construction. It has already been noted, however, that an individual camp is normally very difficult to date through archaeological excavation. Investigations of this kind at the example from this series of campsites at Ythan Wells, underlain by a clavicular camp, revealed stratigraphy that supports the conclusion that the series were left behind by the Severan army in the third century, but a series of radiocarbon dates at the Kintore example has established a Flavian horizon.[31] St Joseph called attention to the point that, as regards the large Roman temporary camps in northern Britain, 'the remarkable uniformity in size' of the two main series of them 'demonstrates how close a relationship existed between the composition of a Roman expeditionary force and the area of its camps'.[32] In so doing, he unwittingly imperilled his own argument, for, as Hanson has shown, the enclosure at Durno enclosed an area some fifteen per cent greater than Agricola's army would have required at Mons Graupius on the most generous estimates.[33] To these objections may be added the additional problem of Bennachie's distance from the Forth, which is surely excessive from the standpoint of the narrative of the *Agricola* as outlined above. It is also problematic from the standpoint of other evidence, as we are about to see. If the dating evidence at Kintore establishes this series of camps as Flavian, rather than Severan, constructions, the fact that they appear to be too large to have been practical for Agricola's army before the battle of Mons Graupius is an important point to which we shall again return later in this study.

EVIDENCE FROM TEXTS, ARCHAEOLOGY AND LANGUAGE

Neither of the predominant methodological approaches to the evidence so far considered has ever located the battle of Mons Graupius at a hill of that name, or even approximating it. A third approach has been to privilege the onomastic evidence of two key place-names contained in our sources, so that, for example, Scottish hills with names that might seem to contain variations of the word *Graupius* might be considered to be potential sites of the battle. Of these, Duncrub on the western outskirts of Dunning in Strathearn was first linked with Mons Graupius by William Watson, who noticed that, as Kenneth Jackson later put it, in rendering spoken Gallic and British words into written form, 'the Romans often confused Celtic *c* and *g*... for some reason, rather unclear'.[34] Watson therefore proposed that Tacitus's *Graup-* could stand for an actual **Craup-*. He argued that this word underlies the specific element

-*crub* in Duncrub, but did not regard this as decisive evidence to overturn the general belief at the time that the battle of Mons Graupius was fought at Raedykes.[35]

Half a century later, to the east of Dunning, the archaeologist Richard Feachem established the presence of a Roman temporary camp, a section of the northern rampart of which, more than 100m in length and 3m in width, remains upstanding in Kincladie Wood to a height of some 60cm. Subsequent aerial reconnaissance by St Joseph revealed that this rampart pertained to a 47 hectare clavicular camp.[36] The Flavian date of this camp has been deduced on the basis of typology with the 46 hectare camp further down the river Earn at Abernethy, where excavation by St Joseph recovered a small sherd of Flavian pottery near the bottom of the foundation trench.[37] Dunning has yet to produce similar evidence of its own of a Flavian foundation, but it continues to be considered 'highly unlikely' that the temporary camps here and at Abernethy are not contemporary, since the recovery of pottery of second-century date from the western entrance of Dunning was from a context that would be consistent with re-use of the site several decades later.[38] There is firm archaeological evidence of such re-use of Roman camps elsewhere in Scotland.[39]

Such a coincidence of a Flavian temporary camp and a place-name related to Mons Graupius is a striking one. It cannot but vault Dunning to the head of the list of potential environs in which to place the battle. This becomes the more necessary when we recognise that neither the narrative of Tacitus nor the current body of archaeological and topographical evidence can provide decisive evidence that Mons Graupius lay in the north or north-east of Scotland. The mistaken view that the battle cannot have been fought south of the Tay has resulted in a protracted exercise in special pleading of various kinds surrounding a second important place-name: that of *Victoria* ('Victory'), named in the Flavian survey. Ptolemy provides lists of *poleis* in the territories of various tribes that are almost certainly to be understood for the most part as the names of Roman strongholds. The names listed in the territory of the Dumnonii seem to demarcate an itinerary passing northwards through Dumnonia [see Map 2]. We have already seen that one of these sites, Alauna, is beyond doubt to be identified as the fort of Ardoch in Strathallan. The next site in the list is called *Lindum*, a name that should relate to a lake or pool, and accordingly the next Roman fort north of Ardoch along the Roman road to the Tay lay at Strageath below Muthill, where the road reached a crossing of the river Earn.[40] From this point the road mounted the Gask Ridge and travelled eastwards along its crest as far as Cairnie Wood (and perhaps further) before descending to the Tay and reaching it either at the Roman fort at Inveralmond opposite Scone, or at *horrea Classis*, the storehouses of the fleet, somewhere on the Firth of Tay at or near Perth.[41] It is here between *Lindum* and the Tay that the Flavian survey placed *Victoria*, with its connotations of marking the site of a major victory.[42] Although Ptolemy understood this to have been the name of a *polis* or settlement, it is possible that he misunderstood the nature of this word written on the map of Marinus of Tyre. There is room for debate in pinpointing the locations of *Lindum* and the Roman naval base on the Tay, but it is beyond doubt that *Victoria* related to a location south of the Tay in Dumnonian territory, and most probable by far a location in Strathearn within sight of Duncrub.

The coalescence of this third stream of evidence with those already mentioned, involving the camp at Dunning and nearby Duncrub, surely locates beyond reasonable doubt the environs within which Mons Graupius must lie.[43] It has been shown that Watson's attempt to take his linguistic argument relating to Duncrub a step further, suggesting a possible meaning for *-crub*, is to be rejected on philological grounds. It cannot follow that 'there is, then, no philological evidence to associate Mons Graupius with Duncrub'.[44] In fact, Watson's primary observation, endorsed fifty years later by Jackson, that '*Craupius* would yield *Crup* in O[ld] Welsh' remains in force, whatever the word might be taken to mean, and despite our inability readily to supply a meaning for it.[45] Historical linguistics of this kind can appear to be arcane (or even sleight of hand) to those unversed in philology. It will be worthwhile to review the case in detail. To begin with, it is to be recognised that Tacitus's *Mons Graupius* represents the latinised form of a native place-name that the Romans will have heard spoken. They had not seen it written – hence our ability to suppose that the word spelled as *Graup-* by Tacitus actually represents a mishearing or mis-rendering of **Craup-*. The name *Mons Graupius* represents, moreover, an assumption on the part of scholars that Tacitus's single reference to the place in the phrase *ad montem Graupium* renders the word *Graupius* in the accusative case, making it into an adjective – 'Graup-ish mountain'. As inflected languages, Latin and the Celtic languages altered the endings of words, like *-ium*, to indicate their function in the sentence. It has been recognised, however, that, given the rules of inflection in Latin, 'notionally it [*Graupium*] could be the genitive plural of a tribal name' rather than the accusative singular that is generally assumed.[46] In that case *Mons Graupium* would be the correct form – 'mountain of (people called) the *Graupes*' – rather than *Mons Graupius*.[47] This is a possibility to which we shall return.

In the centuries following the battle, the Celtic language of the northern tribesmen who fought there began to undergo changes, as languages will over time. The nature of these changes seem, where they can be detected on very slim evidence, to have been largely in line with better-attested changes experienced throughout the whole of the Brittonic-speaking zone that would ultimately give rise to the Welsh and Cornish languages. Seemingly the earliest of these changes of direct interest to us was a shift in how the diphthong *-au-* was pronounced and spelled. If the native word was **Craupios* (matching *Graupius*) and followed this pattern, over time it will have become **Creupios*, the *-i-* having affected the quality of the preceding diphthong.[48] Such 'i-affection' may be exemplified by the pronunciation of the English word 'women', in which the -o- has been 'i-affect-ed', producing the pronunciation 'wimmin'. This new word *Creupios* cannot, however, have further developed into the -crub of Duncrub. On the other hand, the genitive plural of a tribal name *Craupes* would have been *Craupon* (match-ing the alternative *Graupium*), containing no -i-, and would have avoided such i-affection, becoming *Cropon* instead. Next, the linguistic phenomenon known as 'lenition', in which consonants within and at the ends of words become sof-tened in particular ways (eg. the English word 'butter', pronounced 'budder' in North American English), ought to have seen *Cropon* change in pronunciation to *crobon*.[49] Eventually, but still before the early Christian period, the inflected ending forming the last syllable of this word, -on, will have been dropped, as took place in all the Celtic languages (called 'apocope'), such that *Cropon* will have become *Crop*, and finally *Crup* (pronounced *crub*).[50]

It was for this reason, with the corrective point (which he did not make) that *Mons Graupium* must be regarded as the correct form of Tacitus's place-name rather than *Mons Graupius*, that Watson noted that *Mons Graupius* 'is formally identical with *Dorsum Crup*', a place mentioned in the medieval *Chronicle of the Kings of Alba* as the site of a major battle in about 965.[51] Skene described this encounter as 'a battle fought at Drumcrub, in Stratherne', thus attracting Watson's attention to Duncrub, the earliest attested form of which name is *Drumcroube*.[52] As Skene seems to have recognised, however, whereas Gaelic *druim*, a 'spine' (Latin *dorsum*), quite accurately describes the situation of Duncrub on a ridge above the Duncrub burn, Gaelic *dún*, a fortified hill settlement, is more problematic. It may therefore be proposed that in 965 *Druim Crup* referred to the ridge above Dunning upon which Duncrub now stands, and that the latter name represents a subsequent change from *Drumcroube* to *Duncrub*. Such toponymic shifts are very common. There is every likelihood of an associa-tion between this feature and *Mons Graupium*. The place-names are not identical, and the fact that, as Keppie put it, Duncrub 'is rather an insignificant pimple', seems fairly decisive against the possibility that its ridge represents Mons Graupium.[53] But can we locate the latter with the help of Duncrub? One possibility is to follow Ian Smith, who in a self-published pamphlet looked south-west of Dunning and identi-fied Craig Rossie as Mons Graupium.[54] There is another candidate, however, which edges ahead of Craig Rossie as a result of further place-name evidence.

In the early medieval period the Pictish equivalent of Latin *mons* was *monid*, as in Monid Carno, an unidentified eighth-century Pictish stronghold named in a contemporary record made at the monastery of Iona.[55] We would therefore expect that, by the early Christian period, the Pictish name for Mons Graupium would have been something very like *Monid Crop* or *Monid Crup*. We have very few Pictish place-names attested in the Pictish period itself. It happens that we do have an attested place-name from eighth-century Pictland which we must now consider. In 728, according to another contemporary record from Iona, a Pictish king called Elpin was attacked and defeated in battle at a place called Monid

Croib.[56] It is clear that the Gaelic source in which this name was preserved under-stood it to mean 'mountain of the tree' (cróibe) or 'trees' (croeb), but the Gaelic word cróeb has no Brittonic cognate. It may therefore be thought that Gaelic observers at the time, encountering this place-name in its original Pictish form, substituted their familiar word for a 'tree' for a similar but unfamiliar Pictish word. Was this word Crop/Crup? The identity of Monid Croib is almost certain: Moncrieffe Hill. This hill forms the eastern terminus of the Gask Ridge that rises above the north bank of the lower river Earn. The Roman road from Lindum to Victoria ran along the crest of this ridge through what is now Cairnie Wood, opposite which, some 3km to the south, lie Duncrub and the Roman clavicular camp at Dunning. The camp is oriented to 'face' the Cairnie Braes, as this part of the ridge is now known, its two claviculae running parallel to it [see Map 3].[57] If Duncrub was the site of a lower ridge pertaining to a people called *Craupes as we have suggested, it is reasonable that the Gask Ridge can have been a mons named for this same community. In Pictish usage monid could indicate a mountain like Craig Rossie, but it could also indicate more generally an upland pasture of much more modest height. It is interesting that in early Ireland tribes would seem to have been envi-sioned as pertaining to a particular territory under cultivation with its associated mountain or forest.[58] It therefore involves no great leap of faith to suppose that Monid Croib, Moncrieffe, is a gaelicised place-name masking a Pictish place-name *Monid Crop or *Monid Crup, which had once been attached to the whole Gask Ridge rather than merely to its eastern end.[59]

TESTING THE CANDIDACY OF THE CAIRNIE BRAES

Unless and until the foregoing argument may become accepted, we ought to return to the more familiar Mons Graupius in reference to the battle site. The proposition that this feature was the Gask Ridge fits comfortably alongside much of what we know or can deduce about the battle. Certainly it lies far enough to the south to be within reasonable striking distance of Agricola's lightly-supplied troops. It was particularly accessible from the lands watered by the Tay and the Earn and their tributaries, which can have carried Caledonian war-canoes down from Atholl and Breadalbane as far as the foot of Moncrieffe Hill below modern Perth. In the first century the Gask Ridge may be thought to have lain at or near the frontier between Dumnonian and Ueniconian territory, which recalls Maxwell's reasonable suggestion that Mons Graupius ought to have 'lain on or near a frontier between two tribal areas'.[60] Whether one accepts the common view that the Caledonian peoples drew up at Mons Graupius in anticipation of it lying on Agricola's presumptive route, or else the view expressed here that Agricola, perhaps employing the forced march, was engaged rather in oppor-tunistically assaulting a great native hosting, for logistical reasons relating to supply there is every reason to expect the battle to have taken place at or near 'a suitable and well known assembly point'.[61] The latter argument gains a degree of strength, at least in terms of the likelihood that Agricola can have outmanoeuvred Calgacos at this point, from the suggestion that the Caledonian leaders ventured to convene their large multi-tribal hosting on the Dumnonian frontier, within sight of the remains of Agricola's Dumnonian forts, and within striking distance of Roman targets further south. Moncrieffe Hill at the eastern end of the Gask Ridge must be thought very likely to have been a traditional place of assembly as early as the Neolithic epoch, during which its lower slopes were home to a henge.[62] Just beyond the Tay to the north of the hill is Scone, the royal inauguration site of the kings of Alba, which is presumed to have served the same traditional function for at least the later Pictish kings before them. It was also named in the twelfth century as the place of assembly for Gowrie. Just beyond the Earn to the south of Moncrieffe Hill lies Kintillo near Bridge of Earn, in the twelfth century named as the place of assembly for Strathearn,[63] to the east of which is Abernethy, which in the early eighth century was probably the principal church of southern Pictland. It is with good reason, then, that the stronghold of Monid Croib is thought to have been a principal royal centre – a 'capital' of sorts – in southern Pictland, upon a hill that had probably been a focus of ritual activity and tribal assembly for centuries prior to the events of 84, and for centuries to come. As such, the neighbourhood surrounding Moncrieffe Hill ought to have been well served by native route-ways, and these will have facilitated the kind of hosting which Calgacos organised before the battle of Mons Graupius.

From points on the Gask Ridge British observers can have had views not just of Schiehallion away in the distance, the sacred hill of the Calidonii, but also of the Tay and Earn valleys. Having learned of their movements, they will have been able to watch for Roman soldiers marching into Strathearn from the direction of Strathallan and the fort sites of Ardoch and Strageath towards the Tay and the fort site of Inveralmond.[64] It has been suggested above that the Dumnonii had become allies of the Romans in the summer of 80 and that this alliance had been instrumental in forcing Agricola's hand in the summer of 83, resulting in a controversial Roman incursion into north-east Scotland. We have also seen, however, that it is not impossible that the decisive battle of the war can have been fought on the margins of Dumnonian territory. Much depends upon the fate of the Perthshire forts after the events of the previous summer, and whether the Dumnonii of Strathearn, who are suggested here to have been a community called 'Craupes, remained steadfast in alliance with Rome or threw in their lot with Calgacos.

The linguistic evidence linking Duncrub and perhaps Moncreiffe Hill to Mons Graupius, and the evidence that *Victoria* denoted a location along the Gask Ridge road between Strageath and the Tay, enables us to assemble a circumstantial case for Dunning and the Cairnie Braes that surpasses easily that pertaining to either Raedykes or Durno-Bennachie, the other main candidates for the battlefield. Neither of these latter sites can boast a shred of linguistic or onomastic evidence to bolster their candidacy. Neither includes a Roman temporary camp that is as securely dated to the Flavian period, and as appropriate in its dimensions, as the Dunning encampment. This is not to say that their candidacy, nor indeed that of Craig Rossie south-west of Dunning, must be rejected outright. These must rather follow some distance behind Dunning and the Cairnie Braes in the running to secure our confidence. Moreover, it has been argued here, as Hind demonstrated some twenty years ago, that in several key respects the latter location is a more comfortable fit alongside the testimony of the *Agricola* than at least its more northerly rivals. In considering such textual evidence we cannot disregard the implications of the Roman place-name *Victoria*. We are unlikely ever to uncover conclusive proof that the battle of Mons Graupius was fought at one place rather than at another.[65] It is left to us only to weigh the balance of probabilities arising from our different categories of evidence. The devil, as usual, is in the detail, and in particular for the present identification in the position of the river Earn lying between the Gask Ridge and the Flavian temporary camp at Dunning. This is a matter to which we shall return in considering the details of the battle as described by Tacitus. One finds a degree of comfort in Hanson's view that only a reading of the *Agricola* that he would characterise as 'too close and literal' would enable the spectre of a comparable omission to single-handedly disallow the candidacy of Bennachie as Mons Graupius. It is to be acknowledged nevertheless that the candidacy of the Gask Ridge, however strong in other respects, is vulnerable on the matter of the river Earn.[66] It has been observed that 'so far none of the various identifications [of Mons Graupius] put forward are conclusive, for the supporting evidence in each case is deficient in some respect'.[67] If this would seem to hold true for the Gask Ridge, it remains nonetheless the likeliest of the identifications that have so far been put forward.

CHAPTER SIX

Striking Terror

Prelude to Battle

I
t is commonly argued in undergraduate tutorials that tribal Celtic peoples,
faced with Roman expansion (or indeed those in later centuries who faced
similar challenges), ought to have recognised such threats for what they were,
overcome their petty differences and combined their efforts to resist in the interests of defending their common way of life. Tacitus himself observed about the
Britons that 'the greatest advantage for us over such powerful peoples is that they
do not take common counsel' (*in commune non consulunt*).[1] Yet it may well have
been because the Caledonian peoples were showing signs of doing precisely this
in the summer of 83, 'arming even their young men, putting their wives and children in places of safety, and ratifying a conspiracy (*conspiratio*) of tribes (*civitates*)
with assemblies and sacred rites',[2] that Agricola and his officers, despite their various troubles in the previous year, were able to look upon the campaigning season
in 84 with eagerness. What the legate needed desperately that year was a decisive
victory over the Caledonian Britons against whom his prior efforts had brought
him. In that way he might silence his critics in the Senate – those 'cowards in the
council' mentioned by Tacitus. He might also discourage unrest and the wavering
of alliances further south among the peoples he had recently subdued. Inevitably,
we must therefore suspect that Agricola, in order to achieve such ends, will have
tended to exaggerate the significance of the battle of Mons Graupius and the
size of the coalition ranged against him in his dispatches to Domitian and his
later reminiscences – Keegan's 'Bullfrog Effect' – probably more through over-
interpretation and wishful thinking than through egregious fraud.

The characteristic lack of collegial action among the Caledonian peoples
and their tendencies towards skirmishing rather than pitched battle had so far
proven a major obstacle to the possibility of such an engagement.[3] The war was

controversial. Indecisive results and casualties were turning the screws upon Agricola. All the same, the fallout from his campaigning of the summer of 83 had not been entirely discouraging. A coalition was now crystallising under the troublesome Calgacos. The men of the *classis Britannica* had successfully stormed and reconnoitred some of the furthest-flung coastal areas north of the Forth, and Tacitus, here perhaps echoing the claims of an Agricolan dispatch, reports that they had demoralised the natives and created among them a sense of being surrounded by the Romans.[4] We have no way of substantiating this claim or assessing the psychological effects of this strategy. It may have been as effective as Tacitus claims; perhaps that explains why more of the same was planned for the summer of 84. The primary aim of the war-galleys was unchanged: spreading further terror and misery along the coastline of the Caledonian zone and compelling its tribal leaders either to surrender and sue for peace, or else to band together with Calgacos and provide Agricola with the decisive encounter he craved. It has been argued above that it was probably relatively early in the summer that the legate got wind of just such a native hosting and that this was taking place on the lower river Tay, at or near Moncrieffe Hill. Perhaps he owed this information to his fleet, for the Tay is navigable as far as modern Perth below Moncrieffe.[5] It seems to have been the norm in medieval Wales for musterings to be heralded by the sounding of horns.[6] If this were true of first-century northern Britain one may readily appreciate how Roman informants can have become alerted.

Seizing the initiative and swiftly gathering his troops from their winter quarters without making adequate provision for them (*expeditus*), Agricola drove into Dumnonian territory. Caught out, it seems, Calgacos gathered his available strength and moved to Mons Graupius to await his enemy. It has been argued above that his destination is more likely to have been the Cairnie Braes on the Gask Ridge than any of the other candidates put forward to date. We shall proceed on this basis as we explore the events of the battle itself. If one prefers the idea that Calgacos and his allies were not caught out, but came to Mons Graupius and remained there for some time, lying in wait for the Romans, we have seen that they can have been encouraged to do so by their leader's successes of the previous summer, whether or not Roman strategic raiding had been as effective as Tacitus claims. We have also seen that the Caledonian peoples are unlikely to have believed that a war could be regarded as won until they had proven it in massed battle. Whether or not it was intended by Calgacos that battle should take place there, the identification of Mons Graupius as the Gask Ridge would tend to give this hosting a pronounced air of defiance – even foolhardiness – for having been convened on the fringe of Dumnonian territory. Perhaps the native leaders wished to demonstrate to Roman and native alike that they had been anything but cowed or intimidated by the previous year's events. Indeed, it may have been their bravado and their indignation, rather than desperation, which sealed the fate of Calgacos and his allies at the battle of Mons Graupius. In that event, this famous engagement may well have been, at its heart, as much a clash between the political aims, and the fragile and beleaguered reputations, of similar men on either side as a clash between two irreconcilable ways of life.

MAKING CAMP

On or before the day before the battle, Agricola and his army came marching into view from the slopes of Mons Graupius. The column of soldiers marching down Strathearn from the direction of Ardoch and Strageath may have been as much as 15km in length. It ought to have been led by a vanguard consisting of several cohorts of auxiliary infantry and cavalry, and flanked to every side by mounted *exploratores*, some of which scouts may well have been Caledonian-born.[7] In the proposed context, the vanguard will have come to a halt at the site of the Dunning temporary camp, some 3km from the enemy occupying the slopes of the Cairnie Braes. Having chosen this site, the surveyors will have completed marking out the plan for that camp by the time the main body of troops had come up from behind. The many examples of Roman armies encamping at a distance of about 3km from an enemy position suggests that this was something of a routine practice.[8] It is pleasing that the proposed context would seem to reflect this. It may be noted that a rather different approach would have to be contemplated in order to allow Craig Rossie to be Mons Graupius, since a line of march down Strathearn to Dunning, past an occupied Craig Rossie, would have left the right flank of Agricola's forces unacceptably exposed to a British onslaught from the slopes above.

In the meantime, Agricola himself, with his personal guards and his staff officers, ought to have arrived at the new campsite at the head of the main body of his remaining cavalry, followed by the legionary legates and the prefects of the *auxilia*. As the legionary and remaining auxiliary infantry arrived behind him, moving perhaps six abreast, cohort by cohort, legion by legion, followed by a rearguard of more cavalry, Agricola should have given thought to reconnoitring the ground upon which he now expected to fight. Indeed, he probably inspected it himself, though not perhaps exclusively so.[9] Work-parties from the legions now executed the surveyors' plans, cleared the campsite and set about digging the ditch, raising the rampart (part of which still stands in Kincladie Wood), and assembling the camp from its prefabricated components. The rapid and orderly establishment of this temporary city – a microcosm of Roman civilisation – must have been an impressive and provocative sight to behold from the slopes of Mons Graupius.[10]

THE BRITISH POSITION

The quality of the British position must have been obvious to Agricola. It may also have been somewhat familiar. The proposed identification of that position as the Cairnie Braes would tend to arrange Calgacos and his allies roughly between Keirwoodhead above Innerdunning, where the Dunning burn empties into the river Earn, and Bankhead above Forteviot, where the Water of May empties into the Earn. The 47 hectare Flavian temporary camp at Dunning would have been clearly visible from this vantage point. It would seem to have been about here that, twelve-and-a-half centuries later, the Earl of Mar would initially deploy a Scottish army that was to be subsequently outmanoeuvred and decisively defeated on Dupplin Moor above Forteviot by the army of Edward Balliol on 11 August 1332.[11] The proposed British position would therefore seem to have been one that Mar subsequently recognised to be one of strength, and also one where battle could be given. The advantage it provided on that occasion lay in more than the height of the ground, for the river Earn lay as a significant obstacle between Balliol, in his camp at Forteviot, and the Scots above him on the ridge.

There is no mention of such an obstacle, nor of a river crossing, in the battle described by Tacitus. Were we required to regard his account as a complete and meticulous description of the battle, we simply could not accept the proposed identification of the battle site. We are not so required, and shall see that there are at least hints in Tacitus's narrative of the necessary Roman riverine tactics. It is not insignificant, moreover, that, in his own British war forty years before, Aulus Plautius twice encountered the same tactical situation against Caratacos, occupying positions at river crossings, that would face Balliol here at the Earn.[12] A few years later Caratacos would subsequently choose to meet the legate Ostorius at a place in Wales which Tacitus describes as follows:

> The place fixed upon for the struggle was once where approaches, exits, every local feature would be unfavourable to ourselves and advantageous to his own [i.e. Caratacos's] forces. On one side the hills rose sheer; and wherever a point could be reached by a gentle ascent, the way was blocked with stones composing a sort of rampart. Along the front ran a river with a precarious ford, and bands of warriors were in position before the defences.[13]

Caesar too had confronted similar British tactics in his foray into the island a century before this, defeating a native force that had 'advanced to a river with their cavalry and chariots, and tried to bar the way by attacking from a position on higher ground'.[14] There are additional references to pitched battles at fords and river crossings in Welsh poetry of the early Christian period, such as at the battle of *Gwen Ystrat*.[15]

For Calgacos to have taken a position above the north bank of the Earn on the Gask Ridge, making a stand at a river crossing, would in other words have been entirely in keeping with contemporaneous, earlier and later British tactical thinking, such as it was, when facing an invading army. This tends to work further in the proposed site's favour as a plausible Mons Graupius. The river has plainly endlessly changed its meandering course over the passage of the 1,900 years and more since the summer of 84. As was attested in the first *Statistical Account of Scotland*, it 'frequently overflows its banks, and is thereby the occasion of a great damage to the low grounds through which it runs'.[16] That this was also true in the first century is suggested by the place-name *Lindum*, if its identification with the fort at Strageath on the Earn can be accepted. A man who chose to fight a pitched battle along its banks at the proposed location, in other words, was entitled to expect the ground to pose considerable challenges to cavalry. The Earn was fordable in 1332, at one point at least, in the vicinity of Forteviot. In more recent times it was more usual, understandably, to cross the river by way of cobles – flat-bottomed ferry boats – that were maintained more or less where the current Dalreoch and Forteviot bridges now stand.[17] The Earn between these two points cannot have presented more than a trifling obstacle to soldiers who had so recently stormed Anglesey across no less a span of water than the Menai Strait. On that occasion, Agricola had made decisive use of auxiliary troops who 'had swimming experience in their homelands which enables them to take care not only of themselves but of their arms and horses'.[18] One is reminded that Plautius too had won a contested river crossing so wide that he reckoned his legionaries required a bridge, and so relying upon a detachment of auxiliaries 'who were accustomed to swim easily in full armour across the most turbulent streams'.[19] As for Ostorius, according to Tacitus he had been daunted by Caratacos's strong position but gave in to his soldiers, who 'clamoured that no place is impregnable against courage', and, after carefully surveying the ground to assess his enemies vulnerabilities, 'crossed the river without difficulty'.[20] There would therefore seem to be nothing implausible about placing the battle of Mons Graupius in the proposed context, save only in that at first glance it seems a poor fit with Tacitus's narrative.

Tacitus refers to the British host at Mons Graupius as representing 'the combined strength of all their tribes', and numbers it at 'more than thirty thousand armed men', ranging from youths to old men.[21] As a general rule, it is always advisable – no less in the present century than in the first – to greet one-sided reports of the numbers of men involved in any battle with robust scepticism. We have seen that Calgacos and his fellow leaders ought to have been able to summon their kindred-in-arms, and that the Flavian survey suggests that that these co-conspirators included men from as far afield as the Lennox and Buchan (and perhaps beyond). This survey, along with the significance of the Grampians as a frontier in Pictish times and our vigilance for Tacitean hyperbole, discourages us from assuming that Calgacos received decisive levels of support from north of the Mounth. There have long been suspicions that the efforts of Calgacos represent the nascent period of the Caledonian hegemony attested in later Roman sources. Insofar as this theory can have any bearing upon the present discussion, it ought to reinforce our expectations that the war effort mustered against Agricola in the summers of 83 and 84 was largely, but not necessarily entirely, a southern phenomenon.[22]

Leslie Alcock has estimated on measured grounds that the population of the whole of the Caledonian zone will have been on the order of about 27,000 men, women and children in the early Middle Ages, of whom something like 6,000 will normally have been obliged to answer a summons to arms from their individual potentates.[23] Another and more intricate approach to this question, involving calculations of average numbers of persons per medieval parish, would generate a rather more robust number, roughly in the region of 45,000-55,000, the potential practical fighting strength of whom, should one accept for argument's sake Professor Alcock's factor of one fifth of this total, would have been in the region of about 10,000 warriors.[24] It is to be kept in mind that it cannot have been practical to muster every free farmer of a district or kindred for military service, such that musterings organised by individual headmen are likely to have been selective exercises. If Mons Graupius was the Gask Ridge, perhaps only relatively local leaders among the Ueniconian and Dumnonian peoples will have had the freedom to levy something approaching the entire free population of their kindreds and districts. Other tribal leaders of the coalition, having gone beyond the frontiers of their homelands, in some cases over considerable distances, may have been reluctant to muster expeditionary forces that went beyond their own henchmen and kinsmen, with perhaps a selection of other clients. It may be that the 'cross-cutting ties' of kinship, fosterage and clientage within Caledonian tribes, not to mention exchange networks and the practicalities of stock-rearing in close proximity, were sufficient to enable such leaders to pick warriors from among most of the free farmsteaders who would normally be summoned to join a tribal levy.[25] It is to be recalled that Tacitus makes a point of the Calidonii 'arming even their young men', which may be taken as suggestive of the mustering of *fian*-like bands in addition to the adult warriors levied in these different ways.

It would not be surprising, in other words, if the kindreds-in-arms mustered by Calgacos and his Caledonian allies at Mons Graupius, supplemented here and there by larger bodies of levied warriors and *fian*-like bands, represented a sizeable fraction – but still only a fraction – of the total practical fighting strength of the peoples involved in the coalition. For argument's sake, however, one might reasonably suggest that Calgacos did have at his disposal roughly the 10,000 warriors that would have approximated – on the simplistic estimates ventured above – to the combined practical military strength of the Caledonian zone. To judge from the apparent sizes of large composite British coalition armies of the seventh century, such an allowance would not seem unreasonable of itself, especially as there seem to be examples in medieval Wales of universal (more or less) levies in response to full-scale invasion.[26] In order to assemble a host 10,000 strong at Mons Graupius, however, the coalition that gathered around Calgacos would probably have required the support of kindreds-in-arms from outwith the Caledonian zone, such as among the Taixali and the Decantae, or indeed among more southerly or westerly peoples. We have seen that this proposition is not particularly unlikely.

It must be obvious that, as regards the benefit of the doubt, successive acts of generosity, though not undue generosity, are required to allow Calgacos a host even a third of the size of that given to him by Tacitus. Scepticism, then, would seem to be entirely justified. It was not Calgacos, but Tacitus, for whom the notion of total victory at Mons Graupius required all the tribes of the north to have been conquered there *en masse*, who fielded the massive British force at Mons Graupius described in the *Agricola*. This does not prove, however, that there was no large British force, by British standards, at Mons Graupius. The Romans are unlikely to have made particular note of *Victoria* if the engagement had been nothing more than one of a handful of 'insignificant skirmishes' against the northern peoples.[27] We cannot ignore our textual evidence that the battle was a decisive encounter. At the same time we must acknowledge the good grounds for believing that Tacitus, perhaps following Agricola himself, transformed it into something impossibly cataclysmic. Prior scepticism has been fuelled by the fact that Agricola believed he could decisively overcome the host of Calgacos with 11,000 auxiliaries – a decision which (should the foregoing analysis be accepted) would seem to have been entirely reasonable.[28] In fact, it is notable that our analogical estimates of the size of the native force at Mons Graupius produce a number roughly equal to the estimated size of Agricola's auxiliary infantry force.

According to Tacitus, as we have seen, the legate's forces at Mons Graupius consisted of some 13,000-14,000 auxiliary infantry and cavalry all told, and, it is supposed, between 4,000 and 7,000 legionary troops. It is difficult to believe that Calgacos can seriously have expected a force of perhaps 10,000 Caledonian warriors to outfight and overcome a Roman army of such a size. Had he convinced himself, based upon his prior successes, that divine forces were on his side and would see him through to victory? The argument is worth raising again that Agricola and his army, by marching light and in haste, had managed to catch the Caledonian peoples in the middle of a great assembly further downriver that was never intended to lie in wait for the Romans, and may indeed have been a prelude to an invasion of their own. Parallel examples suggest that it is not impossible, in such a scenario, that the gathering natives knew nothing at all about Agricola's advance upon them until the Romans hove into view further up Strathearn.[29] In any event, and for whatever reason, a decision to stand and fight will have been taken, reflecting the likelihood that massed battles were the normal method through which such peoples sought to decide their wars.[30]

THE EVE OF BATTLE

No doubt there was some form of exchange between the legate and Calgacos in which both men resolved to fight – not a foregone conclusion – and win the looming battle. It is to be expected, though Tacitus does not mention it, that both leaders had recourse to augury as part of their preparations for the imminent engagement. The Roman priest known as a *haruspex* sought for omens in the flight patterns of birds, or by the careful inspection of the entrails of an animal put to death for the purpose. Famously, the Romans were fascinated and appalled by eyewitness reports that, for very important matters, the Gallic augur, known as a *vatis*, might seek for omens in the death throes of a human being – particularly a prisoner of war – stabbed to death for that single purpose.[31] We cannot be sure that Caledonian peoples followed this Gallic practice, or indeed in the taking of heads as trophies also attested in Gaul.[32] If they did so, it seems inescapable that the necessary executions and mutilations may have been performed upon Romans or Roman auxiliaries or collaborators taken as hostages in the successful Caledonian actions of the previous summer.

Like Gallic nobles of the previous century, the more powerful Caledonian leaders will have proceeded to the field of battle attended by a personal body-guard of henchmen, if a comparatively small one.[33] They will have been further surrounded by their kindred-in-arms, and in some cases by additional warriors who had come out of an obligation to render military service. *Fían*-like bands are likely to have fought as units unto themselves, distinct from these kindreds-in-arms. According to Roman sources from the late Republican period, the Gallic warrior normally equipped himself with a shield the height of a man, and, being a man of substance, was attended by a shield-bearer, normally a client.[34] According to Tacitus, however, the British forces at Mons Graupius had only small targes (*breves caetrae*; *parva scuta*), and both Pictish sculpture of later times and evidence from medieval Wales support the veracity of this observation.[35] Leaders can therefore have had no practical need of any shield-bearer, though this is no guarantee that no parallel attendants existed, especially as the *daryanogyon* or shield-bearer is attested in medieval Wales.[36] Similarly, although Gallic warriors are described as having worn tall and elaborate helmets, there is no hint of this in Tacitus, nor indeed in Pictish sculpture, where helmets are conspicuous by their absence.[37] Indeed, one of the tablets discovered at Vindolanda on Hadrian's Wall has been interpreted as stating that the typical native British warrior, patronisingly called *Brittunculus* or a 'little Briton', was *nudus*, 'unprotected by armour' or even naked.[38] Whether this was strictly true, or whether armour of a kind was worn but was regarded disparagingly by the Romans, ought perhaps to be left an open question. It seems that in early Christian times northern British warriors commonly protected themselves with a leather cuirass, but it is uncertain whether armour of this kind was as common in the first century. In that event we might even expect tribal headmen like Calgacos to have had access to a mail cuirass.[39]

Like the Gauls, on the other hand, who according to Roman commentators fought with swords as long as spears,[40] the native warriors at Mons Graupius, according to Tacitus, wielded 'huge swords' (*ingentes gladii*; *enormes gladii*) with blunt tips rather than sharpened points. These, according to Tacitus, would prove unwieldy and unequal to the task of swordplay with Roman-equipped soldiers at close quarters.[41] Nothing like such a blade dating from the Iron Age has ever been found in Scotland, where known swords are fairly slender weapons. Pictish sculpture suggests that the early medieval counterparts of Calgacos's Caledonian warriors afoot tended to wield short blades. Perhaps it was an appreciation for the Roman *gladius* that occasioned this later preference for smaller and lighter swords. Much better attested from Iron Age Scotland are the spears that will have been the weapon of choice for the vast majority of the warriors in any northern British tribal army of the first millennium. A *Gododdin* elegy describes the weaponry of a Uotodin host in early Christian times with the following lines: 'crimson their swords, let their blades stay uncleansed; lime-white shields and four-sided spear-points'.[42] Only the foremost warriors of a tribe are likely to have had the means and licence to carry a sword. Roman sources mention Gallic spears 'twisted in their entire length, so that a blow not only cuts, but mangles the flesh, and withdrawal tears the wound open',[43] as well as 'a special kind of javelin' called a *madaris*.[44] The javelin, like the spear, is well attested from Iron Age Scotland, and also later in Pictish sculpture. Tacitus makes it plain that the Caledonian warriors used javelins (*teli*) of some description to great effect at Mons Graupius, but otherwise fails to speak of the spears that surely predominated among Calgacos's men on the day.

The Roman auxiliary infantryman – the legionaries did not fight at Mons Graupius – was usually much more heavily armoured and equipped than these British warriors. Technology must always have influenced the outcomes of clashes between Roman and Briton, though not to the exclusion of others. Agricola's auxiliary soldiers will typically have been protected by a metal cuirass weighing in at some 12-15kg, an iron helmet with protective cheek-, neck- and brow-guards, and a flat oval or oblong shield over a metre long and half as wide, and some 10kg in weight. Although such military accoutrements will not have been uniformly present among Roman auxiliaries, the contrast is quite stark to the almost complete lack of such defensive equipment among their Caledonian enemies at Mons Graupius. Their javelins were not the heavy legionary *pila*, but instead weapons more on a par with the lighter British *teli*, and the spear carried by each soldier is also unlikely to have differed greatly from British examples. A Roman general with ability and well-trained men would not hesitate, in the right conditions, to pit light infantry against such heavily equipped soldiers and expect such skirmishers to be effective. Heavy infantry were, however, a foe quite beyond the scope of a Caledonian kindred-in-arms before the advent of Roman armies.[45]

According to Tacitus, Agricola's auxiliaries wielded swords that paled in comparison to the size and weight of the *enormes gladii* of the enemy, and this was to prove an advantage, and not a detriment, in the fighting of that day. He therefore seems to have envisioned auxiliaries armed with the short, stabbing sword (*gladius*), some 40-50cm in length, carried by legionary soldiers. This is a problem, as auxiliary soldiers tended to carry weaponry typical of their homelands, including swords that, on the whole, were of the longer, thinner sort typical of swords from the Caledonian zone. One solution to this problem would be to posit that Agricola took the highly unorthodox step of arming his auxiliaries with *gladii* for the Caledonian war, training them to fight accordingly. This seems quite unlikely. It is less problematic to conclude that here Tacitus's account becomes confused, effectively transforming the auxiliaries who fought at Mons Graupius into legionary soldiers equipped with *gladii*, thus furnishing his readers with a familiar battle narrative rather than a strictly accurate one.[46] We shall see that elsewhere he seems again to lose track of the fact that the battle of Mons Graupius was not fought by legionaries. These problems are important reminders that Tacitus on his own is not an infallible witness as regards his description of the battle, and that the proposed identification of the battle site need not be unduly compromised by the details of his testimony.

In dogging the movements of the Roman army overland in the previous year, Calgacos may have been emulating the examples of Caratacos and Uenutios. There is no evidence that he developed innovative tactics for effectively over-coming the advantages enjoyed by the Romans in terms of equipment, or that he proved willing or capable of adapting his military experience to face such a foe. Of itself this is insufficient evidence to prove that his skills of generalship were contemptible. The British force gathered at Mons Graupius was a conglom-erate of kindreds-in-arms and, probably, *fian*-like bands, reflecting the societies that produced them. It is certainly to be doubted that these companies possessed the necessary discipline and organisation to execute ingenious or even moder-ately innovative co-ordinated tactical plans, had any been available.[47] The military achievements of the previous summer, if they are to be attributed to him, indicate that Calgacos possessed generalship skill in respectable measure. It seems unlikely that he can have risen to the prominence he enjoyed at the head of the tribal coalition of 84 unless he also possessed considerable skill at manipulating and fortifying mentalities and morale among those who looked to him for leadership. There were practical limits, however, to what his captaincy, however skilled, could achieve in the face of the nature and organisation of his host.

His opposite number at Mons Graupius had considerable experience of warfare in Britain. There can have been few legions anywhere in this period with as much combat experience as those in Britain, so that it may be suggested that the native warriors at Mons Graupius were faced with seasoned veterans whom even their fellow Romans ought to have regarded as some of the sturdiest soldiers anywhere in the empire.[48] Agricola and his officers are likely to have built up an awareness of the tactical options that were and were not open to such men as Calgacos; no doubt they planned their own battle accordingly. The influence of Tacitus once moved scholars to regard his father-in-law as having been a general of significant genius. More recent evaluations of Agricola's generalship have helpfully stripped it of its Tacitean veneer, but it is possible to take such deconstruction too far. He emerges from the evidence as a capable commander. He was well versed in

orthodox military methodology and the mechanisms of Roman military organisation whereby a general's strategic and tactical planning were translated into
action. It is true that episodes of genius are difficult to establish with a great deal of
confidence, but there is considerable room for doubt as to whether there was ever
much call for such genius. Where familiar and mainstream plans of action were
sufficient to secure victory, these must always have been preferable to unneces-
sarily innovative and complex approaches. In other words, like Calgacos, Agricola
may have been more capable a general than circumstances allowed for or required
in his best-evidenced encounters. Moreover, his leadership skills are difficult to
measure once the evidence is shorn of his son-in-law's hyperbole. Perhaps he was
not as moral, self-disciplined and inspirational a figure to his men as he appears
in the *Agricola*. At the least it would seem that his leadership was not a significant
detriment to their mentalities and morale, and it may do him an injustice to
assume that Tacitus's exaggerations of his personal qualities were entirely baseless.
Not all the subjects of glowing eulogies are contemptible people.

THE BRITISH DEPLOYMENT

On the day of the battle, according to Tacitus, the British vanguard took up
a position on the level ground at the foot of Mons Graupius. At present the
amount of such ground lying between the foot of the Cairnie Braes and the
river Earn varies. Rising up the slope of the hill behind the vanguard, which
we might understand to have consisted in the main of *fian*-like bands with their
superior organisation, energy and fighting ability, Calgacos had arranged the
rest of his host, 'for show,' writes Tacitus, 'and in order to strike terror'.[49] Perhaps
it would be unfair to Tacitus if we did not entertain the idea that the success of
this spectacle lies in part behind what has been regarded here as an inaccurate
estimate of the size of the native host. As it stands, the Jesi manuscript describes
Calcagos's men here as *convexus velut insurgerent*, 'rounded as they were rising
up'. Ogilvie suggested the emendation *conexus*, giving a sense of being in close
formation rather than rounded formation.[50] Interestingly however, the Cairnie
Braes form a convex slope, somewhat akin to an amphitheatre, over a distance
of perhaps 3km between Keirwoodhead to the west and Bankhead to the east
[see Map 3]. This too may be regarded as an additional point in favour of the
proposed identification.

Tacitus places native charioteers on the plain (*campus*) between the two hosts.
Campus is an apt word for application to the stretch of land to the south of the
Earn below the Cairnie Braes. These warriors, according to Tacitus, were making a great show of 'noise and rapid movement'.[51] Such a spectacle appears
indeed to have been one of the major functions of the war chariot in a combat
situation. According to Roman sources, Gallic war chariots in the time of the
conquest were drawn by two horses and contained a warrior and his charioteer,

seemingly one of his henchmen,[52] and no doubt one whom he regarded as being particularly reliable. We have only one other account of how war chariots were deployed in Britain, dating from more than a century before the battle of Mons Graupius and relating to observations made at the opposite end of the island. Caesar had been confronted by Britons 'driving all over the field' in chariots, 'hurling javelins' and generally making as great a show of themselves as they could in an attempt to overawe the enemy. Caesar was suitably impressed by these chariot-eers. Knowing that an account of them would be of interest to his readers back home, he noted that 'by daily training and practice they attain such proficiency that, even on a steep incline, they are able to control the horses at full gallop and to check and turn them in a moment; they can also run along the chariot-pole, stand on the yoke, and get back into the chariot as quick as lightning'.[53] Tacitus seems to imply that, at Mons Graupius, British charioteers put on a similar display of razzle and dazzle. In early Christian times, long after the chariot had become obsolete in northern Britain, a *Gododdin* elegy suggests that comparable battle-field ostentation was still being displayed by one Uotodin warrior who 'on the day of conflict would perform a feat on a white stallion'.[54]

The war chariot was clearly as much a psychological weapon as anything else. That being said, Caesar recognised its tactical potential as well. He noted that, once such displays of daring and prowess were over, the warriors left their chariots and fought on foot, their charioteers remaining behind to enable them to move from place to place with the mobility of cavalry, or to disengage more quickly than other footmen.[55] Being portable platforms for the casting of javelins, war chariots no doubt served a particularly useful purpose at the outset of an engage-ment. Perhaps at Mons Graupius the chariot-borne warriors attempted to disrupt the Roman advance from the marching camp by peppering the auxiliaries with javelins. Like Plautius forty years earlier,[56] Agricola dealt with these chariots as his first order of business, ordering them to be engaged and dispersed by his auxil-iary cavalry, probably Gallic and British horsemen, even while his infantry were advancing towards the foot of Mons Graupius. In this the cavalry were successful, thus clearing the way for an unobstructed advance. It would seem, however, that a running engagement of some description ensued, no doubt with exchanges of javelins, whence both the British charioteers and their mounted foes would return to affect the course of the battle to come. The air will have been filled with the sounds of instruments like those Gallic examples described by Diodorus as 'trumpets… of a peculiar and barbaric kind, which produce a harsh, reverberat-ing sound suitable to the confusion of battle'.[57] The Deskford carnyx, a Scottish national treasure, is an example that leaps to mind, but it ought to be pointed out as well that Pictish sculpture contains images of Picts sounding trumpets of a far more prosaic kind in hunting scenes. It is possible that the more 'peculiar' carnyx was reserved for battle. It may be worth recalling the 'weird spectacle' confronted by Suetonius Paulinus at the crossing of the Menai Strait in 60. That had consisted of 'black-robed women with dishevelled hair like Furies, brandishing torches' and 'druids raising their hands to heaven and screaming dreadful curses'. Such displays seem to have been characteristic of British warfare in this period. Their effect upon Roman soldiers was probably different than upon native forces. They were probably never completely ineffective, however, in making an impression even upon the disciplined fighting men of Rome, who for all their training remained human beings with human emotions.

In the last moments leading up to the battle, according to Tacitus, among the Caledonians 'the boldest warriors stepped to the fore',[58] very much in keeping with Gallic and German battle practice which Tacitus will have known well enough from his readings. The *Gododdin* elegies, moreover, speak of a Uotodin prince of early Christian times who 'set his picked men in the vanguard, set a stronghold at the fore', and contain a number of appreciative references to warriors of the period who were inclined to manoeuvre themselves into foremost positions when battle was joined.[59] There seems little reason, in other words, to disbelieve Tacitus on this matter of detail. This was the time when the henchman who enjoyed hospitality and influence in the service of his lord was expected to 'earn his mead'. Such were the expectations of an elite culture that held bravado and repute in such high regard. There is much suggestion in early Welsh poetry that warriors might rely upon mead and wine to summon up the necessary resolve to meet these expectations. It has been suggested that one result of this tendency of the warriors in such hosts to cluster behind a relatively small number of men of renown – perhaps renown as old as their days as young *fian*-like warriors – may have been that each kindred-in-arms assumed a wedge-shaped formation that may have been many 'ranks' deep, with its best and most precocious warriors positioned at the forward apex of the wedge.[60] Looking again to later native evidence, the Aberlemno battle scene depicts three ranks of Pictish footmen facing a charging Bernician horseman, and places a sword-wielding warrior in the foremost position, with two ranks of spearmen behind him. Similarly, early Welsh poetry describes northern British warriors fighting 'close-ranked' or with 'ranks closed for battle', speaking of such formations as shield-walls and comparing them, bristling with spears, to palisaded ramparts.[61] Such deep formations ought to have been attractive in ill-disciplined companies, for it would have made it functionally very difficult for the forward ranks to run away. On the other hand, unlike a Roman cohort they must have been next to impossible to manoeuvre about a battlefield once they had formed up, whatever their leaders' tactical talents may otherwise have been. That being said, it seems that in medieval Wales household warriors were deployed within a potentate's forces in such a way as to take maximum advantage of their savvy, courage, and experience.[62] Those warriors of this kind who may have been present, and had not been placed in the vanguard or reserved by their potentate as his personal bodyguard during the fighting, might in other words have been formed into a rearguard to discourage those in front of them from flight. Certainly this seems an unlikely role for *fian*-like bands of vigorous young warriors who are likely to have been most valuable as shock troops.

AGRICOLA'S BATTLE-PLAN

Having ascertained the disposition of the British host, Agricola will have held a council (*consilium*) of war with his legionary legates and the prefects in command of his auxiliary cohorts, in order to explain his battle-plan.[63] His intention, according to Tacitus, was to advance upon Mons Graupius with 8,000 auxiliary infantry, perhaps a dozen cohorts or more consisting in each case of the retinues of potentates recruited from various peoples, flanked to either side by 3,000 cavalry, also auxiliaries, probably consisting on each flank of about six *alae* of Gallic and southern British troopers.[64] By this period, as Tacitus's description indicates, the Batavi in particular had acquired a particularly robust reputation as auxiliary infantry. Calgacos gained no particular advantage from his adversary's decision to place his faith in these allies rather than in his citizen soldiers.[65] Indeed, if there was to be a river crossing involved, these auxiliaries may well have posed a much greater threat to the British forces than did the Roman legionaries.

As indicated above, Tacitus's testimony contains clues to suggest that such a crossing did take place at Mons Graupius, despite the fact that he does not explicitly mention one. He maintains that Agricola, despite concerns about the possibility of becoming surrounded, struck first against Calgacos with a mere six cohorts. This plan strikes one as rather odd until the battle is placed into the proposed context, in which the river Earn lay in the way of Agricola's infantry, advancing upon the Gask Ridge from the south. The opening assault described by Tacitus was spearheaded by Tungrian and Batavian auxiliaries. These men from the Low Countries were renowned as specialists in wetland combat like those upon whom Roman legates were accustomed to rely in winning riverbanks held by hostile British and other forces. It may be, in other words, that Tacitus's vague indication that these cohorts launched the assault upon Mons Graupius reflects a tactical situation – namely a river crossing – that he otherwise fails to mention or describe. Catherine Gilliver's examination of the circumstances under which first-century Roman generals are known to have deployed auxiliary infantry rather than legionaries in the line of battle has shown that in every other case the Romans were forced to fight across marshy ground or river crossings.[66] In that event, it is necessary to presume either that he was somehow ignorant of this important detail, which seems unlikely, or else, as seems more likely, that he chose to omit it for some reason that is difficult to ascertain. Various explanations might be posited, each as plausible and impossible to verify as the next, and each revolving around the likelihood of uncomfortable facts whose omission can have been made without peril to, or even to enhance or protect the reputation of Agricola.

Whatever the explanation may be, the point to be made, or rather reinforced, is that Tacitus's failure to mention something is not decisive proof that it did not take place. This is especially true in our own case where we have other evidence to place the battle within the proposed context, and where Tacitus otherwise hints, however tangentially, that it was fought there.

According to Tacitus's information, the Roman approach to Mons Graupius would begin, as has already been mentioned, at their encampment, within which Tacitus sets the legate's rousing and fabricated pre-battle speech to his restless troops.[67] It is likely enough that swift marching with light supplies had rendered his men somewhat wearier and hungrier than was usual upon campaign, but if the legate harboured any specific concerns about this Tacitus does not mention them. His legionaries, between 4,000 and 7,000 strong, he would keep in reserve, 'drawn up before the rampart' (pro vallo),[68] and so, in the context of Dunning, some 3km from the foot of the Gask Ridge. If this seems rather further back than ought to have been advisable, perhaps we ought not to place undue stress upon this point. One need hardly point out that this strategy of relying entirely upon auxiliary troops to win the battle, while in keeping with the proposed context of the fighting, is at complete odds with the rousing oration placed into Agricola's mouth by Tacitus only moments before. His words are quite explicitly given as if they were intended to fire the hearts of citizen legionaries and not those of German and other auxiliaries. We have already seen another instance of this kind of blurring in Tacitus's narrative. The point is thus underlined that, while in all likelihood Agricola did address his auxiliaries, perhaps unit by unit, before he committed them to battle,[69] these exact words, like those of Calgacos, are a fiction. They were intended to inspire and impress readers in the salons of Rome, and not the men who fought and died at Mons Graupius.

With this in mind, it is necessary to recall that, in the Agricolan speech, Tacitus has the legate urge his legionaries to 'prove to your country that her armies could never have been fairly charged with protracting war or with inciting rebellion'. We have regarded this above as a key statement in the *Agricola* which reveals much about the political and personal context within which Agricola was operating in the summer of 84. It has been suggested as a result that, by electing to rely upon his auxiliaries at Mons Graupius, the legate, perhaps even following imperial advice on this point, was seeking to avoid the prospect of sustaining further legionary casualties in this controversial war. As Tacitus himself puts it, perhaps in reference to a decision of just this kind, 'great would be the virtue of a victory secured without shedding Roman blood'.[70] Against such a background it may be suspected that his observation that the legionaries were kept *pro vallo*, and so well out of the action, exaggerates the actual distance that was maintained between the auxiliaries and the legionaries kept in reserve. We have seen that the legate was entirely justified in the proposed tactical context in placing his confidence in his Batavian and Tungrian auxiliaries rather than in his legionaries, and also that a force of 13,000 or 14,000 auxiliary troops should have been much smaller in size than the undisciplined native force at Mons Graupius. Nevertheless, their exclusion from glorious battle and the opportunity for vengeance must have sorely stung the legionaries of IX *Hispana* in particular. If he felt he could not trust them to show the necessary restraint to remain out of the fight, this too could explain why Agricola may have taken the decision to hold his legionaries unusually far in reserve.

Whether or not Agricola was duly impressed by the sounds and the spectacle of a large British host working itself up in preparation for battle, he seems at least to have been impressed by the size and situation of the men arranged against him. We have reduced their numbers to a third of those provided by Tacitus, but may presume that this was still the largest single native force the legate had faced in all his years of campaigning in Britain. Concerned about the prospect of his advancing auxiliaries becoming enveloped or encircled, facing attack from 'in front and on the flanks', the legate 'widened the order of battle' (*diductis ordinibus*).[71] This is to say that his battle-plan involved extending the frontage of his advancing soldiers by increasing the amount of space that normally separated individual cohorts and prevented their convergence upon one another – gaps that were maintained even after battle had been joined.[72] We have seen that Calgacos may at most have had fifty per cent more men at his disposal than Agricola's 8,000 auxiliary infantry, and in that event the legate's strategy suggests that the native forces were fairly dispersed. Indeed, it is to be recalled that Caratacos, having deployed along a river, had concentrated his forces against Ostorius at the most obvious fording places. Perhaps Calgacos now did the same.

The plan alarmed several of the officers, says Tacitus, who advised their commander, probably during the *consilium*, that the line of battle would be so extended that it would be best to bring up the legionaries to supplement it.[73] Agricola overruled this idea. Perhaps he would have been hesitant to do so, thus placing his faith in the cavalry he intended to deploy to protect his flanks, had there been much prospect of the native host being sufficiently flexible to make the necessary tactical adjustments to exploit the proposed disposition of the auxiliaries. This is not the first time in the *Agricola* that Tacitus portrays his father-in-law as having stout-heartedly ignored the admonitions of nervous nay-sayers. One suspects in each case that it is mostly a literary device intended to shore up Agricola's reputation, and in this case to exaggerate the fearsome look of Calgacos's army. Agricolan reminiscences affected by 'the Bullfrog Effect' may also underlie this aspect of Tacitus's presentation. In addition to affording him the opportunity to demonstrate the bravery and tenacity of his father-in-law, the idea that he was brazen can also have served to challenge accusations that Agricola was insufficiently motivated to bring about a quick end to his northern war. It has been suggested above that Domitian himself may have been among those who advised the legate to risk no shedding of Roman blood in bringing the controversial war to a conclusion. If there is anything in this suggestion, it might be thought that the underlying point here – that Agricola would not back down from the decision to fight the battle with auxiliaries even when it began to look foolhardy – had its origins in an Agricolan dispatch that had depicted the legate as an obedient and loyal follower of his emperor.

It is uncertain how much space the Romans would have required to arrange themselves in the intended way. It has been estimated that a dozen cohorts arranged side by side will have presented a frontage rather less than about 3,400m long. As Agricola apparently extended the necessary gaps between the cohorts in his line of battle in order to protect his flanks, its frontage was probably at about this notional maximum of 3,400m, in which each gap would be as wide as the frontage of an individual cohort.[74] It is some 3km between the Water of May on the east and Balgour on the west, facing the arc of the Cairnie Braes from the south bank of the Earn. Once again, the proposed context for the battle is a pleasing fit with these rough calculations.

When the *consilium* was concluded and the plan of battle established, Agricola returned to his tent. After a time a red standard (*vexillum*) was raised above it, and the legate emerged in his symbolic red cloak. Here was the signal that his troops had been awaiting. The time had come for the auxiliaries upon whom the battle-plan depended to take up their weapons and begin formation for the final advance upon the enemy. In the meantime, many of them are likely to have had recourse to drink to help steel their nerves.[75]

1 Modern monument on the site of Trimontium, the Roman installation at Newstead, with Eildon Hill in the background.

2 Two peaks of Eildon Hill, viewed from the third, from which Trimontium derived its name.

3 View across modern Perth from the Moncrieffe Hill hillfort; the pointed peak in the furthest distance at the centre of shot is Schiehallion.

4 Schiehallion, viewed from 'the Queen's View' on Loch Tummell.

5 View south down Strathtay from the King's Seat hillfort, Dunkeld.

6 The river Devon.

7 Dumyat Hill, viewed from Craigrie, Clackmannan.

8 Dumyat Hill, rising above Abbey Craig and the Wallace Monument.

9 The site of the Roman installation at Raedykes.

10 View of Stonehaven Bay from Raedykes.

11 Bennachie, viewed from the site of the Roman installation at Durno.

12 Upstanding remains of Roman ramparts at Ardoch.

13 Upstanding remains of Roman ramparts at Ardoch.

14 Upstanding remains of Roman ramparts at Ardoch.

15 The site of the Roman installation at Strageath.

16 View along the Roman road leading from Strageath and along the Gask Ridge.

17 The site of the Roman installation at Dunning; it lay between the roadway running from left to right in the centre of shot, and Kincladie Wood at the far side of the modern field. The Gask Ridge lies beyond in the background.

18 Upstanding remains of Roman rampart at Kincladie Wood, Dunning. The interior of the camp lay to the left of shot.

19 Upstanding remains of Roman ramparts at Kincladie Wood, Dunning, looking outwards from the camp.

20 Craig Rossie, viewed from the site of the Roman installation at Dunning.

21 The Cairnie Braes section of the Gask Ridge, in the centre of shot, viewed from a distance.

22 The Cairnie Braes above Dalreoch, viewed from the site of the Roman installation at Dunning.

23 The Cairnie Braes above Forteviot, viewed from the site of the Roman installation at Dunning.

24 The Cairnie Braes above Dalreoch, viewed from the south above Baldinnies.

25 The Cairnie Braes above Forteviot, viewed from the south above Baldinnies.

26 The Cairnie Braes above Dalreoch, viewed from the south at Baldinnies.

27 The Cairnie Braes above Forteviot, viewed from the south at Baldinnies.

28 View south up the Dunning burn from Baldinnies, to Kincladie Wood in the middle distance.

29 The river Earn at Forteviot Bridge.

30 The convex lower slopes of the Cairnie Braes.

31 The convex lower slopes of the Cairnie Braes at a distance.

32 View south from the Cairnie Braes towards Dunning, the sheen of modern agricultural works of which is visible to centre-right. The Roman installation lay to the left of the village.

33 View south from the Cairnie Braes towards Dunning, at the centre of shot. The Roman installation lay to the left of the village.

34 View of the river Earn from the Cairnie Braes; the sheen of modern agricultural works of Dunning is visible to centre-right.

35 View of the river Earn from the Cairnie Braes; the sheen of modern agricultural works of Dunning is visible to centre-left.

36 View of
the river Earn
from the
Cairnie Braes;
the sheen
of modern
agricultural
works of
Dunning
is visible to
centre-right.

37 The hillfort
at Moncrieffe
Hill, viewed
from the north
across the river
Tay.

38. The Moncrieffe
Hill hillfort.

39 View westwards from the Moncrieffe Hill hillfort along the Gask Ridge.

40 Aberlemno battle scene.

CHAPTER SEVEN

Bringing Matters to a Decision

The Battle of Mons Graupius, AD 84:
An Impressionistic Reconstruction

The Roman advance upon Mons Graupius will have halted several times in order to allow the line of auxiliaries, formed up in their cohorts, probably three ranks deep, to correct inevitable drift within the ranks as they made their way over the irregular terrain leading to the British position [see Map 4].[1] The possibility has been mentioned that their approach was also hampered by the efforts of war chariots before these became dispersed by Agricola's cavalry. At present, the ground separating Dunning from the river Earn is drained by several burns, and this may well have been the case in 84 as well. The longer the frontage of this advance, the more difficult it would have been to maintain a straight line. Accordingly, Tacitus notes that the auxiliaries did not finally execute the planned widening of their line until after their advance had already begun. The precise character of this manoeuvre is not known to us. The sense of anticipation on both sides must have grown more acute with each successive pause, with a cacophony of shouts, Caledonian whoops and blaring horns growing alongside it.

At last, according to Tacitus, Agricola dismounted and joined the infantry to fight among them. He does not mention his father-in-law's personal bodyguard, which will have consisted of several hundred soldiers, probably auxiliaries.[2] To have done so would have been to shatter the illusion of the brave general imperilling himself in his zeal to come to blows with the enemy. Throughout his description of the battle, Tacitus implies that Agricola remained entirely disengaged from the mêlée, surveying the progress of the fighting and issuing supplementary directives. These were presumably carried by a member of his staff to the relevant prefects commanding the auxiliary cohorts. The idea that Agricola fought alongside his infantry is therefore to be doubted.

THE EXCHANGE OF JAVELINS AND THE QUESTION OF THE EARN

As the protracted line of auxiliaries, its way now clear of war chariots, closed to missile range, perhaps as far as 60m or as near as 30m from the enemy, there was probably a resounding relay of shrill Roman battle horns. At this signal, Calgacos and his allies will have been confronted with the sight of the shouldering of some 3,000 javelins in the front rank of Agricola's army, and perhaps as many as 8,000 in all three ranks.[3] Possibly there were already British javelins in the air when the subsequent order came for the Roman soldiers to loose their own. There is no mention of British archery at Mons Graupius. In the proposed scenario, Agricola's troops, raising their *teli*, were faced with crossing the Earn through 'a dense shower of javelins' before they could engage the enemy in close-quarters fighting.[4] Perhaps this explains why Tacitus gives the impression that the Caledonian peoples and their fellow conspirators had rather the better of the Roman auxiliaries in this first exchange of missiles. After all, he says the same thing of Caratacos and his allies in their earlier battle against Ostorius at a river crossing, where 'so long as the struggle was carried on by missiles, most of the wounds and numerous casualties fell to our own side'.[5] Though not as heavily equipped as their legionary comrades, Roman auxiliary infantry were well protected by cuirass, helmet and long shield. Under normal circumstances they would not expect to suffer remarkable losses as a result of even dense and sustained missile fire.[6] The proposed river crossing, on the other hand, in an echo of the earlier encounter, would have furnished Calgacos and his allies with the kind of advantage of position that could account for their good showing at this stage of the fighting. Under normal circumstances, Roman infantry sought swiftly to close the distance to the enemy, charging headlong with voices raised, in order to take maximum advantage of the disruption their javelins had caused among the enemy ranks. This does not seem to have happened at Mons Graupius. A river crossing like the one proposed here can have slowed the Roman advance sufficiently to allow for the kind of sustained barrage of British javelins described by Tacitus. This may be taken, in other words, as a further hint in support of the proposed scenario, despite the fact that Tacitus does not explicitly place a river at the foot of Mons Graupius.

Calgacos, it would seem, was better prepared than those earlier British leaders who had not expected Plautius to attempt his river crossing, and was charier of his enemy. His warriors now showed steadiness and skill, Tacitus says, in parrying incoming Roman *teli* with their great swords and small shields. In the proposed setting, we might expect that the auxiliaries sought to take maximum advantage of this disruptive power of their javelins in covering as best they could the necessary river crossing. British shields penetrated by javelins will usually have been rendered useless where the javelin stuck fast and could not be withdrawn. All the while native warriors, whose effective killing range at some places will have been greater than that of the auxiliaries for having the advantage of higher ground, 'poured on us a dense shower of javelins'. It seems as though the native forces were seeking to achieve a degree of 'blanket fire' until such time as the auxiliaries could close the distance to the enemy, hampered, it has been argued, by the need to cross the Earn in order to do so. The Aberlemno battle scene depicts a rearward rank of Pictish skirmishers armed only with a javelin. It is possible that the British ranks at Mons Graupius included groups of similar men, perhaps youths in the main, upon whom native leaders relied for weakening and disheartening an advancing foe.[7] One imagines, if their ranks were as deep as has been suggested above, that the risk of 'friendly-fire' casualties was rather high.

We have seen that it was only six of Agricola's infantry cohorts that now moved forward 'to bring matters to a decision through hand-to-hand swordplay'. Four of these, perhaps a little fewer than 2,000 men all told, were Batavi, 'the most conspicuously courageous of all the German peoples of Gaul' and much renowned for their *ésprit de corps*.[8] The other two, probably just under 1,000 strong, were Tungri, another German people from the west bank of the Rhine.[9] We have already seen that these details too are a good fit with the proposed scenario involving a crossing of the river Earn at the foot of the Cairnie Braes [see Map 5]. Depending upon the breadth, depth and character of the river on that day two millennia ago – and the Earn is today notoriously changeable in its character – such a crossing may have been fraught with great danger. Had the Romans been facing an enemy that shared their discipline and organisation the danger would have been greater. Here again, as with the legate's decision to increase the gaps between his cohorts, it is doubtful that Calgacos's host possessed the tactical versatility to make the kinds of *ad hoc* adjustments that might have enabled it to exploit such vulnerabilities as significant gaps in the line of advance that are likely to have briefly arisen in a river crossing. As things stood, the developing situation does not seem to have occasioned tactics from Agricola other than the very rudiments of infantry warfare: the straightforward advance intended to drive through the enemy ranks.

Controversial tactics on Agricola's part at this point, or notable valour on the part of other men than the legate, are two possible explanations among many for the proposed omission of a crossing of the Earn from Tacitus's account of the battle of Mons Graupius. He does not even pretend that Agricola himself, unlike Ostorius, was personally involved in this initial assault upon the British position, nor that he made any great show of personal prowess or bravery at any point in the battle once it was joined. He says only that the German auxiliaries, having endured heavy fire in the exchange of javelins, now acquitted themselves admirably. It cannot be doubted that the spectacular sight and boisterous noise of the British front line of renowned warriors tested their nerve as they advanced upon it. Roman soldiers, save for at their initial charge, were expected to fight in silence, listening for the orders and encouraging words of their officers.[10] If the cohorts were arranged into three ranks, as we have proposed above, it is likely that the prefects preferred to place their most reliable soldiers in the forward and rearward ranks. Soldiers of more questionable or unproven character will have been in the second rank, where they could take heart from the men before and behind them.[11] In other words, the first exchanges of sword-play at Mons Graupius will have been between some of the most skilled and steady swords-men in either host. On the Roman side, these included those who, like legionary centurions, were expected to lead their individual units into battle from the front rank and initiate the forward push by forcing their way into the gaps left by fallen enemies – an act which required particular nerve.[12] If a river crossing were involved as proposed, the principal objective of these captains will have been to drive the enemy vanguard back from the north bank of the Earn and, perhaps, to bring about a general panic among the natives.

CONSPICUOUSLY COURAGEOUS

Not for the last time, at least as Tacitus portrays it, the momentum of the bat-tle of Mons Graupius now changed hands as these Roman auxiliaries surged into the British line. The *Gododdin* elegies speak of 'the crash of shields as loud as thunder' in battle in early Christian times, and make many references to the shields of the foremost men in combat being rent asunder.[13] The noise must have been horrific as the Batavi and Tungri made the most of their auxiliary training, striking enemy warriors in the face or head with their heavy shields and hacking with their swords or lunging with their spears at those who were unbalanced, stunned, or downed, thus 'scattering those who stood on the level ground' and forcing their way up the lower slopes of the hill.[14] We have seen that Ostorius, having resolved to cross his own river to fight Caratacos and his allies, launched the assault only 'after surveying the ground to discover its impenetrable and its vulnerable points'.[15] It would be surprising if Agricola too had not located these particular cohorts in such a way within his line of battle as to exploit some aspect of the ground or the deployment of the British host through their initial foray. Given their expertise at riverine combat, perhaps these men had been deployed so as to carry out crossings of the river at points well away from the most obvious fordable spots, and where Calgacos's forces may accordingly have been thinner. As Tacitus portrays it, the British swordsmen, despite being skilled with their small shields and their awkward and unwieldy blades, proved no match for the quick and versatile Roman *gladius*. The unlikelihood that Agricola's auxiliaries were armed with these swords has already been mentioned, and it seems more likely that there was no great disparity between the arms and equipment on either side at Mons Graupius. The advantages enjoyed by the men from the Low Countries who fought for Rome lay rather in their drilling and training, and in their mail cuirasses which were well suited to protect them from the cutting action of the thin native swords, if not from injury from the force of a heavy sword blow. The heavy Roman shield could present a soldier with difficulty in parrying a succession of swift strikes, but this was not problematic at Mons Graupius where the blows probably came at generous intervals.

The effects of these first few minutes of the engagement, with all the accompanying clamour of battle-cries, clashing iron, shield blows and agonised voices, are likely to have had a tremendous psychological effect upon Calgacos's coalition army. It has been observed that its forward units at the foot of Mons Graupius, whose main task may have been to resist a river crossing, are likely to have assumed wedge-shaped formations with some of the most renowned and talented warriors in the entire host foremost of all. In normal circumstances of native warfare, the sight of the best and boldest warriors of the kindred, standing their ground against the enemy, will have served to hearten the men of lesser renown positioned behind them. The valour of these great fighters served to stiffen the resolve of their kinsmen, acting as a counterbalance to their lack of discipline. On this occasion, however, it is to be expected that the opposite effect was achieved. Waves of shock and disbelief will have reverberated through the British ranks as these conspicuous and famous men, the flower of the host, fell or gave way in their individual fights with Batavian and Tungrian infantrymen.

When the skeletal remains of people killed in hand-to-hand combat are recovered by archaeologists, the number of severe wounds some single individuals are seen to have sustained can be quite astounding. The scene at the battlefield of Mons Graupius can only have been one of indescribable horror. There is no reason to suspect early Welsh poets of particular exaggeration where they say 'I saw blood-spattered men surrender their weapons', or that 'long biers bore men drenched in blood' after a battle.[16] It seems that at Mons Graupius the bloody German onslaught pushed forward with great, even excessive pace. Roman infantry were trained to move slowly and steadily forward once they had engaged the enemy, in order to minimise the potential for disorder as individual soldiers sought to pick their way among the mutilated dead and dying. However, as Goldsworthy has observed,

> it is always easier to cope with fear when doing something, rather than passively enduring it... The urge to get the thing over with... instinctively quickened the advance. In a sense, a quick pace...was a symptom of fear as much as a means of frightening the enemy.[17]

At Mons Graupius such an impetuous surge might have had decisive effects upon British morale and discipline. It might even have been the result of particular orders from a legate who, in the proposed context, desired above all else to facilitate a crossing of the river Earn by his remaining auxiliary cohorts, perhaps six or so in number. On the other hand, it can only have hastened the onset of weariness in men bearing a burden in armour and equipment that may have been in excess of 25kg, whether or not they may be thought to have made the proposed river crossing. It also placed them in greater and greater danger of becoming cut off, surrounded and overwhelmed.

EAGER RIVALRY

At some point, and presumably at a prearranged signal from the horns, the remainder of Agricola's auxiliary infantry, some 5,000 strong, surged forward themselves to engage the enemy with swords. Until this point they may still have been under fire from enemy javelins. Now they 'joined with eager rivalry in cutting down all the nearest of them'.[18] It would have been a standard motivational strategy on Agricola's part if he made the most of rivalries between his different auxiliary cohorts.[19] In the proposed context, as we have seen, it may be that the legate held these men back at the most obvious fording places, until such time as he had ascertained that the north bank of the Earn had been won by the Batavian and the Tungrian cohorts. The language of the *Agricola* suggests that this was achieved mere moments after these cohorts had engaged the enemy. This may be an exaggeration or telescoping of events, or it may be more or less accurate.

Now the fight was on in earnest all the way along the Roman frontage, seemingly some 3km and more in length. Tacitus says of it that the Roman troops advanced so quickly and fiercely that they left men in their wake that had only been wounded, and in some cases, men that had not been wounded at all.[20] If this is not just fanciful storytelling, it would seem that in some places, as their foremost and bravest warriors fell, the British ranks probably broke and ran rather than wavering. One is left with the impression of a rather confused, even chaotic scene as the battle unfolded before Agricola and Calgacos. The legate's infantry, seemingly moving more quickly and incautiously than was advisable, were pressing up the slopes of Mons Graupius and deeper into the enemy ranks, impelled by the bravest and most reckless soldiers. Confusion and ill discipline are entirely typical of combat in every era. Dio speaks of a similarly confused mêlée after Plautius's auxiliaries had forced their way across a contested river, and how that legate, taking advantage of the disorder, ordered a body of legionaries led by the future emperor Vespasian to storm across the river to support them.[21] Auxiliary cohorts like those that fought at Mons Graupius may have been more prone than their legionary counterparts to get into disorder, lacking the superior levels of legionary discipline necessary to maintain a measured pace in combat.[22] In any case, studies have shown that in the extreme stress of combat most men will lose immediate sight of their leader's objectives and training and simply fight for their lives, and perhaps those of those nearest them.[23] Perhaps it was in this phase of the fighting that Aulus Atticus was killed, a prefect in command of one unnamed cohort, thus becoming, according to Tacitus's report, the sole notable Roman casualty on the day. The prefect ought to have been encouraging and directing his men from horseback, watching for conspicuous acts of prowess, bravery and cowardice and perhaps calling for a more measured and disciplined performance. Tacitus reports that he was slain when his 'youthful ardour and ferocious horse had borne him into the enemy'.[24]

BRITISH COUNTERMEASURES

To add to the general disorder at this point in the battle, British charioteers now drove into the fray, still being pursued by the auxiliary cavalrymen who had driven them from the field in the opening phase of the battle. 'These at first spread panic,' says Tacitus, further confirmation that the war chariot, however obsolete by this date in the wider European context, remained an efficacious weapon of war under the right conditions – in this case through poor, if perhaps desperate tactics. Even as Roman auxiliaries, Gallic horsemen tended to be high-spirited and ill-disciplined,[25] and in pursuing the charioteers into the mêlée like this no doubt they and their British colleagues caused Agricola some consternation. The snapshots provided by Tacitus are a welcome reminder that the soldiers and warriors who struggled against one another at Mons Graupius, however well trained, were human beings fighting for their lives. They might exhibit uncertainty, confusion, questionable judgement and fear, as well as courage and character, in their determination to survive.

The tide of the battle was turning once again, but this shift in momentum was not to last. Tacitus says that the war chariots and horses 'were soon impeded by the press of men and by the unevenness of the ground'.[26] Nevertheless the charioteers had done enough and the battle, which had been going against the British coalition, had now entered a new phase. The vagaries of Tacitus's language here do not allow us fully to appreciate the nature of the charioteers' contribution to the battle of Mons Graupius. It is possible that they simply drove into the fighting in search of their lords afoot, and inadvertently disrupted the Roman surge. It is also possible, however, that they did so in a deliberate and desperate attempt to impede that surge, striking across terrain and into a combat situation quite unsuitable to their usual modes of fighting in order to lend support to their faltering comrades. At any rate, their war chariots, which relied above all else upon mobility to remain effective, now became inextricably bogged down at the heart of the fray. Tacitus comments upon the unseemliness of the scene as these vehicles confounded the Roman advance, observing that 'the fighting had nothing of the look of a cavalry action, for men and horses were carried along in confusion together, while chariots deprived of guidance, and terrified horses without drivers, dashed wherever panic urged them, whether sideways or in direct collision against the ranks'.[27] In sniffing at the charioteers and their unattractive and seemingly either accidental or desperate contribution to the fighting, Tacitus is able to gloss over the effectiveness of their efforts.

The spirited initial advance of Agricola's auxiliaries was now apparently peter-
ing out. On the lower slopes behind them lay a scene of devastation, with living
and dead British casualties, among them some of the most famous and celebrated
warriors of the Caledonian zone, interspersed with fallen and wounded auxiliary soldiers, horses and ruined chariots. No doubt weariness was setting into
their limbs, to the advantage of the more lightly equipped natives. This, combined
with the unorthodox intervention of the British charioteers, may have required
the prefects to call for a degree of regrouping within their cohorts. In the proposed context, the terrain too may well have played an important part in bringing
the Roman advance to a halt. It has already been mentioned that the battle of
Dupplin Moor was fought in the same neighbourhood in August 1332, and here
too the fact of becoming 'impeded by the press of men and by the unevenness of
the ground' was to prove a key factor in the outcome of the fighting. As Ranald
Nicholson put it in summarising contemporary descriptions:

> The first Scottish attackers... advanced on foot. As these approached they were
> harassed by an incessant flight of arrows from the English archers... Nevertheless,
> when the antagonists came to close quarters and Scots and English were fighting
> with their pikes firmly fixed against one another, the Scots at first had the advantage:
> the fall of the ground favoured them... But as the arrows of the English archers
> took toll of the Scots and their foremost men were pushed forward against the
> spears of the defenders, the initial onslaught soon lost its order and its momentum.
> Before long, the Scottish flanks, upon which the archers directed most of their fire,
> were driven under a hail of arrows to converge upon the Scottish centre. Unable
> to make headway, hemmed in on either side by the pressure of the arrow-riddled
> troops on either flank, the men-at-arms of the Scottish centre soon lost array... The
> configuration of the ground meant that access to the enemy could be gained only
> through a narrow glen. At the far end the first Scottish battalion was held in check...
> and thrown in upon itself through the execution made by the English archers... At
> this juncture, Mar, with his hastily arrayed and unwieldy host... charged down the
> narrow pass but failed to communicate their own impetus to their unfortunate
> compatriots in front. These were borne down one upon the other. Whoever lost his
> footing fell never to rise. Confused and panic-stricken more through the pressure
> of their comrades than by the arms of the enemy, the Scots clambered over one
> another to escape being trodden underfoot and suffocated.[28]

It does not seem possible to place the battle of Dupplin Moor at the Cairnie
Braes, yet the circumstances of the Scottish army in that engagement seem haunt-
ingly familiar to those encountered by the British host at Mons Graupius. For
despite their inferior equipment and discipline, some British forces yet remained
in position above the stalled Romans on the slopes of that hill. Seemingly
a significant part of the host, these men, according to the rather embroidered

account of Tacitus, still 'occupied the tops of the hills and were idly scorning our fewness'.[29] Their resolve at this point may have been unexpected, and a cause for concern for the Romans if they had expected them to break and run.

It is not portrayed in this way by Tacitus – who was anxious to present a dramatic narrative and to convince his readers that a crucial Agricolan command decision secured his victory – but, in having decimated and humiliated the cream of Calgacos's fighting force, the Romans had probably already won the battle of Mons Graupius. If a change in the tide of battle was now in the air, it is likely that only the character of the legate's victory remained at stake. That being said, the auxiliaries had advanced remarkably and even recklessly quickly. The possibility may therefore be raised that Calgacos had formulated a battle-plan in which his forces would intentionally give way, intending to draw the enemy into a vulnerable position and administer a decisive counter-stroke. This seems extravagant, but not impossible. In any event, having forced their way across the Earn and thence up the Cairnie Braes, advancing cohorts of Roman auxiliaries would have found themselves entering the hollow formed by the convex slopes of the ridge arcing between Keirwoodhead and Bankhead. With enemy warriors rising above them to either side, such cohorts would clearly have been in a compromised position in the proposed setting. Yet so too would have been the British warriors fighting at or near the front line, for so long as the men behind and above them continued to stand their ground while the Romans continued to push forward, these men, like the Scots at the battle of Dupplin Moor, will have been in increasing danger of becoming crushed in 'the press of men'.

There is nothing particularly ingenious or inspired about what happened next. Presumably at an order or signal from Calgacos, or perhaps a deputy, these reserve British kindreds-in-arms began to descend gradually (paulatim) from the heights [see Map 6].[30] The use of the plural colles, 'hills', is interesting here in the proposed context of convex slopes, which would surely have given the Romans the sense of enemies advancing from colles rather than from a single collis. If his society did not demand of Calgacos that he lead his kindred in battle from the front, fighting alongside them as a figure of courage, protection and inspiration in the face of an enemy with as formidable a reputation as the Roman army,[31] it seems likely that the leader of the coalition was still alive at this stage of the engagement. Tacitus tells us nothing of his fate after battle was joined. We can deduce from this only that he was not captured and taken prisoner. From a vantage point among his kin, fighting for his life, his capacity to direct the movements of his reserves on the slopes above him will have been non-existent. As coalition leader, however, he may have been expected to lead rather from his chariot, moving about from kindred to kindred, band to band, giving whatever heart and direction he could to as many of these as could be reached. In that event, the vantage point thus available ought to have been sufficient to call for the commitment of his reserves at what was deemed to be a crucial moment. The burning, but insoluble question must be whether the spirited

Roman advance up the slopes of Mons Graupius caught Calgacos off guard, or whether it played into his hands. There seems to be no reason entirely to reject the possibility that Agricola's soldiers were permitted to drive rapidly forward as part of a rudimentary battle-plan. The conglomerate British host was probably unable to execute much else in the way of tactical manoeuvre, however, even if Calgacos was blessed with considerable military genius.

A legate's personal participation in the fighting might have been interpreted by his men as proof of desperation or crisis. Agricola was therefore allowed by his military culture to oversee the progress of battle from a rearward position that was ideal for the marshalling and commitment of reserves at the optimum time, and to the optimum point of impact.[32] One should therefore not overstate the vulnerability of Agricola's men at this point, even in the context of the Cairnie Braes and the unlikely event of a shrewd Caledonian battle-plan. At the same time one feels that the pivotal moment of the battle of Mons Graupius was now upon its protagonists. It has already been suggested that his reserves are unlikely to have been able to win the battle for Calgacos at this stage. Nonetheless, a decisive counter-strike forcing a Roman retreat ought to have salvaged much of the situation by bringing about an inconclusive result. On the other hand, Agricola now had the opportunity to transform a victory into a rout.

RIDE TO VICTORY

Placed in the proposed context, the commitment of the British reserve forces to battle at Mons Graupius may, as we have seen, be thought to have been ordered by Calgacos when the Roman troops had pressed into the convex slopes between Keirwoodhead and Bankhead, with banks of native warriors arranged above them to either side and ahead. The impression made by Tacitus that, executed with deftness, this might have been a grim development in terms of Roman casualties, seems entirely understandable in such a context. Yet, as the *Agricola* describes it, this was no deft late counter-strike, nor even a frenzied charge calculated to overwhelm or drive off the enemy, of the kind that had successfully defeated Roman armies in the later stages of some past battles.[33] It was instead a rather slow-footed advance that seems to have challenged Agricola little. Whether this crucial lack of pace was the result of an excess of caution or fear, or perhaps of an inability on the part of these kindreds-in-arms to advance in good order without drifting together and impeding one another's progress, must remain forever unclear to us. The proposed context of the Cairnie Braes, with their convex shape, augments the terrible possibility of a Dupplin-like disaster, in which the British warriors below became pressed together as their countrymen pushed down from the slopes behind them from either flank. It is a scene that has been played out with tragic results in recent years on the terraces of football grounds and the general admission seating areas of musical events. We cannot know to what extent it may have been played out at Mons Graupius, nor how many of the native dead were killed by the crushing weight of their own great army.

Most of the men involved in this fateful British advance were probably warriors whose regular fighting days were long behind them, who may be envisioned, as they were by Tacitus, as ill suited to face Romans in battle. By now they will have seen many warriors of renown slain or driven off by Agricola's troops. Neither can we be certain that Calgacos himself was still alive at this point, nor that these reserves had the benefit of any coherent central direction at this stage of the battle. One can but forgive them their inadequate performance at this stage of the fighting – perhaps with disastrous results for their own side – and observe that few assemblages of tribal warriors of this kind had much hope of out-finessing a drilled, disciplined and organised Roman army. In descending into the mêlée at this point rather than scattering from the slopes of Mons Graupius, these men demonstrated the kind of consummate courage and sense of honour that their society rigorously required of them. Those who were to be slain as a result died as they had lived. It is unlikely that the tribal poets of their peoples soon allowed audiences to forget them.

Agricola's counter-strike as these kindreds-in-arms descended slowly from the heights was crucial to the immediate significance of the battle of Mons Graupius, if not to its outcome. It may also be overdone by Tacitus. As he presents it, the enemy seemed to have been insufficiently circumspect. His companies had over-committed themselves and left their flanks and rear vulnerable to the legate's reserve cavalry. No doubt the surviving British leaders found it effectively impossible at this stage to co-ordinate and control the movements of this composite tribal host, as men who had as yet been denied the opportunity for glory and retribution found themselves at last within striking distance of a vulnerable enemy. At the same time, although the Gauls seem to have been accomplished horsemen with the capacity – and not least horses of the required size and training – to give battle on horseback, there is little evidence to suggest that this was also the case of the natives of northern Britain. It was precisely because their native ponies stood only twelve hands in height that the Caledonian peoples relied upon chariots rather than cavalry,[34] and they probably had little experience in developing battle-plans that took sufficient account of mounted troops. Whatever the precise explanation, which probably involved a number of different factors, Agricola now seized his chance. He had remained particularly vigilant, Tacitus says, in the event the enemy made to surround his army. Now he deployed his reserve horsemen, who in the proposed context will have had to make their way across the Earn at a ford that was not now defended. As the British reserves descended the hill to overwhelm the enemy, they suddenly found themselves outflanked by four auxiliary cavalry squadrons (*alae*), each of which consisted of something in the region of 500 troopers [see Map 6].[35] If it has been correctly deduced above that the slow-footed advance of the British reserves speaks of a lack of co-ordination and order, a cavalry charge would have been particularly effective as a countermeasure. 'Thus', says Tacitus, 'the enemy's design recoiled onto himself'. At the critical moment in the battle, he had played into Agricola's hands, and had been decisively and disastrously outmanoeuvred by what have fairly been described as 'textbook tactics' that ought not to impress us overmuch save in their execution.[36] Tacitus implies that Agricola had anticipated at the outset of the battle that the enemy would attempt to outflank his army. The reader is thus invited to infer that he also devised some stratagem that had successfully masked his capacity to strike decisively with his reserve cavalry, then struck in this way when the need arose. We cannot, however, escape the possibility that Tacitus here exaggerates the importance of his father-in-law in securing the victory at Mons Graupius.

Perhaps Agricola, had he now found himself in his enemy's position, momentarily disadvantaged but possessing the higher ground, equitable numbers and well-trained Roman troops, could have salvaged the situation even now. A year before, the men of *legio* IX *Hispana* had managed to keep their wits about them when their camp had been surrounded and assaulted by some of the very same British warriors, one supposes, who now lay dead at Mons Graupius. Despite the gravity of their plight, IX *Hispana* had stood their ground, placed their faith in their fortifications and their training, and lasted the night. The warriors of the Caledonian peoples and their allies, however valiant and experienced in the right battle conditions, and despite their great prowess and fear of ignominy, simply did not possess sufficient amounts of that kind of discipline or morale. Even for Roman soldiers, the sight and thunder of 2,000 armed horsemen bearing down upon them was very intimidating. For men who may never before have witnessed horses being used for shock action, the spectacle must have been quite dreadful. We may be sure that as Agricola's horsemen, advancing at the trot, gave rein to their mounts to charge, they made the most of their fearsome appearance. A cavalry charge against infantry was primarily a psychological weapon. Infantry with the nerve to stand against one will find that horses will not normally allow themselves to be ridden into a solid wall of men.[37] Such a charge was intended, however, to shatter such morale. Faced with this great crisis of confidence, having already seen many of their best and bravest warriors slain, and now having no reserves behind them to prevent their flight, the natives panicked. It clearly did not matter to them that a hillside is hardly ideal terrain for horsemanship. The shock value of Agricola's cavalry charge had worked its magic. Perhaps 'the press of men' too exerted an influence in panicking his enemies.

Unless we are to postulate – as well we might – a Dupplin-like disaster on a similar scale, most of the British dead are likely to have been killed in flight from the battlefield. It is impossible to estimate how many were slain or injured in the fighting itself. All that may be observed is that the number of Roman dead suggests the possibility that this phase of the battle may not have been particularly lengthy. In fact, Tacitus furnishes us with no evidence to suggest that the battle of Mons Graupius will have been longer in duration than about fifteen minutes. Were it any more lengthy, one would expect a lull in the fighting, about which Tacitus says and implies nothing.[38]

A GREAT AND HORRENDOUS SPECTACLE

The battle of Mons Graupius was over. The rout was on. All that remained to be determined now was the number of fleeing youths and men of all ages Agricola's 2,000 auxiliary horsemen would be able to cut down in pursuit before the natives managed to take shelter in the woods. Such merciless brutality is hideous to contemplate twenty centuries later. In the emotionally charged atmosphere of battle, it was the inevitable consequence faced by any contemporary army in rout. It was a particular danger for a force like Calgacos's, which lacked the training, discipline and organisation to disengage cannily, and in good order, from the heat of battle.[39] A scattered enemy was particularly vulnerable to cavalry, and could suffer terrific losses. The plight of the fugitives becomes all too clear when one bears it in mind that Agricola's auxiliary cavalry, some *alae* of which had already caused trouble for their comrades afoot, could not be relied upon to exhibit disciplined restraint, even had Agricola been of a mind to order it.

At the sight of the Britons in flight, the auxiliary infantry, no doubt with a great deal of jubilation, will have been ordered to cluster into their individual cohorts. This allowed first the four *alae* already committed, and then the rest of the reserve cavalry, to surge between them and beyond, up the hill, bent on riding down the enemy.[40] No doubt in places horses and infantry impeded one another. In the previous year, the British attackers of IX *Hispana* had successfully avoided a rout in their withdrawal from that engagement, with inconclusive results for both sides. Now 'there was a great and horrendous spectacle in the open spaces' separating the hill from the forests, says Tacitus. The auxiliary horsemen were chasing down fugitives, butchering, taking captives, and, in some cases, massacring those captives.[41] The murder of such hostages is more grist to the mill in favour of a battle fought relatively early in the campaigning season. At the end of the season, as we shall see, Agricola showed himself keen to take and keep hostages from the native peoples of northern Britain. On the other hand, the earlier in the season the battle was fought, the more of a hindrance would have been large numbers of captives. Given the pressures the legate was experiencing in the Senate, such hindrances probably could not be entertained. That being said, no doubt some of this is embroidery on Tacitus's part. A modern audience might expect such atrocious behaviour to be played down or denied by commentators. In the salons of Rome such scenes were regarded not as shameful atrocities, but as glorious proof of their city's might and the favour of the gods. Yet we need not doubt that all this and more was visited upon the Britons as they scattered from the battlefield with the thunder of hooves behind them. In a memorable phrase,

Maxwell suggests that 'it was no more difficult, and probably a lot less hazardous, than pig-sticking'.[42]

And so the natives of the Caledonian zone and their allies from further afield paid the terrible price extracted from any vanquished force by their conquerors in this and many other periods, Roman, Celtic or otherwise. There seems to have been nothing uniquely savage about the victors' behaviour in the wake of Mons Graupius. Certainly, and with good reason, they expected no less violence to have been their lot had the tables been turned. *Gododdin* elegies, for example, celebrate one Uotodin warrior of the early Christian period who 'would show no mercy to those he pursued', and another, of whom it is said that 'whomever he overtakes will not escape'.[43] The trend was general at the time and remained so for a very long time. Roman soldiers were known sometimes to choose suicide over surrender and the horrors, real or imagined, that came with capture by enemies.[44] It is worthwhile to underline the fact that most of the slaughter of this phase of the engagement was carried out by cavalrymen who were probably Gallic and southern British auxiliaries, and not by Romans as such with a particular taste for Celtic genocide. If the Gask Ridge was Mons Graupius, as we have supposed, escape from this carnage will not have been an easy prospect. It lay in the main back over the convex slopes of the ridge. The ascent will have been a challenging prospect for the weary and disheartened, if also for a mounted horse. Thence, a man might flee northwards, making for the crest of the ridge and the descent towards Methven Moss, where horsemanship would have been difficult. He might also flee in a more westerly direction across Dupplin Moor towards the woods at Perth (the Pictish toponymic element *pert* denoted an overgrown place) on the lower Tay. The distances involved are considerable. Twelve-and-a-half centuries later Edward Balliol and his army would rout a Scottish army on Dupplin Moor that also found escape from mounted pursuers very difficult.[45] Not surprisingly, Tacitus reports that, in some cases, men whose panic or despair got the better of them gave up all hope and simply charged headlong at Agricola's troopers, 'giving themselves up to death'.[46] No doubt some preferred honourable suicide to the disgrace of flight, or hoped to enable others to escape the catastrophe by sacrificing their own lives. Others will not have been able to think in such rational ways. Their plight makes for grim reading.

We are told in the *Agricola* that some native companies, perhaps *fían*-like bands, managed to carry out something like an orderly withdrawal after the greater body of the British host had scattered or fallen. Rallying in the woods, Tacitus reports, they opportunistically assailed incautious Roman pursuers, like the Uotodin warrior whose elegy proclaims that 'when everyone else was in retreat, you would attack; may glory come to you because you would not flee'.[47] Perhaps Calgacos and his own household retinue, if he had one, were among these stalwart few. The pursuit of a scattered enemy was always likely to leave all but the most disciplined of horsemen vulnerable to counter-attacks by companies of infantry in tight formation.[48] The scene is thus set for Tacitus to allege that, as a result of this situation, 'serious loss would have been sustained' on the Roman side had the legate, 'who was everywhere at once', not mounted his horse and ridden ahead, managing to rein in and organise the pursuit.[49] The moderation thus implied is inconsistent with the allegation that the native host suffered thirty times the number of casualties than the Romans, and we know that a general's directives might be ignored by his men in the euphoria of victory.[50] It is to be suspected that Tacitus here attempted to make a great deal of very little. Neither does the back-and-forth image of the battle put forward by Tacitus particularly prepare one for such lopsided casualty figures as those presented in the *Agricola*. At least twice during the engagement the momentum of the fighting as described seems to have favoured Calgacos and his fellow conspirators. As already observed, we may, and indeed must, suspect that this impression was accentuated by Tacitus for dramatic effect, to make the victory at Mons Graupius seem more hard-won than is likely to have been the case.

As usual, the pursuit of fugitives from the battle went on until nightfall. As darkness descended, the Romans, 'gladdened by the victory and the spoils, enjoyed a night of elation'.[51] For more than a few, this joy will have been diluted by the loss of comrades or serious, and in some cases crippling, injuries requiring the attentions of the doctors. Once Agricola had managed to restore his jubilant troops to order, the hunt for British fugitives had become a calculated, almost mechanical business. Where the woods were dense, the legate dispatched a body of infantry-men and dismounted troopers to scour the undergrowth for enemies in hiding. Otherwise, he relied upon mounted horsemen to chase down stragglers and to wreathe and search through thinner stands of trees.[52] Only now, according to Tacitus, when it became clear that they would catch no more incautious Romans unawares in the woods, did the last of the native warriors cannily melt away 'into the shelter of extensive and pathless wilds'.[53] The engagement was over. As the Romans retired wearily to their encampment, which we have identified here as the temporary camp at Dunning on the other side of the river Earn, their sentries looked on as, 'amid the mingled wails of men and women', Britons wandered the battlefield 'to drag away the wounded and call for those thought uninjured'.[54]

Long before the field was given over to natives seeking their loved ones, their bodies were probably looted by Roman auxiliaries looking for booty. Amid the slaughter vividly described by Tacitus lay, according to him, some 10,000 native dead. Whether or not one accepts this number is an act of faith. We have seen that Agricola is likely to have ensured that his victory had a suitably decisive look in his dispatches to the emperor, and Tacitus may have exaggerated this impression still further himself. The vast majority will have died in the rout that followed the mêlée itself. Certainly the general idea conveyed by Tacitus that one-third of the host assembled by Calgacos were slain in the battle and in the subsequent rout seems entirely reasonable. In that event there would have been about 3,000 men killed on the native side, a number very much in line with decisive defeats in the handful of comparable major military engagements known to have taken place between Welsh and Norman forces.[55] To place such losses in the context of our foregoing demographic estimates, the total number of younger and older warriors slain will have been something like six per cent of the total population of the Caledonian zone. It will also have been something like a third of the combined fighting strength of that region under normal circumstances. The figure is decisive. Of course, many, and perhaps most of those slain will not have been adult warriors at the peak of their powers. The more elderly and youthful tribesmen, whom Tacitus makes a point of including among the native forces, are likely to have made up the bulk of the casualties. Moreover, it would probably be inaccurate to envision the Caledonian zone itself as being denuded of six per cent of its population, since a significant proportion of those killed at Mons Graupius may have come there from further afield, as we have seen. It also bears consideration, although Tacitus does not mention it, that a native host on campaign may have been supported by a substantial train of women, servants and slaves,[56] substantial numbers of whom can have fallen victim to the rampaging enemy in a rout. The presence of such non-combatants seems particularly likely if, as proposed, Agricola had marched north to disrupt an aggressive hosting, and this consideration may serve to explain why there seem to have been so many native youths and elders present at Mons Graupius. Nevertheless, a reasonable estimate of the number of native casualties produces a very impressive and terrible total when viewed in context. The point is thus underlined that Agricola, however much Tacitus embellished his account of things to make the necessary point, may well have been justified in perceiving his *victoria* over Calgacos as a master stroke for Rome.

CHAPTER EIGHT

Devastation and Silence

Aftermath of Battle

Agricola reported the loss of 360 men at Mons Graupius. The fallen were probably gathered by the surviving members of their units for cremation, the legate making a point of honouring their sacrifices.[1] It ought to have been very difficult for him to misrepresent this total to any significant degree, however concerned he had been about limiting the number of casualties in the battle. In other words, each cohort will on average have lost about thirty men, about six per cent of its notional complement of 480. Of course it is highly unlikely that casualties were borne in equal proportions across the entire length of the Roman line. Perhaps the six Batavian and Tungrian cohorts that led the advance sustained a higher proportion of the overall losses than the others.

It is a simple fact that their military technology tended on the whole to enable Roman armies to cause more deaths among enemy troops than they themselves sustained in close-quarters combat. The British sword is far less likely to have killed armoured Roman soldiers than to have broken bones or bruised soft tissue with heavy blows. We ought probably to expect there have to been something in the region of 1,000 or more Romans wounded on top of the number of dead given by Tacitus. In that event roughly a fifth of those who marched upon Mons Graupius will have been either killed or wounded.[2] It will be noted that, using the modified figures proposed above, the Romans may be thought to have lost about one soldier for every ten native warriors they had slain. This is obviously very far removed from Tacitus's three soldiers for every hundred natives, but it still represents decisive victory. It is to be expected that Agricola was careful to attend and honour the wounded. In the days that followed his victory, the legate, no doubt greatly elated and relieved, probably recognised, decorated and otherwise rewarded men for gallantry in an exuberant parade.[3] Perhaps he also made a show of dishonouring the cowardly, or even demoting those officers who had wavered when presented with his battle-plan.

THE TRAIL OF THE FUGITIVES

News of the battle and its outcome spread rapidly throughout the Caledonian zone. According to Tacitus, the natives had begun deserting and burning their own dwellings and settlements, withdrawing with their households into hiding, no doubt in most cases making for the shelter of higher ground.[4] Unless these and other vignettes are entirely the products of Tacitus's imagination, it is to be presumed that his father-in-law sent scouting parties riding out into the Caledonian zone after the battle, and subsequently began to receive reports of abandoned native dwellings. It may have been over-interpretation of such evidence that lay behind Tacitus's more sensational observation that 'some of them vented their rage upon their wives and children, as if in pity for their lot'.[5] It would seem presumptuous, however, to deny the possibility that some native freeholders, overwhelmed by desperation and despair, did indeed commit atrocious acts of violence upon their own families, like those who had taken their own lives at Masada some eleven years earlier. Tacitus reports as well that the fugitive Britons do not seem to have remained in one place for very long.[6] It may be observed that behaviour of this kind, including the abandonment of settlements in favour of mobility and the removal and concealment of goods and cattle, would seem to reflect the precautions that one would expect of peoples who anticipated exposure to the ravages of an invading army.[7]

There is a certain suggestion here that the natives were not entirely unfamiliar with such misery and the emergency measures it necessitated. Since ravaging is likely to have been the principal element of warfare between kindreds, no doubt each household, kindred and community had its contingency plan, ready to put in place when trouble arose. Here and there, says Tacitus, the natives still dared 'to take counsel together', at which meetings 'the appearance of their dearest ones sometimes touched them, and sometimes roused their wrath', though in the end they had always dispersed.[8] It seems unlikely here again that the Romans can have borne witness to such scenes themselves. Tacitus may therefore have fleshed out the basic point that Agricola received intelligence in the aftermath of his great victory that native assemblies were still taking place. It is to be expected that it was customary for a British community vanquished in battle to concede that the war had been won by the enemy, and to sue the latter for peace on honourable terms, rather than to press on with the struggle.[9] In that event, if Agricola were receiving intelligence relating to native gatherings, it would seem possible that these were being called to discuss and prepare for formal acts of submission to the Romans, and not to plan further military operations against them.

It is the claim of Tacitus that all these things took place literally overnight, while the legate and his soldiers had been celebrating a victory that they recognised had won them the controversial Caledonian war. It has already been suggested, however, that Tacitus had reasons for wishing it to appear that the battle of Mons Graupius had taken place towards the end of the summer of 84 rather than towards the beginning. In this way he sought to absolve Agricola from blame for further native hostility in northern Britain, as well as to accentuate the battle's climactic function in the *Agricola*. Thus, when Tacitus says that on the day following the battle the Romans gazed from their camp upon a landscape of 'devastation and silence everywhere, forsaken hills, houses smoking in the distance, and no one visible to the *exploratores*',[10] we are entitled to believe that he has telescoped weeks of British and Roman activity into the space of a single momentous night. It is more likely instead that, with mounted *exploratores* 'dispatched into every part' of the country,[11] the legate moved on from Mons Graupius, weeks of campaigning still ahead of him. Perhaps he pushed in the first instance to the mouth of the Earn, encamping at Abernethy until he could make contact with the *classis Britannica* to arrange for supplies. It may have been in divisions that his army crossed the Tay and proceeded further north, perhaps engaging in a systematic plundering of the countryside along the way.

At the end of the season, having established that there would be no British regrouping or counter-attack, Agricola 'led the army back' into the territory, or indeed 'march' (*finis*), of the Boresti (*in finis Borestorum exercitum deducit*). This people do not seem to have been mentioned in the Flavian survey and their 'march' continues to elude detection. The narrative of the *Agricola* implies that it was after accepting hostages from them that Agricola led his army southwards in a series of deliberately slow marches through the lands of tribes newly conquered after Mons Graupius.[12] This implication suggests that the Boresti were among the northernmost of the peoples made subject to the authority of Rome by Agricola. The school of thought that has linked *Boresti* with *boreas*, the Graeco-Latin name of the north wind, has much to commend it.[13] On the basis of the archaeological evidence of Flavian forts in northern Britain discussed below, representing the occupation that came with conquest, the Boresti ought to have dwelt in Angus or the Mearns as Hanson and others have suspected,[14] being at a guess a Uacomagian people. The Mearns, indeed, where the Mounth draws nearest to the sea and which in Pictish times was frontier country between northern and southern zones, would seem to be a good fit with the notion of a *finis*. Here, moreover, Agricola can easily have monitored the North Sea coast, perhaps even from the site of the temporary camp at Raedykes, and made contact with his naval commanders.[15]

If Mons Graupius was the Gask Ridge, one would therefore envisage a scenario in which Agricola and his army, perhaps divided into smaller divisions, marched and ravaged north-eastwards for some weeks after the battle. Sending

out and welcoming back *exploratores*, they would seem to have halted some distance beyond the Mearns – perhaps indeed as far north as the Spey. They then
returned thence 'back' into the lands of the Boresti, probably in the Mearns, 'it
having been learned', says Tacitus, 'that the trail of the fugitives was uncertain,
but that the enemy were not at all being massed together' (*incerta fugae vestigia
neque usquam conglobari hostis compertum*).[16] In the intervening time, the legate is
likely to have received the submissions of a succession of native leaders. A steady
accrual of hostages, plunder and tribute provides one potential explanation for
the overly large series of temporary camps north of the Mounth. It is possible that
the legate also caused some of his men to build 'glen-blocking forts' along the
highland fringe while he was negotiating peace terms and awaiting the reports of
the *exploratores*.[17] It seems that no hostile force could be located, and that Agricola
and his *exploratores* were relying almost entirely upon intelligence, in the pursuit
of which they are likely to have been assisted by native informants. This recalls
the likelihood that the *exploratores* included, or perhaps largely consisted of British
horsemen for whom the prospect of speaking with native northerners was a
straightforward one.

As the summer was drawing to a close, probably in August, Agricola led his
legions, hostages and baggage-train southwards. Tacitus describes this return
march back to winter quarters as a slow procession contrived 'so as to overawe
the new peoples by such deliberate progress.'[18] This was the culmination not just
of all his peacemaking efforts that summer, but indeed of his various efforts in
northern Britain over the course of the previous four summers as well. It was
his last opportunity to enjoy and exploit his great victory. In Borestian territory
the army had been rejoined by the *classis Britannica*. Agricola now gave its commander (*praefectus*) a detachment of men, and ordered him to 'sail around Britain'
harrying and terrorising the coastal areas for a final time.[19] Enjoying favourable
weather and the satisfaction of having established a fearsome reputation amongst
the northern Britons after two seasons of work along their shores, the war-
galleys of the provincial fleet, having fulfilled the orders received by their prefect,
had finally returned to base, possibly at Richborough (*Rutupiae*) in Kent.[20] The
Caledonian war was over.

CHAPTER NINE

Thoroughly Tamed

Roman Conquest in Northern Britain?

U pon receiving news of the victory at Mons Graupius from the dispatches of his legate in Britannia, the emperor Domitian, according to Tacitus, responded with official pleasure. He ordered the customary *ornamenta triumphalia*, the nearest a man of Agricola's background could come to the full triumphal honours that were reserved for the emperor himself.[1] The proposition has been challenged that Domitian also honoured the victory by issuing the commemorative coin minted in or after September 84, upon which is depicted a cavalryman riding down a swordsman on foot. The contrary argument rests mainly upon Tacitus's claim that the battle took place at the end of the campaigning season, about which doubts have been expressed above.[2]

DOMITIAN AND AGRICOLA

Agricola's son-in-law would have his readers believe that these were empty gestures – that behind closed doors the insecure Domitian was envious of Agricola's military glory and regarded it as a threat to his own personal prestige.[3] Perhaps it was so. In the context of Roman politics, forty-four has been described as 'mortifyingly young to retire from affairs'.[4] The stagnation of Agricola's once buoyant career upon his return to Rome from Britannia smacks of a begrudging, even resentful emperor. But in 98 Tacitus had his own grudges against the assassinated Domitian. He was writing in part, moreover, to pander to similar grudges among his fellow senators, and we must therefore tread with caution in assessing his handling of the hated emperor's career.

Domitian does not seem to have become the monstrous despot reviled by Tacitus and his colleagues until some years after the termination of Agricola's proconsular

legateship in Britannia, giving Tacitus's protestations an air of anachronism.[5] There
is a real air of ambiguity about Domitian's attitude towards Agricola, insofar as it can
be reconstructed and examined alongside the emperor's behaviour towards men
who were certainly among his inner circle.[6] We have already seen that the emperor,
under a certain amount of pressure from Agricola's detractors in the Senate, may
have harboured reservations about the legate's motives and justification for prosecuting and continuing his controversial Caledonian war. He may indeed have looked
upon it as a waste of resources, effort and men. In fairness to Domitian, however, no
indictment was ever brought against Agricola, and it has been suggested above that
it may well have been his emperor's support that prevented it from happening.

It would arguably have been a reasonable precaution on the emperor's part to cool
somewhat the heels of a man who had now shown himself capable of manoeuvring
around imperial directives and savvy enough to rationalise having done so. Where
there is little other evidence to suggest that Domitian was convinced that Agricola
also posed some kind of threat to him, or harboured particular ill will towards his
emperor, we cannot afford to trust Tacitus implicitly on the point. Had it been so,
the emperor is unlikely to have allowed Tacitus's father-in-law to die in his bed.
Indeed there are several hints to the contrary, supporting the idea that Domitian was
not particularly hostile towards Agricola. The senatorial career of Cornelius Tacitus
himself, the advancement of which depended in part upon his association with, and
the personal influence of, his wife's father, suffered no perceptible ill effects in the
80s and 90s. Indeed, Tacitus seems rather to have flourished under Domitian, even at
the latter's most obsessive.[7] The primary credit for his son-in-law's success probably
belongs elsewhere – not least in the merits of Tacitus himself. It would nevertheless
seem noteworthy that a senator so closely associated with Iulius Agricola should
have enjoyed such favour at a time when, according to the allegations of the *Agricola*,
the emperor hated and feared the victor of Mons Graupius.

Tacitus's allegations thus seem rather implausible. By cultivating the spectre of an
imperial grudge, he affixes his late father-in-law with what the post-Domitianic
Romans regarded as a badge of honour.[8] The reality is likely to have been a great
deal less sinister. Even deprived of the dark overtones in which Tacitus dresses it up,
imperial ambiguity towards a man like Agricola could go a long way towards sink-
ing a formerly buoyant career. We have deduced above that Agricola's meteoric
ascent to the consulship had owed much to the patronage of such heavyweights
in the new Flavian political arena as Petillius Cerialis and Vespasian himself. If that
is so, it is no great surprise that he would seem to have ceased to be a high flier
without the benefit of such gusts of wind. He would not be the only senator who,
having enjoyed the good graces of Vespasian and Titus, watched his career take a
noticeable turn for the worse after the accession of Domitian. It must have been
difficult for a man who had formerly been the beneficiary of institutional favouritism to adjust to this new situation of relative indifference on the emperor's part.
One can readily understand how Agricola, from his vantage point, might even

have regarded indifference as ill favour or hostility as Tacitus suggests. To this point, his success in the political arena had not stemmed from his intrinsic talents as a politician, proven in the imperial court and the Senate. Instead, it was owed to having chosen to back Vespasian's bid for the principate at a critical time, whose subsequent gratitude was the most significant single factor in Agricola's political life. If he was forced to fall back upon his own skills and talents to win political success upon his return to Rome from Britannia, his failure to win it may simply reveal a relative lack of such skills and talents.

It has been argued cogently that Agricola, as his son-in-law portrays him, was ill suited to the task that lay before him. He had built up no record of impressive performances in the Senate. Indeed, he apparently had no particular skill or love for oration, and little taste for political intrigue, and the fading of his star upon his homecoming probably reflects this.[9] Neither does the man described by Tacitus sound like someone with great skill as a self-publicist, or in reciprocating the cut-throat shenanigans by which his own critics had recently sought to discredit him. Instead, in the end, as Tacitus himself observes, Agricola 'drank deeply' (*penitus hausit*) of the opportunity for peace and quiet in his retirement.[10] One is put in mind of Maternus, a character in Tacitus's *Dialogue on Orators* written several years after the *Agricola*. Like Agricola, this character 'took the first step on the path of fame' during the principate of Nero, and emphatically renounces oratory (*eloquentia*):

The retinue that attends you when you go outside, and the crowd of morning callers, have no charms for me… I find in uprightness a readier protection for my personal standing and my peace of mind than in eloquence… The gain-getting eloquence now in vogue, greedy for human blood, is a modern invention, the product of a depraved condition of society… The age of bliss, on the other hand – the golden age, as we poets call it – knew nothing of either accusers or accusations; but it had a rich crop of poets and *vates* who, instead of defending the evil-doer, chanted the praises of those that did well… Nor should I hesitate to contrast the poet's lot in life and his delightful literary companionships with the unrest and anxiety that mark the orator's career… For my part I would rather have the seclusion in which Virgil lived, tranquil and serene, without forfeiting either the favour of the Divine Augustus or popularity with the Roman people… May I no longer have anything to do with the mad racket and the hazards of the forum, or tremble as I try a fall with white-faced Fame. I do not want to be roused from sleep by the clatter of morning callers or by some breathless messenger from the palace. I do not care, in drawing up my will, to give a money-pledge, through anxiety as to what is to happen afterwards, for its safe execution. I wish for no larger estate than I can leave to the heir of my own free choice. Some day or other the last hour will strike for me as well, and my prayer is that my effigy may be set up beside my grave, not grim and scowling but all smiles and garlands, and that no one shall seek to honour my memory either by a motion [in the Senate] or by a petition [to the emperor].[11]

It has already been noted that Tacitus embarked upon his literary career, the first work of which being the *Agricola*, after souring on oratory. Maternus here speaks for Tacitus himself, but one wonders to what extent he also speaks with the voice of the author's late father-in-law upon his homecoming from Britannia.

Agricola seems to have expected a second consulate upon his return to Rome, followed by another, less strenuous, opportunity for proconsular legateship in the province of Asia. The legateships of the wealthy provinces of Asia and Africa were much sought after, and it was normal for a man of consular rank in that period (unless he could count on preferential treatment) to be faced with a wait of between ten and twelve years after his consulate before finally becoming eligible to seek such an appointment.[12] Having been afforded a very lengthy tenure of office in Britannia, Agricola ought not to have expected an immediate subsequent appointment. As things turned out, he did not receive the consular *fasces* for a second time, living only ten years after his victory over Calgacos and dying in August 93. Although these were the years of Domitian's infamous reign of terror, Agricola was perhaps a victim of an enigmatic epidemic that seems to have claimed other senators in these years.[13] The emperor had not forgotten him. Domitian's own physicians visited him during his last illness – not necessarily with the ulterior motives implied by Tacitus – and the emperor made a public show of his sorrow at the news of Agricola's passing.[14] It seems he died resentful, an ambitious man frustrated by the inactivity of this last decade of his life, and by what he regarded as the squandering of his achievement in northern Britain by a disinterested regime.

Having been denied an earlier opportunity to resume his public life, it would seem that Agricola's lack of stomach for high-risk politicking and intrigue, made manifest, as Tacitus relates, in the time of Nero, discouraged him from doing so in the last years of his life after Domitian's principate had entered a state of crisis in 89. Tacitus points out that, when the opportunity was at last made available to him in this period, his father-in-law, uneasy about the political climate of the times, declined it.[15] The decision was true to form, at least as Iulius Agricola is portrayed by his son-in-law in the *Agricola*. Unless we are to take Tacitus at face value in his allegation that the offer was never a sincere one, it seems that the increasingly desperate and suspicious Domitian was willing in these years to breathe life into Agricola's flagging career. This surely implies something about the extent to which the emperor believed this stalwart supporter of the Flavian dynasty could be trusted in this time of crisis, whatever indiscretions he may have been thought to have committed in prosecuting his Caledonian war.

DOMITIAN AND BRITANNIA

As regards Britannia itself, Domitian would seem to have been as ambiguous in his attitude towards the Agricolan conquests north of the Forth as he was towards the man who had won them. If it is accepted that the emperor had never directed the legate to pursue them in the first place, there is little reason to think that they ever held much appeal to him. To judge from the archaeological evidence of Flavian fort-building, the gains in question consisted principally of the territories assigned above to the Uenicones and the Uacomagi. From Stracathro on the river North Esk to the river Tay, the Romans erected a sequence and network of forts ideally situated for surveillance of human and other traffic passing up and down a series of highland glens. These must have been major routeways linking the Caledonian peoples of the lowlands with those of the rugged interior, as well as with peoples living further north and west to the other side of the highland massif.[16] To the south of the Tay, this network of installations was continued as far as the river Clyde. It has been suggested above that the Flavian survey of northern Britain be taken as indicating that these lowland peoples of Menteith, Strathearn, Gowrie and Angus had been represented at Mons Graupius. A case is there for the making that the Romans situated their forts across these regions in such a way as to apply pressure to highland peoples by monitoring their interactions with these lowland tribes, with the real or avowed intention of 'protecting' these latter groups from any further warmongering against Rome or her British allies.

In a short phrase in his *Histories*, the relevant detailed books of which do not survive to inform us further, Tacitus observes both of these conquests and of Domitian's attitude towards them that Britannia was 'thoroughly tamed (*perdomita*) and immediately let go (*statim omissa*)'.[17] However one wishes to understand *perdomita*, it is worth emphasising that there is as yet no archaeological evidence to suggest that the zone north of the Grampian highlands was permanently occupied by the Romans in this or any other period. Perhaps Tacitus addresses this point, however, by observing in the speech given to Calgacos that 'beyond us there is no *gens*, and nothing indeed but waves and rocks'.[18] The circumstances surrounding the subsequent withdrawal of the army from the Caledonian zone may have raised doubt in Tacitus's disgruntled mind that Rome would have exhibited the political will in the 80s to subdue a rebellious Britannia, had Calgacos managed to secure a victory over Agricola and incite an uprising of Boudican proportions. At any rate, in intimating that, from Calgacos's perspective, what was at stake at Mons Graupius was 'liberty for the whole of Britain', and that the battle had represented western Europe's last chance to avoid a future of Roman dominion, since after Agricola's victory nothing lay beyond Rome's grip 'but waves and rocks', Tacitus was engaging in hyperbole of the first order.[19] That being said, it is possible that the desolation of the lands that Agricola had left untrammelled was adopted by Tacitus from an Agricolan exaggeration in the first instance, by which the legate had sought to underline the decisiveness of his victory.

Although clearly not *perdomita* in the traditional sense of the notion, northern Britain had now experienced conquest on a scale that would seldom be witnessed again in any subsequent episode of medieval or modern Scottish history. Behind their double line of forts, at Inchtuthil on the river Tay, near its confluence with the river Isla, the Romans now set about the construction of a new legionary fortress near the foot of Strathtay, which must have been the main route from Atholl into the coastal lowlands of Angus and Perthshire. Here would be housed the legion to which would be charged the ongoing protection and subjugation of the Uacomagi and the Uenicones – and probably the Dumnonii and the Uepogeni as well, if the latter existed in this period – and preserving the terms of the Agricolan and subsequent treaties that now bound these peoples to Rome. Yet Domitian had misgivings about this whole venture. Archaeologists continue to conduct an increasingly detailed autopsy into what Hanson has called 'the anatomy of withdrawal' from the Caledonian zone in the Flavian period. The post-mortem suggests that, after a half-hearted attempt to maintain a permanent occupation of the installations already discussed, there followed a decisive reversal of imperial policy within about five years of the battle of Mons Graupius, as trouble flared up along the Danube.[20] Agricola was still alive to witness these developments from afar in his retirement. The most striking and evocative evidence comes from Inchtuthil, where, famously, the construction of the massive legionary fortress was abandoned even before it had been completed. Unlike Tacitus, whose regard for Agricola did not allow him to view this episode as anything but a calamity and a slight to his father-in-law's honour, Domitian is unlikely to have exhibited much hesitation in giving the order to evacuate northern Britain. One suspects, moreover, from Tacitus's narrative, that his was the majority view in Rome at the end of the first century. Neither the spectre of British opposition, to whatever extent it existed, nor the difficult highland terrain of northern and western Scotland can have presented themselves to the Romans as especially intimidating obstacles to the permanent occupation of the Caledonian zone envisioned by the Flavian fort-builders. Like the career of the senator who had achieved it, the conquest of northern Britain could not, however, endure imperial indifference and the lack of political will inspired by this refusal to be bothered.[21]

GLORY, CONQUEST AND SUBJUGATION

Neither this first withdrawal, which Domitian seems to have been careful to dress up as a redeployment of resources in the wake of total victory in the north,[22] nor the fluctuating frontier of the next generation or two, greatly concerns us here. Our interest lies in assessing the significance of the battle of Mons Graupius, and the view, based upon the fact of these withdrawals, that 'in the end... Calgacus won, for it was the Romans who pulled back into central Scotland'.[23] Do subsequent developments illustrate that the battle of Mons Graupius was essentially a futile waste of human life, having 'neither checked the course of Roman occupation of North Britain nor altered the pattern of local native society'?[24] Or has 'the anatomy of withdrawal', conducted almost entirely on the basis of archaeological excavation, skewed our perceptions of the significance of Agricola's victory over Calgacos in the summer of 84?

For the people of Rome, as we have seen, the victory provided the occasion for *ornamenta triumphalia* in honour of Agricola's achievement. In the longer term, wars against the peoples of the Danube, the fall and assassination of Domitian and the rise of a new imperial order served to distract attention away from the comparatively minor affairs of the province of Britannia. Moreover, for all his efforts to secure it, victory at Mons Graupius brought decidedly little to Agricola himself in terms of his subsequent career. In some ways, given the controversies surrounding the Caledonian war, the entire episode may well have done his public life more harm than good. No doubt there were some Roman officers, and particularly prefects of the auxiliary cohorts and *alae* that did the actual fighting and dying at Mons Graupius, for whom having participated in the campaigns of the Caledonian war and the battle itself served to bolster reputations and advance political careers. For these men, and for countless soldiers who had distinguished themselves at Mons Graupius, the battle had not been an exercise in futility, whatever the subsequent withdrawal may have entailed. Viewed from the perspective of the imperial court and Roman high society, the engagement may well struggle to seem particularly significant. Viewed from the perspectives of individual soldiers and other participants, however, Mons Graupius takes on rather a different appearance.

If this is true of the Roman side, it ought to be no less true of the native side. The *Gododdin* elegies furnish us with powerful testimony to the fact that even a famous rout was capable of producing subject matter for the court poet in the early Christian period. Even Tacitus acknowledges native acts of courage and prowess surrounding the battle of Mons Graupius. It is to be expected that individual reputations, and even the prestige of entire kindreds, derived profit from the engagement for some time to come among the Caledonian peoples and their allies. We do not know whether Calgacos himself survived the fighting. Neither can we assume, if he lived, that defeat at the hands of the Romans, given their track record in first-century Britain as a whole, must have resulted in an insuperable blow to his prestige. Certainly the personal excellence of Caratacos, and that of Uenutios, had proven capable of weathering reverses in wars against Rome. Perhaps in British society the willingness to fight a powerful enemy counted for something, whatever the outcome might be.

As regards the wider societies to which the native combatants at Mons Graupius belonged, the central question to be addressed is whether the subsequent abandonment of military sites in the Caledonian zone requires there to have been a corresponding abandonment of everything that Agricola had achieved there by besting Calgacos at that engagement. The Romans did not make war to control land as such, but to control peoples.[25] In the immediate aftermath of his victory, Agricola made treaties with vanquished tribes in the Caledonian zone who ought to have been keen to make peace after their defeat and two seasons of Roman plundering. The dismantling of installatons in their territories must be significant and suggestive of ongoing redeployment of Roman forces both within Britannia and across the breadth of the empire.[26] That permanent bases of operations for large bodies of soldiers do not seem to have been maintained for long north of Dumnonian territory is not proof, however, that the terms of these treaties were now forgotten by either side. It cannot be a certainty that a controlling Roman presence of a significant, but archaeologically elusive, nature was not cultivated and maintained by successive legates in Britannia after Agricola.

Centuries later, the seventh-century Bernician hegemons Oswig and his son Ecgfrith, whose home territory straddled the ruins of Hadrian's Wall, would prove entirely capable of subjugating peoples of the Caledonian zone, Argyll, and the British territories between the Clyde and Solway, exacting tribute and other obligations from them, while exerting political and cultural influence upon them. This they achieved not, as a rule, through the permanent occupation or colonisation of these lands, but rather through a combination of largesse and intimidation stemming from seemingly infrequent military operations. Ecgfrith, for example, would appear to have been able to maintain a tributary grip upon areas of the Caledonian zone for the better part of fifteen years as a result of a single overwhelming military victory.[27] It would be most unwise of us to presume that Romans, unlike Bernicians, had to occupy native territory permanently with bodies of soldiers in order to subjugate British peoples or apply various sorts of effective pressure to them. A strong case can be made that such occupation – conquest 'proper' – was their preferred method of controlling subject peoples, but other options must always have been open to them.

The problem to be addressed here is not one that is unique to the Flavian period in northern Britain. It relates instead to the ongoing status of northern British peoples throughout the provincial period. Archaeological investigation has established fluctuations of the frontier between the provincial and extra-provincial populations of the island of Britain during these four centuries, and outlined the occupation history of many key Roman installations in northern Britain. How the history of Roman occupation may relate to the history of Roman subjugation is open to question, however, and far more difficult to ascertain by archaeological means. Archaeology has so far failed to show that any Roman military site north of the Hadrianic wall was permanently occupied from Agricola's time onwards. Surely this fact cannot, on its own, be taken as proof that the Roman administrations of Britannia did not enjoy the kind of influence over the activities of northern British peoples that can have justified a belief among the provincials that northern Britain was under their control. 'Control' is, after all, a difficult concept to measure by empirical means. Perhaps the occasional reminder of Rome's might was sufficient to cow most of the Caledonian peoples for extended periods of time.

Increasingly, 'conquest' and 'subjugation' mean different things to different scholars. At issue would seem to be the ability of the Romans after the battle of Mons Graupius to affect 'the pattern of local native society' in territories in which they had chosen to forego permanent occupation. The occupation history of their military sites in these territories would seem emphatically to rule out that particular kind of conquest, which had already begun to transform vast areas of southern Britain into Roman provincial territory. There seems to have been no introduction of colonial settlements and no onset of the principal examples of that process of imbalanced cultural exchange between Romans and natives that we call 'romanisation'. Yet archaeologists cannot rule out subjugation to Roman authority involving intimidation, close scrutiny, disarmament of local groups in accordance with *pax Romana*, and formal acts of exchange that saw Roman subsidies travel into the north and the payment of tribute by particular northern peoples. It is impossible to ascertain from the archaeological record, for example, that Roman operatives, including collectors of such renders and distributors of such subsidies, were not regularly to be found in Perthshire and Angus in the generations following Agricola's victory over Calgacos. Neither can the archaeo-logical record easily detect such operatives as may have lived for extended periods among the northern natives at native settlement sites.[28] It is certain only that elite material culture in northern Britain was awash with Roman material from the Flavian period onwards,[29] and that within a hundred years of the battle of Mons Graupius, northern Britain had become a different place than it had been when Agricola had marched his army through it, whether one considers politics, economics, or the social fabric.

It is possible to overstate the latter case. Few large-scale socio-economic phenomena like changes in settlement or population patterns, or even in the shape and structure of native societies, may be profitably attributed to a single cause like the presence of the Romans.[30] A compelling case has been made, all the same, that ongoing contact with the Romans brought new economic opportunities to the peoples of northern Britain, probably revolving around acquisition of surpluses in slaves and other commodities for exchange, the pur-suit of which may have resulted in increased levels of social differentiation within and between native populations.[31] Within a hundred years, the Calidonii would emerge from this dynamic period as a coherent people within which, accord-ing to Dio, such peoples as the Uenicones and the Uacomagi had 'merged', leaving their old names behind.[32] It seems likely that Roman influence was the spur for this process of 'ethnogenesis' that saw northern British peoples adopt Caledonian identity. Whether such influence came in the form of the threat of military intervention, imbalances of exchange that favoured particular poten-tates, kindreds and peoples, or changing economic currents arising from what Britannia could supply and demand, it would seem the Calidonii adapted to such circumstances.

It is intriguing that the Gask Ridge may be seen as having lain in the frontier zone between this new Caledonian *gens* and the Maiatai, another similar *gens* that emerged at about the same time, no doubt as a result of similar processes.[33] Having thus coalesced, both of these new confederate peoples would endure for centuries, in some form, beyond even the end of Roman authority in Britannia. It must strain credulity to suggest that Agricola's victory at the battle of Mons Graupius was solely responsible for ushering in the indicated processes, or for the ethnogeneses of the Calidonii and Maiatai of subsequent centuries. At the same time it must strain credulity to allow it no role at all in these developments arising in large part from Roman activity in Britannia.

CHAPTER TEN

Final Thoughts

This study has no hope of becoming, and is not intended to be, the final word on Agricola, Calgacos, their respective operations in northern Britain, the battle that they fought at Mons Graupius, the location of that hill, or the significance of what happened there. On these matters much remains to be asked, investigated and disentangled. The study of Flavian Scotland before and after the battle will continue apace. Attitudes towards Agricola, Calgacos and their activities will not remain static as the surviving evidence is assessed and re-assessed in the light of new theories like those put forward here, and is occasionally built upon through new discoveries. Maxwell has observed that, whatever the actual significance of 'the bloody field of Mons Graupius':

> the Scottish nation has long since taken to its breast the gallant, if foolhardy, North Britons who made their stand against the might of Rome… Not without reason, its antiquaries have viewed the shadows cast back in time by Bannockburn, Flodden Field, and Drummossie Muir.[1]

The embracing of such battles in this way, and the criteria according to which they become added to such a list, invariably reveal more about the embracer than the battle itself. However enthusiastic one might be about the battle of Mons Graupius, the wider questions surrounding the Flavian occupation of northern Britain that followed it, the abandonment of sites, and the significance of such abandonments for the Roman impact in northern Britain would seem to be of greater importance than the rather narrower question of Agricola's particular contribution. Yet one suspects nevertheless that Mons Graupius will continue to loom large in the field, even if it fails to dominate it.

Even more, perhaps, than the location of Mons Graupius, the veracity of Tacitus's narrative surrounding his father-in-law's Caledonian war seems to be particularly controversial at present. None of us is capable of avoiding our own subjectivity in assessing the evidence before us. It will always be tempting to indict Tacitus on the basis of his own. It has been observed recently that 'cases of scholars who declare evidence from other disciplines inadmissible when it is incompatible with hypotheses formed on the basis of sources from their own subject (even where scanty) abound',[2] and recent imprecations that we dispense with the *Agricola*'s evidence where it contradicts an archaeological model can smack of this kind of thinking. In the foregoing chapters, and in particular in the attempt to locate Mons Graupius, an attempt has been made fairly to interact with the different categories of evidence that are available to us in seeking to understand the relevant events. There can be no denying that the weighing of such evidence is an extremely delicate operation. It may be illustrative of this point that, as regards the location of the battlefield, the present author has found that minute shifts in his reading of the evidence have inclined him to change his mind more than once during the course of his deliberations. It is therefore not surprising that neither those who would like Calgacos to have won the battle of Mons Graupius (thus casting Tacitus as a scurrilous liar) nor those who would like there to have been no such person and no such battle (thus casting Tacitus as a scurrilous liar), find themselves unable to make a case, so vulnerable is the *Agricola* to such extreme appraisals of its historical value. The kind of decisive evidence that can emphatically rule out particular interpretations of Tacitus's *laudatio* rarely exists, allowing for a fertile environment for competing theoretical models of varying degrees of likelihood. It therefore seems unlikely that the field of study surrounding the battle of Mons Graupius will run short of competing and con-tradictory theories any time soon. As Ramsay MacMullen observed, 'nothing is more difficult to control than our sense of what is likely'.[3] If this investigation seeks to establish anything, it may be that it seems unwise to privilege *a priori* any particular category of evidence over others. It seems particularly unwise for the evidence of philology, for example, to be dismissed by non-philologists simply because they do not understand or 'believe' it, or to set Tacitus to one side as an utter fiction in order to make way for the flowering of archaeological theories unconstrained by contemporaneous textual evidence. If such views strike one as more critical of archaeologists than of others, this is not to be taken as a general complaint. Instead, more than anything else, it reflects the understandable domi-nance of archaeologically driven models in this particular field of study.

It has not been without caution or tentativeness that the Gask Ridge has been identified here as Mons Graupius, the muir of a community called *Craupes*, and the temporary Roman encampment at Dunning as the point from which Agricola marched upon it. This is not to say, however, that this identification has been made idly. That the battle was fought in Strathearn seems, on the available tex-tual, archaeological, linguistic and toponymic evidence, to be beyond reasonable doubt. The hints that nudge the Gask Ridge ahead of such alternative locations as Duncrub and Craig Rossie are of rather a different and less certain order, but are not inconsiderable for all that. In 1970, Feachem, having decided that Mons Graupius was Duncrub, lodged his wish 'to see a suitably inscribed pylon in memory of Calgacus and his British confederates on the summit of the hill at Duncrub as a counterbalance to the huge granite altar lauding the invaders' achievements at Trimontium'.[4] Ten years later, in a more circumspect paper, Lawrence Keppie spoke on this theme to the Scottish Archaeological Forum, remarking that 'perhaps a statue to the Caledonian Vercingetorix will be raised to mark the site of Scotland's earliest recorded battle; but in my view it would be premature to organise a public appeal for funds, until we can be more sure where it should be set up'.[5] Twenty-five years further on still, the pockets of Scotland remain safe, for this study has been unable to establish the identity of Mons Graupius with anything like the degree of certainty that would justify such a gesture. Only time and further work will determine whether it has moved us a step closer towards such an identification. It is the way of things that each new candidate seeking to be identified as Mons Graupius finds itself under relentless fire as soon as it raises its head above the parapet. The Gask Ridge, like every other candidate, has its obvious aiming points for critics. Time will tell whether it will develop additional, perhaps fatal, vulnerabilities, or whether solutions will be found to its existing problems. The same is true, of course, of those other candidate sites that have been deemed here to be more problematic than the site that has been preferred. There is every likelihood that intriguing cases remain to be made on behalf of as yet unappreciated additional locations, including those associated with as yet undiscovered temporary camps. The candidacy of Bennachie has exemplified this very phenomenon, springing up from nothing as a result of a chance discovery. The enthusiasm with which Bennachie has been embraced as Mons Graupius is nevertheless somewhat surprising,[6] given the compelling criticisms of the evidence adduced in support of it, raised almost immediately it was put forward, by some of the heaviest hitters in the field of Roman archaeology in Scotland. If this study serves only to underline the point that the jury is still out, its author can hardly find himself disappointed.

MAPS

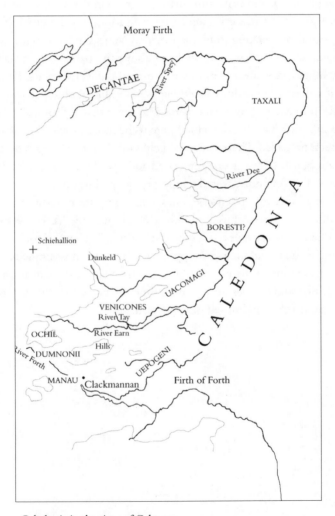

Moray Firth

DECANTAE

River Spey

TAXALI

River Dee

BORESTI?

CALEDONIA

Schiehallion

Dunkeld

UACOMAGI

VENICONES
River Tay

OCHIL
River Earn

Hills

River Forth

DUMNONII

UEPOGENI

MANAU • Clackmannan

Firth of Forth

1 Caledonia in the time of Calgacos.

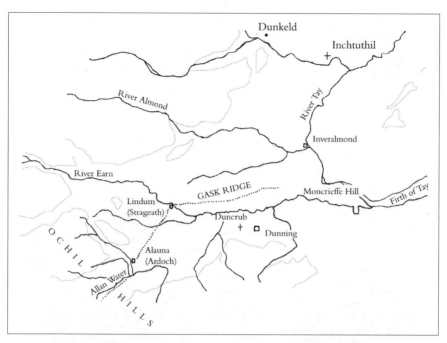

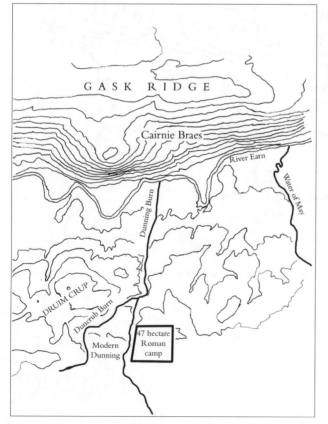

Above: 2 Strathearn and the Gask Ridge.

Left: 3 The Dunning Camp and the Cairnie Braes.

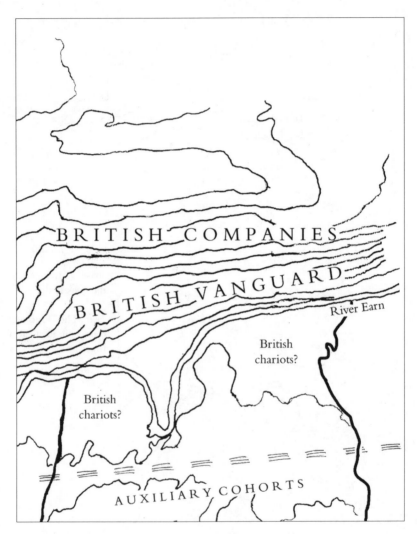

4 The Roman approach to Mons Graupius in context.

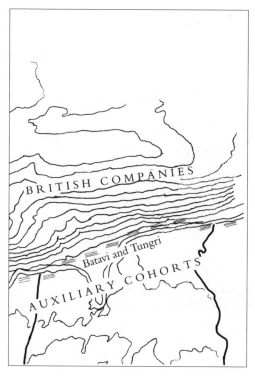

5 The Roman advance in context.

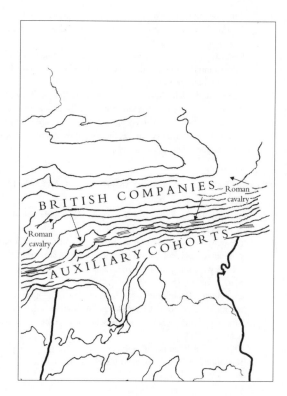

6 The British counter-strike in
context.

Notes

ABBREVIATIONS

AT   Annals of Tigernach. W. Stokes (ed.), *The Annals of Tigernach*, Vol. 1. (Felinfach, 1993).
AU   Annals of Ulster. S. Mac Airt and G. Mac Niocaill (eds), *The Annals of Ulster (to A.D. 1131)* (Dublin, 1983).
PSAS *Proceedings of the Society of Antiquaries of Scotland.*

A CHRONOLOGICAL NOTE

1   The cases have been reiterated respectively by R.M. Ogilvie and I. Richmond (eds), *Cornelii Taciti: De Vita Agricolae* (Oxford, 1967), 317-20, and W.S. Hanson, *Agricola and the Conquest of the North* (London, 1987), 40-45.
2   Ogilvie and Richmond, *Agricola*, 318-19; Hanson, *Agricola*, 43-44. That Hanson's objections fail to undermine Richmond's disquiet is outlined by G. Maxwell, *A Battle Lost: Romans and Caledonians at Mons Graupius* (Edinburgh, 1990), 9-11.
3   Ogilvie and Richmond, *Agricola*, 319-20; L. Keppie, 'Mons Graupius: the search for a battlefield', in *Agricola's Campaigns in Scotland: Scottish Archaeological Forum* 12 (1981), 79-88, at 81. Hanson, *Agricola*, 42, and Maxwell, *A Battle Lost*, 115, object on questionable grounds, since the battle of Mons Graupius may have occurred earlier in the season than Tacitus suggests.
4   Ogilvie and Richmond, *Agricola*, 319.

CHAPTER ONE: AN EXPRESSION OF FILIAL PIETY

1   Tacitus, *Agricola*, §§1-2; for the death of Agricola, see *Agricola*, §44. All textual references to the *Agricola* in this study are to the edition of Ogilvie and Richmond, *Agricola*. It is deduced that the text was composed, or at least largely completed, during, or perhaps very shortly after, the principate of Nerva, from Tacitus's positive treatment of that emperor, who 'did not leave a happy memory behind him'; R. Syme, *Tacitus*, Vol. I (Oxford, 1958), 12, 19.
2   Syme, *Tacitus* I, 19.
3   Ogilvie and Richmond, *Agricola*, 80-87, trace the history of the Jesi text, which was discovered in the fifteenth century at Hersfeld, and is thought to have been produced at the Frankish monastery of nearby Fulda, where it would seem to have been known to Adam of Bremen in the eleventh century.
4   Ogilvie and Richmond, *Agricola*, 1-6, 31-80, 317-35, represent the posthumous contribution of Richmond, prepared for final publication by Ogilvie.
5   Hanson, *Agricola*, 40-45,

6   Maxwell, *A Battle Lost*.

7   Syme, *Tacitus* I, 2.

8   Tacitus, *Agricola*, §§2-3.

9   As suggested by Syme, *Tacitus* I, 119, perhaps on a similar reading of the introduction to the *Agricola*.

10   Syme, *Tacitus* I, 7, 90.

11   Tacitus, *Agricola*, §4.

12   Tacitus, *Agricola*, §6.

13   Tacitus, *Agricola*, §§13, 17.

14   Tacitus, *Agricola*, §§2-3, 7, 39-45.

15   Tacitus, *Agricola*, §2.

16   Syme, *Tacitus* I, 135.

17   Tacitus, *Agricola*, §13. Tiberius and Claudius are also mentioned here.

18   Tacitus, *Agricola*, §21.

19   Tacitus, *Agricola*, §30.

20   On Tacitus's military tribunate, see A.R. Birley, *Tacitus: Agricola and Germany* [henceforth *Agricola*] (Oxford, 1999), xxii.

21   Syme, *Tacitus* I, 176; on our uncertainty about Tacitus's career between his praetorship in 88 and his consulate in 97, and our inability to draw firm conclusions from his writings, see *idem*, 68.

22   Syme, *Tacitus* I, 190.

23   Syme, *Tacitus* II, 621-24.

24   On Tacitus's first legateship, see T.A. Dorey, 'Agricola and Domitian', *Greece and Rome*, 2nd series 7 (1960), 66-71, at 70. Hanson, *Agricola*, 15-16, is in my view excessively cautious about the extent to which Tacitus will have relied upon Agricola as a source.

25   Tacitus, *Agricola*, §24 ('I have often heard him say that a single legion with a few auxiliaries could conquer and occupy Ireland…').

26   Syme, *Tacitus* II, 765. Paulinus's known (but lost) memoir dealt with campaigns in Mauretania rather than in Britain, but it may be thought likely that he also wrote about his British campaigns.

27   Plutarch, *De Defectu Oraculorum*, 18, in F.C. Babbitt (ed.), *Plutarch's Moralia*, Vol. V (London & Cambridge, 1936).

28   For a recent summation of the evidenciary value of Tacitus's works, see B. Hoffmann, 'Tacitus, Agricola and the Role of Literature in the Archaeology of the First Century AD', in E.W. Sauer (ed.), *Archaeology and Ancient History: breaking down the boundaries* (London & New York, 2004), 151-65.

29   By way of illustration, we know that Tacitus was taken to task on a passage of his *Historiae*, and agreed to omit it from a recitation, though not from the text; see Syme, *Tacitus* I, 120.

30   As reviewed by Ogilvie and Richmond, *Agricola*, 21-31; this aspect of the work is regarded as grounds for scepticism by Hanson, *Agricola*, 16-17, though less so by the still cautious Maxwell, *A Battle Lost*, 2-3.

31   On the *Dialogus* and Tacitus's abandonment of oratory, see Syme, *Tacitus* I, 104-111; on the historio-graphical character of the *Agricola*, see *ibid.*, 121-25, and Ogilvie and Richmond, *Agricola*, 11-20.

32   M. Henig, 'Togidubnus and the Roman Liberation', *British Archaeology* 37 (September 1998), aroused criticism and support of varying degrees of utility within the archaeological community; reasoned and balanced criticism was offered by W.S. Hanson's letter to the editor of *British Archaeology* 40 (December 1998). The unconvincing archaeological arguments are dropped in M. Henig, *The Heirs of King Verica: culture & politics in Roman Britain* (Stroud, 2002), 66-67, in favour of an argument based upon the unlikelihood that native leaders would have given battle to the Romans; for a more balanced analysis of this complex question, see S. Davies, *Welsh Military Institutions, 633–1283* (Cardiff, 2004), 111-35.

33   Henig, *Heirs of King Verica*, 67, seems now to be prepared to accept an 'insignificant skirmish' at Mons Graupius.

34   J. Keegan, *The Face of Battle* (London, 1976), 31.

CHAPTER TWO: A MAN KEEN ON ADVANCEMENT

1   Tacitus, *Agricola*, §44.

2   Ogilvie and Richmond, *Agricola*, 1-2.

3   Tacitus, *Agricola*, §4.

4   Tacitus, *Agricola*, §4.
5   Strabo, *Geographica*, iv.1, in H.L. Jones (ed.), *The Geography of Strabo*, Vol. II (London & New York, 1923).
6   Ogilvie and Richmond, *Agricola*, 2.
7   Tacitus, *Agricola*, §4; his appraisal of Graecinus is corroborated by ancient references to his writings, see Ogilvie and Richmond, *Agricola*, 2-3. On contemporary political attitudes towards philosophy, see Syme, *Tacitus* I, 39-40.
8   As proposed by Syme, *Tacitus* I, 20.
9   Syme, *Tacitus* I, 64. The title *laticlavius* refers to the *latus clavus* ('broad stripe'), the purple stripe that men of senatorial birth were entitled to wear on their tunics to denote their rank.
10   Tacitus, *Agricola*, §5. B. Dobson, 'Agricola's Life and Career', in *Agricola's Campaigns in Scotland: Scottish Archaeological Forum* 12 (1981), 1-13, at 1-2, has raised doubt that *electus quem contubernio aestimaret* places Agricola in Paulinus's personal staff.
11   Tacitus, *Agricola*, §5.
12   Tacitus, *Annales*, xii.36, in J. Jackson (ed.), *Tacitus: the Annals*, Vol. III (London & Cambridge MA, 1951); Tacitus, *Historiae*, iii.45, in C.H. Moore (ed.), *Tacitus: the Histories*, Vol. 1 (London & New York, 1925).
13   Tacitus, *Annales*, xii.40.
14   Tacitus, *Annales*, xii.36.
15   Tacitus, *Annales*, xii.39.
16   Tacitus, *Annales*, xii.31.
17   Tacitus, *Annales*, xii.31.
18   Tacitus, *Annales*, xiv.31.
19   Tacitus, *Annales*, xiv.29-30. On preferring Tacitus's explanation of the uprising to that of Cassius Dio, see Syme, *Tacitus* II, 762-65.
20   Tacitus, *Annales*, xiv.31-32.
21   Dobson, 'Agricola's Life and Career', 2.
22   Tacitus, *Annales*, xiv.32.
23   Tacitus, *Historiae*, ii.25.
24   Tacitus, *Annales*, xiv.33-37.
25   Ogilvie and Richmond, *Agricola*, 3.
26   Tacitus, *Annales*, xiv.33.
27   Tacitus, *Agricola*, §16.
28   Tacitus, *Annales*, xiv.31-32.
29   Tacitus, *Agricola*, §19.
30   Tacitus, *Agricola*, §19.
31   Syme, *Tacitus* I, 25-29.
32   Tacitus, *Agricola*, §13.
33   Tacitus, *Annales*, xiv.32.
34   Tacitus, *Agricola*, §21.
35   Tacitus, *Agricola*, §5.
36   Tacitus, *Agricola*, §5.
37   Tacitus, *Agricola*, §7.
38   On Agricola as the 'herald' of Trajan, see Syme, *Tacitus* I, 58.
39   Tacitus, *Agricola*, §5.
40   Tacitus, *Agricola*, §6.
41   Syme, *Tacitus* I, 21.
42   Tacitus, *Agricola*, §6.
43   Tacitus, *Agricola*, §6.
44   Tacitus, *Agricola*, §§6, 9; on the origins of Tacitus, see Birley, *Agricola*, xx-xxi.
45   Tacitus, *Agricola*, §6, outlines these years of Agricola's career.
46   On Hanson's view of Agricola's early career that 'nothing had occurred which would have marked him out as special in any way' (Hanson, *Agricola*, 36), see below.
47   Dobson, 'Agricola's Life and Career', 2-3.
48   Tacitus, *Agricola*, §6-7.
49   The case is summarised by Hanson, *Agricola*, 37-38.
50   Tacitus, *Agricola*, §7.

51   S. Frere, *Britannia: a history of Roman Britain* (3rd edn, London, 1987), 75, though legionary disposi-
     tions are a matter for dispute.

52   A.K. Goldsworthy, *The Roman Army at War* 100 *BC–AD* 200 (Oxford, 1996), 13-14, 28; it was com-
     mon for the first cohort to be an over-strength unit of more than 480 men.

53   Tacitus, *Agricola*, §7.

54   Syme, *Tacitus* I, 169.

55   Goldsworthy, *The Roman Army at War*, 29-30.

56   Tacitus, *Agricola*, §7.

57   Dobson, 'Agricola's Life and Career', 3.

58   Tacitus, *Annales*, xii.40; Tacitus, *Historiae*, iii.45.

59   Tacitus, *Historiae*, iii.45.

60   Tacitus, *Historiae*, iii.78-80.

61   Tacitus, *Agricola*, §17.

62   Tacitus, *Agricola*, §8.

63   Tacitus, *Agricola*, §17.

64   For an interpretation of the archaeological evidence pertaining to the Roman conquest of the
     Brigantes, see Hanson, *Agricola*, 60-65.

65   Tacitus, *Agricola*, §8.

66   Tacitus, *Agricola*, §9.

67   Tacitus, *Agricola*, §8.

68   Tacitus, *Historiae*, iii.45.

69   Tacitus, *Agricola*, §17.

70   Tacitus, *Agricola*, §9.

71   Tacitus, *Agricola*, §9.

72   Syme, *Tacitus* I, 67; a 'suffect' consulship was one that was conferred to supplement the number
     of consuls who had earned their offices through the annual elections. Hanson, *Agricola*, 36, argues
     about Agricola's early career that 'nothing had occurred which would have marked him out as spe-
     cial in any way'; for a contrary view that focuses upon Agricola's backing, see Dobson, 'Agricola's
     Life and Career', 3-5.

73   B.W. Jones, *The Emperor Titus* (London & Sydney, 1984), 79-86.

74   Tacitus, *Agricola*, §9.

CHAPTER THREE: ANOTHER ISLAND

1   Tacitus, *Agricola*, §22; on the Celtic name of the river Tay and Roman spellings of the same, see
     A.L.F. Rivet and C. Smith, *The Place-Names of Roman Britain* [henceforth *PNRB*] (London, 1981),
     470. Ogilvie and Richmond, *Agricola*, 57, and Hanson, *Agricola*, 84-85, consider the archaeological
     evidence relating to the route taken by Agricola northwards from Brigantia.

2   Tacitus, *Agricola*, §22.

3   Tacitus, *Agricola*, §10. For a review of the textual evidence relating to Caledonia, see J.G.F. Hind,
     'Caledonia and its Occupation under the Flavians', *PSAS* 113 (1983), 373-78.

4   W.J. Watson, *The History of the Celtic Place-Names of Scotland* [henceforth *CPNS*] (Edinburgh &
     London, 1926), 19, established the plausible associations between Ptolemy's *Varar Eiskhusis* and the
     river Beauly, formerly (and in Strathfarrar still) known as Farrar, and between Ptolemy's *Lemannonios
     Kolpos*, and the Lennox (Gaelic *Leamhnacht*); see also Rivet and Smith, *PNRB*, 387, 485-87.

5   J.C. Mann and D.J. Breeze, 'Ptolemy, Tacitus and the tribes of north Britain', *PSAS* 117 (1987), 85-91,
     at 91; for a rebuttal, see G.W.S. Barrow, 'The tribes of North Britain revisited', *PSAS* 119 (1989), 161-
     63.

6   Hind, 'Caledonia', 373-75.

7   Watson, *CPNS*, 20; Rivet and Smith, *PNRB*, 289-91. *Alba* meant 'the island of Britain', rather than
     Scotland, when the Gaelic place-name *Druim Alban* (Adomnán's *dorsum Britanniae*) was first coined.

8   AU 873.8; Watson, *CPNS*, 21.

9   Tacitus, *Agricola*, §23.

10   Watson, *CPNS*, 20-22; see also Rivet and Smith, *PNRB*, 250, 289-92. I am grateful to Alex Woolf for
     assistance and thoughts on these points.

11   Tacitus, *Agricola*, §27.

12   Ogilvie and Richmond, *Agricola*, 43; the case is made in detail by Rivet and Smith, *PNRB*, 245.

13   Rivet and Smith, *PNRB*, 140; Hanson, *Agricola*, 90–91, suggests that there may be a corresponding archaeological zone corresponding to Dumnonian territory.

14   Watson, *CPNS*, 103; on the potential significance of Clackmannan, see J.T. Koch, 'The Stone of the *Weni-kones*', *The Bulletin of the Board of Celtic Studies* 29 (1982), 87–89, at 88. Craigie affords impressive views across the plain of the Forth.

15   Watson, *CPNS*, 438.

16   Rivet and Smith, *PNRB*, 342–43.

17   P. Sims-Williams, *The Celtic Inscriptions of Britain: phonology and chronology*, c. 400–1200 [henceforth *CIB*] (Oxford & Boston, 2003), 378; on the date, see p. 363.

18   R.G. Collingwood and R.P. Wright (eds), *The Roman Inscriptions of Britain*, Vol. 1 (Oxford, 1965), §191.

19   The ethnonym is discussed by Koch, 'Stone of the *Weni-kones*', 89, who suggests however that the Uepogeni supplanted the Uenicones in Fife.

20   Rivet and Smith, *PNRB*, 140; on the name *Uacomagi*, see *ibid.*, 484–85. *Uenicones* seems to appear as *gwynngwn* in 'Aneirin', *E Gododin*, I. Williams (ed.), *Canu Aneirin* (Cardiff, 1938), l. 83; see Koch, 'Stone of the *Weni-kones*', 87–89.

21   Ogilvie and Richmond, *Agricola*, 43; both Hanson, *Agricola*, 119, and Maxwell, *A Battle Lost*, 25, have followed suit, though the maps presented by both include Gowrie in Uacomagian territory. Mann and Breeze, 'Tribes of northern Britain', 90, and D.J. Breeze (again), 'Agricola in the Highlands?', *PSAS* 120 (1990), 55–60, wish to place the Uacomagi in Strathspey, but it is a more natural reading of Ptolemy to place this people 'above' and between the Uenicones 'toward the west' (i.e. south) and the Taixali 'toward the east' (i.e. north), and so south of the Grampian massif; this has been appreciated by Hanson, *Agricola*, 117–20. The river Spey (*Tuesis*) would, in that event, be erroneously assigned to the Uacomagi in Ptolemy's *Geography*, on which see below.

22   Most readings of Ptolemy place the Uenicones in Fife, but Rivet and Smith, *PNRB*, 128, make a strong case for believing that the one place-name associated with them, the Roman port facility at [*H*]*orrea* [*Classis*], lay north of the Tay; following this view, Koch, 'Stone of the *Weni-kones*', 88, suggests that *Maen Gwynngwn*, the 'stone of the Uenicones', was located on the Tay. Even if an identification with Carpow is preferred, as it was by Ogilvie and Richmond, *Agricola*, 44, this would hardly preclude its association with a Gowrie people on the opposite bank of the Tay.

23   Watson, *CPNS*, 108. The Pictish regnal list in the Poppleton manuscript, M.O. Anderson, *Kings and Kingship in Early Scotland* (Edinburgh & London, 1973), 245, gives the clearly connected name *Círcenn*, while Fordoun, on the Bervie Water in the Howe of the Mearns, was evidently situated in *Mag Círcinn*, which ought to have denoted 'the heartland of Círcenn' (*mag*, literally a 'plain', tending to have a particular meaning in the early Middle Ages). *Círcenn*, literally 'ridge-head', would therefore seem to denote the Mearns, and it may therefore be suggested that the name conveys the sense of 'foremost part of Círech'. It was as *an Mhaoirne*, the *mormaer*'s district, anglicised as 'the Mearns', that Mag Círcinn was to become known by the tenth century (Watson, *CPNS*, 110–11); this name indicates that in Pictish times Mag Círcinn became the base of operations of a *mormaer*, and this may support the suggestion that it had formerly been the base of operations of the Pictish king of Círech. Perhaps it was also the tribal heartland of the Uacomagi.

24   Koch, 'Stone of the *Weni-kones*', 89, has pointed out that the ethnonym *Uepogeni* is probably connected with a Pictish personal name (variations of *Vipoig Namet*, Anderson, *Kings and Kingship*, 246); one wonders whether the Pictish personal name *Ciric* (*Chronicle of the Kings of Alba*, Anderson, *Kings and Kingship*, 251) is connected with the gaelicised *Círech*, and indeed whether the hypothetical Neo-Brittonic form of Uenicones (**Guincon*) underlies the Pictish personal name rendered *Finguine* in Gaelic sources.

25   Rivet and Smith, *PNRB*, 140–41.

26   Rivet and Smith, *PNRB*, 136, 138. If the Uacomagi are placed in the southern Pictish zone, the river Spey has been erroneously assigned to them in Ptolemy's *Geography*, where the river Dee (*Devana*) is mistaken as the name of a *polis*; Rivet and Smith, *PNRB*, 140. The thirteenth-century tract *De Situ Albanie* speaks of the Dee and the Spey as defining Mar and Buchan, one of the historic regions of Scotland, Anderson, *Kings and Kingship*, 243.

27   Hind, 'Caledonia', 376; on the names *Decantae* and *Taixali* see Watson, *CPNS*, 18–19, 22–23; Rivet and Smith, *PNRB*, 330, 463–64.

28   Although he has a great deal to say about Caratacos in his *Annales*, Tacitus makes no mention of him at all in the *Agricola*; one therefore wonders how Calgacos was portrayed in the lost books of his

Historiae that covered the Flavian period.

29   Tacitus, *Agricola*, §29.

30   K.H. Jackson, 'The Pictish Language', in F.T. Wainright (ed.), *The Problem of the Picts* (Edinburgh, 1955), 129-66, at 160, suggests that we call this language 'Pritenic'.

31   Diodorus Siculus, *Bibliotheca Historica*, v.28, in C.H. Oldfather (ed.), *Diodorus of Sicily*, Vol. III (London & Cambridge MA, 1939); Strabo, *Geographica*, iv.4.

32   Diodorus Siculus, *Bibliotheca Historica*, v.28.

33   Tacitus, *Agricola*, §11.

34   Diodorus Siculus, *Bibliotheca Historica*, v.28.

35   Caesar, *De Bello Gallico*, v.14, in H. J. Edwards (ed.), *Caesar: the Gallic War* (London & New York, 1917).

36   Diodorus Siculus, *Bibliotheca Historica*, v.27; see also Strabo, *Geographica*, iv.4.

37   Athenaeus, *Deipnosophistae*, iv.36, in C.B. Gulick (ed.), *The Deipnosophists: Athenaeus*, Vol. II (London, 1928).

38   M. Gluckman, *Politics, Law and Ritual in Tribal Society* (Oxford, 1965), 86-87.

39   These two types of tribal leader are contrasted by Gluckman, *Politics, Law and Ritual*, 116-17.

40   I. Armit and I.B.M. Ralston, 'The Iron Age', in K.J. Edwards and I.B.M. Ralston (eds), *Scotland After the Ice Age: environment, archaeology and history*, 8000 BC–AD 1000 (Edinburgh, 2003), 169-93, at 176.

41   Caesar, *De Bello Gallico*, vi.15; see also Davies, *Welsh Military Institutions*, 37-38.

42   Goldsworthy, *The Roman Army at War*, 44, 54, 56; on the *teulu*, see Davies, *Welsh Military Institutions*, 14-49.

43   Davies, *Welsh Military Institutions*, 22-26.

44   Davies, *Welsh Military Institutions*, 17.

45   Davies, *Welsh Military Institutions*, 19-20.

46   I. Armit, *Celtic Scotland* (London, 1997), 43.

47   Gluckman, *Politics, Law and Ritual*, 124-25.

48   Armit and Ralston, 'The Iron Age', 178.

49   Armit and Ralston, 'The Iron Age', 176-79.

50   Athenaeus, *Deipnosophistae*, iv.37; Caesar, *De Bello Gallico*, i.9.

51   The *fían* is discussed by K. McCone, *Pagan Past and Christian Present in Early Irish Literature* (Maynooth, 1990), 203-7. The quotation is from *Togail Bruidne Da Derga*. I am grateful to Alex Woolf for suggesting that the institution be raised for consideration in this context.

52   'Taliesin', *Arwyre gwyr katraeth gan dyd*, I. Williams (ed.), *The Poems of Taliesin* (Dublin, 1968), poem II, ll. 1-2, 6, 11, 28. Readers will find the J.P. Clancy translation of the poem in T.O. Clancy (ed.), *The Triumph Tree: Scotland's earliest poetry AD 550–1350* (Edinburgh, 1998), 79-80, both accessible and accurate. See also Davies, *Welsh Military Institutions*, 64-65.

53   D.N. Dumville (ed.), *Míniugud Senchasa Fher nAlban*, §§35-36, 43, in D. N. Dumville, 'Ireland and North Britain in the Earlier Middle Ages: contexts for *Míniugud Senchasa Fher nAlban*' in C. Ó Baoill and N.R. McGuire (eds), *Rannsachadh na Gàidhlig* 2000 (Aberdeen, 2002), 185-211; L. Alcock, *Kings and Warriors, Craftsmen and Priests in Northern Britain AD 550–850* (Edinburgh, 2003), 157, notes that the greatest 'great halls' could probably accommodate feasts that numbered a little more than 100 participants.

54   Davies, *Welsh Military Institutions*, 23-24.

55   As Goldsworthy, *The Roman Army at War*, 46, puts it upon reflection, 'tribal armies were not supple, manoeuvrable forces, but clumsy masses capable only of open battle or an ambush on a grand scale'.

56   Davies, *Welsh Military Institutions*, 36.

57   Caesar, *De Bello Gallico*, v.11.

58   Tacitus, *Annales*, xii.33.

59   Tacitus, *Agricola*, §30.

60   Tacitus, *Agricola*, §15.

61   Tacitus, *Agricola*, §21.

62   Tacitus, *Agricola*, §10.

63   Tacitus, *Agricola*, §13.

64   Caesar, *De Bello Gallico*, v.20-21, vi.12.

65   Caesar, *De Bello Gallico*, iv.21.

66   Tacitus, *Annales*, xii.37.

CHAPTER FOUR: WHEN SHALL WE HAVE AN ENEMY?

1   Tacitus, *Agricola*, §18.

2   Dobson, 'Agricola's Life and Career', 5.

3   Maxwell, *A Battle Lost*, 8; on the expectations that went with Agricola's age, see Syme, *Tacitus* I, 10-11, 67-68.

4   Hanson, *Agricola*, 69-83.

5   Maxwell, *A Battle Lost*, 8.

6   Tacitus, *Agricola*, §20.

7   Goldsworthy, *The Roman Army at War*, 114.

8   Syme, *Tacitus* I, 34; Birley, *Agricola*, xxii.

9   Tacitus, *Agricola*, §20.

10   Ogilvie and Richmond, *Agricola*, 4-5; Hanson, *Agricola*, 36.

11   Syme, *Tacitus* I, 45.

12   Tacitus, *Agricola*, §17.

13   Tacitus, *Agricola*, §18; Hanson, *Agricola*, 83, and Maxwell, *A Battle Lost*, 12, dismiss the idea of an Ordouician genocide. For an interpretation of the wider archaeological evidence pertaining to the Roman conquest of the Ordouices, see Hanson, *Agricola*, 47-48, 50-54.

14   Tacitus, *Annales*, xiv.30.

15   Tacitus, *Annales*, xiv.30.

16   Tacitus, *Annales*, xiv.30.

17   Tacitus, *Agricola*, §18.

18   Tacitus, *Agricola*, §18.

19   Hanson, *Agricola*, 65. For an interpretation of the archaeological evidence pertaining to the Roman conquest of the Brigantes, see Hanson, *Agricola*, 59-68.

20   Syme, *Tacitus* I, 122.

21   Tacitus, *Agricola*, §34.

22   On Tacitus's employment of speeches as a narrative device, see Syme, *Tacitus* I, 192-93.

23   Syme, *Tacitus* I, 3, 7, 17-18, 35, 49-50, 78. Frontinus seems to have died *c.*103, to be replaced in the priestly college by the younger Pliny.

24   Tacitus, *Agricola*, §23.

25   Something along such lines was proposed by A.R. Burn, *Agricola and Roman Britain* (London, 1953), 105; the view that Agricola's fortification of the Forth-Clyde isthmus related to imperial orders has been current ever since.

26   See Hanson, *Agricola*, 69-70 for a consideration of the role which Bassus would seem to have shouldered on Agricola's behalf.

27   A.R. Birley, *The Fasti of Roman Britain* (Oxford, 1981), 213, 404.

28   Jones, *Titus*, 149.

29   Tacitus, *Agricola*, §23; for considerations of the nature and extent of these efforts, see Ogilvie and Richmond, *Agricola*, 57-59.

30   Hanson, *Agricola*, 89, who goes on (93, 96-107) to challenge the view that these conquests were quick and easy.

31   I disagree here with Hanson, *Agricola*, 107, 115, and Maxwell, *A Battle Lost*, 14-15, who follows Hanson on this point.

32   Jones, *Titus*, 154-55. The ancient sources were preoccupied with the possibility that Domitian bore some responsibility for Titus's death.

33   For an example, see Syme, *Tacitus* I, 79.

34   See for example Burn, *Agricola and Roman Britain*, 105; Dobson, 'Agricola's Life and Career', 7-8.

35   The vagaries of Tacitus's language (*Agricola*, §24) have invited much controversy as regards this campaign. It was formerly the preferred model (e.g. Burn, *Agricola and Roman Britain*, 124) that it brought Agricola across the Firth of Clyde into Argyll; Hanson, *Agricola*, 93-96 provides a detailed consideration of the evidence that it was indeed conducted into south-west Scotland.

36   As it was put by Burn, *Agricola and Roman Britain*, 105, 'much in the tone of his biography, it has often been recognised, becomes easier to understand if it is taken to be in part an apologia for one who ended by becoming a somewhat controversial figure'.

37   So Dobson, 'Agricola's Life and Career', 6.

38   Burn, *Agricola and Roman Britain*, 124; Syme, *Tacitus* I, 14-15. See also Ogilvie and Richmond,

Agricola, 4 ('among the frontiers that of Britain counted for least in Imperial policy').

39 Dobson, 'Agricola's Life and Career', 9.

40 Hanson, *Agricola*, 112; Dorey, 'Agricola and Domitian', 67.

41 Hanson, *Agricola*, 84-85, challenging the traditional view (e.g. Burn, *Agricola and Roman Britain*, 96-97) that an advance was also made northwards from Luguvalium, modern Carlisle. On the name *Coriosopitum*, see Rivet and Smith, *PNRB*, 322-24.

42 For a discussion of these two tribes and their territories, see Rivet and Smith, *PNRB*, 138-40. It seems that the Nouantae too were an early Christian people, appearing in *E Gododin*, l. 824, as *gwyr enouant*, 'men of *Nouant*'; J.T. Koch, *The Gododdin of Aneirin: text and context from Dark-Age North Britain* (Cardiff & Andover, 1997), lxxxii-lxxxiii.

43 For a discussion of Tacitus's evidence, see J.G.F. Hind, 'Summers and Winters in Tacitus' Account of Agricola's Campaigns in Britain', *Northern History* 21 (1985), 1-18, at 5-9.

44 Tacitus, *Agricola*, §24. The first-century tribal surveys which form the basis of Ptolemy's treatment of Ireland and northern Britain, and the account of the Ravenna *Cosmography*, may have been conducted in this period of relative hiatus in 81 and 82.

45 Hanson, *Agricola*, 176-77; I agree here with Dobson, 'Agricola's Life and Career', 8.

46 Tacitus, *Agricola*, §24.

47 Tacitus, *Agricola*, §41.

48 Syme, *Tacitus* I, 100.

49 Hanson, *Agricola*, 115.

50 On Tacitus's quaestorship, see Birley, *Agricola*, xxii. As an advocate – indeed the pioneer – of the earlier Agricolan chronology, Birley dates the relevant events accordingly. If one accepts his reconstruction but prefers the later chronology, Tacitus will have been elected quaestor in 81 and held office in 82, under Domitian. It bears mentioning, however, that his later association of his elevation with Titus, rather than Domitian, may not be strictly accurate, since it would not be particularly surprising if he sought to distance himself from the latter emperor.

51 Tacitus, *Agricola*, §39.

52 Syme, *Tacitus* I, 28.

53 Syme, *Tacitus* I, 32.

54 Hanson, *Agricola*, 120.

55 I.G. Smith, *The First Roman Invasion of Scotland: a geographical review* (Edinburgh, 1987), 14-18, puts forward a reasonable case for reading the Flavian survey as implying that these Dumnonian fort-sites were built prior to the battle of Mons Graupius. Hanson, *Agricola*, 120-21, allows for this possibility, but elsewhere (*ibid.*, 108-13) shows that it remains uncertain on archaeological grounds which Flavian forts were begun during Agricola's legateship, and which were founded subsequently. Maxwell, *A Battle Lost*, 20-21, is more guarded about seeing Agricolan forts north of the Forth.

56 Tacitus, *Germania*, §33.

57 Tacitus, *Agricola*, §18.

58 Tacitus, *Agricola*, §§16, 22.

59 Hanson, *Agricola*, 135.

60 Caesar, *De Bello Gallico*, v.20.

61 Tacitus, *Agricola*, §25.

62 A likelihood that emerges from the division of the force into three later in the summer; see Maxwell, *A Battle Lost*, 31.

63 Tacitus, *Agricola*, §25 (*saepe iisdem castris pedes equesque et nauticus miles mixti copiis et laetitia sua quisque facta, suos casus adtollerent, ac modo silvarum ac montium profunda, modo tempestatum ac fluctuum adversa, hinc terra et hostis, hinc victus Oceanus militari iactantia compararentur*).

64 Tacitus, *Agricola*, §25 (*aperto maris sui secreto ultimum victis perfugium clauderetur*).

65 Hanson, *Agricola*, 127; for discussions of these camps, see Ogilvie and Richmond, *Agricola*, 62-64; Hanson, *Agricola*, 121-27. On the depth of penetration into northern Britain implied by Tacitus's narrative, see Hind, 'Summers and Winters', *passim*, including the map at 6; see also Ogilvie and Richmond, *Agricola*, 44-45. It is difficult to reconcile the thesis that the events of 83 took place between the Forth and the Tay with the testimony of the *Agricola*; see Maxwell, *A Battle Lost*, 26-33.

66 For a general discussion of such camps, see Goldsworthy, *The Roman Army at War*, 111-13.

67 Goldsworthy, *The Roman Army at War*, 113.

68 Hanson, *Agricola*, 178. It seems likely that some unknown *praefectus castrorum* is deserving of whatever praise these camps may deserve.

69 Maxwell, *A Battle Lost*, 82. Hanson, *Agricola*, 122-23, regards 'the methodology whereby camps are divided into groups… and the groups, in turn, assigned to specific campaigns' as one that 'does not stand up to detailed critical examination'.

70 Tacitus, *Agricola*, §25. The manuscript tradition is not unanimous in using the plural *castella* here; I follow Ogilvie's preference for *castella* over *castellum*; see Ogilvie and Richmond, *Agricola*, 241.

71 Goldsworthy, *The Roman Army at War*, 52-53; Davies, *Welsh Military Institutions*, 39.

72 Smith, *First Roman Invasion*, 22.

73 S.S. Frere, 'The Flavian Frontier in Scotland', in *Agricola's Campaigns in Scotland: Scottish Archaeological Forum* 12 (1981), 89-97, at 89-91; see also Hanson, *Agricola*, 121.

74 Goldsworthy, *The Roman Army at War*, 25-26.

75 Davies, *Welsh Military Institutions*, 89.

76 Hanson, *Agricola*, 95.

77 Frere, 'Flavian Frontier', 95.

78 Tacitus, *Agricola*, §25; Maxwell, *A Battle Lost*, 31, makes the case for the division of the Roman army along legionary lines.

79 Tacitus, *Agricola*, §25.

80 Tacitus, *Agricola*, §33; Goldsworthy, *The Roman Army at War*, 105-06.

81 Goldsworthy, *The Roman Army at War*, 114.

82 Strabo, *Geographica*, iv.4.

83 Ogilvie and Richmond, *Agricola*, 65.

84 Goldsworthy, *The Roman Army at War*, 106.

85 Goldsworthy, *The Roman Army at War*, 33-37.

86 Tacitus, *Agricola*, §26.

87 Goldsworthy, *The Roman Army at War*, 58, observes, for example, that Gallic auxiliary horsemen could make unreliable scouts.

88 Davies, *Welsh Military Institutions*, 141-42.

89 The desire to locate this marching camp roused scholarly effort comparable to that devoted to the location of Mons Graupius. Ogilvie and Richmond, *Agricola*, 64, suggested that the fort called *Victoria*, which Richmond identified as Strageath, was named for this victory; commemoration of Mons Graupius seems more likely.

90 Tacitus, *Agricola*, §26.

91 Tacitus, *Agricola*, §27 (*coetibus et sacrificiis conspirationem civitatum sancirent*). For similar doubts regarding Tacitus's triumphant discussion of this skirmish, see Hanson, *Agricola*, 176.

92 Goldsworthy, *The Roman Army at War*, 53.

93 That we may take such a view of the native achievement in the summer of 83 is put forward by D.J. Breeze, 'Why did the Romans fail to conquer Scotland?', *PSAS* 118 (1988), 3-22, at 7, and again, more forcefully, in *idem.*, *Roman Scotland: frontier country* (London, 1996), 97.

94 Hind, 'Summers and Winters', 9-10.

95 Maxwell, *A Battle Lost*, 44; this supersedes such reconstructions as Burn, *Agricola and Roman Britain*, 147; P. Marren, *Grampian Battlefields: the historic battles of north east Scotland from AD84 to 1745* (Aberdeen, 1990), 8, 11, 13.

96 Hanson, *Agricola*, 96.

97 Tacitus, *Agricola*, §28.

98 Tacitus, *Agricola*, §27.

99 Tacitus, *Agricola*, §29.

100 Tacitus, *Agricola*, §29.

101 Tacitus, *Agricola*, §29; on auxiliary recruitment, see Goldsworthy, *The Roman Army at War*, 69.

102 Syme, *Tacitus* I, 14.

CHAPTER FIVE: AD MONTEM GRAUPIUM

1 Hanson, *Agricola*, 129.

2 Maxwell, *A Battle Lost*, 72-90, surveys past attempts to locate the battlefield.

3 Tacitus, *Agricola*, §29.

4 On this presumption, see Ogilvie and Richmond, *Agricola*, 65; J.K. St Joseph, 'The camp at Durno, Aberdeenshire, and the site of Mons Graupius', *Britannia* 9 (1978), 271-87, at 282; Hanson, *Agricola*, 130-31.

5   Tacitus, *Agricola*, §§33-34.

6   Goldsworthy, *The Roman Army at War*, 45, 56.

7   Syme, *Tacitus* I, 23.

8   Ogilvie and Richmond, *Agricola*, 65; Hanson, *Agricola*, 128.

9   Maxwell, *A Battle Lost*, 98.

10 Hanson, *Agricola*, 129-30, 136-37.

11 Tacitus, *Agricola*, §38.

12 Hanson, *Agricola*, 143, agrees, in another context, that we ought to be vigilant for such adjustments that Tacitus may have made in order to avoid anticlimax.

13 Hind, 'Summers and Winters', 11.

14 Hanson, *Agricola*, 163-65; Maxwell, *A Battle Lost*, 113-16.

15 Tacitus, *Agricola*, §29; on the Roman summer, see Ogilvie and Richmond, *Agricola*, 318.

16 Tacitus, *Agricola*, §29.

17 Hind, 'Summers and Winters', 11-12.

18 Goldsworthy, *The Roman Army at War*, 90-92.

19 Hanson, *Agricola*, 127, though Hanson elsewhere (p. 128) downplays this point and places much stock in the battle of Mons Graupius having taken place late in the season, e.g. pp. 41-42 on the subject of Agricolan chronology.

20 Goldsworthy, *The Roman Army at War*, 91-92.

21 Maxwell, *A Battle Lost*, 44; see also Hind, 'Summers and Winters', 13; Smith, *First Roman Invasion*, 38.

22 Tacitus, *Agricola*, §38.

23 Ogilvie and Richmond, *Agricola*, 64.

24 Ogilvie and Richmond, *Agricola*, 64.

25 Tacitus, *Agricola*, §35.

26 Maxwell, *A Battle Lost*, 84-87.

27 Hanson, *Agricola*, 130-34; Maxwell, *A Battle Lost*, 93-96.

28 St Joseph, 'The camp at Durno', 277-87. Durno has similarly eclipsed Knock Hill and the Pass of Grange north-east of Keith, where the circumstantial case is similar to, if rather increasingly weaker than, that relating to Raedykes; see Maxwell, *A Battle Lost*, 94-101.

29 Maxwell, *A Battle Lost*, 104-10, offers a favourable but cautious overview; see also Marren, *Grampian Battlefields*, 18-19.

30 St Joseph, 'The camp at Durno', 279.

31 G. Maxwell, 'The Evidence of the Temporary Camps', in *Agricola's Campaigns in Scotland: Scottish Archaeological Forum* 12 (1981), 25-54, at 40; Hanson, *Agricola*, 131-34; Maxwell, *A Battle Lost*, 108-09. I am grateful to Fraser Hunter for reminders regarding the Kintore evidence.

32 St Joseph, 'The camp at Durno', 279.

33 Hanson, *Agricola*, 135-36; the problem was raised earlier by Keppie, 'Mons Graupius', 84, but not to the same level of detail.

34 Watson, *CPNS*, 56; for Professor Jackson's thoughts, see R. Feachem, 'Mons Craupius=Duncrub?', *Antiquity* 44 (1970), 120-24; J.K. St Joseph, 'Air Reconnaissance in Britain, 1969-72', *The Journal of Roman Studies* 63 (1973), 214-46, at 120n. Another example of a voiceless Celtic consonant appearing as a voiced Latin consonant occurs in *Britannia*, which began with a *P-* in British.

35 Watson, *CPNS*, 56; for a summary of the different views of the etymology of this word, see Rivet and Smith, *PNRB*, 370-71.

36 Feachem, 'Mons Craupius=Duncrub?', 218-19.

37 St Joseph, 'Air Reconnaissance in Britain, 1969-72', 219-20. Maxwell, *A Battle Lost*, 18-19, reviews the strong case for seeing the Abernethy marching-camp as an Agricolan installation.

38 A.J. Dunwell and L.J.F. Keppie, 'The Roman Temporary Camp at Dunning, Perthshire: evidence from two recent excavations', *Britannia* 26 (1995), 51-62.

39 I owe this information to personal communication with my colleague Eberhard Sauer, in reference to unpublished conference discussions.

40 Here I follow the argument put forward by Smith, *First Roman Invasion*, 17, as against the identification of *Lindum* (Drumquhassle) proposed by Rivet and Smith, *PNRB*, 393. On the meaning of *Lindum*, see Rivet and Smith, *PNRB*, 391-92.

41 Rivet and Smith, *PNRB*, 372-73, suggest 'an unlocated Roman fort near Monifieth', while Smith, *First Roman Invasion*, 17-18, suggested Friarton or Carpow.

42 Smith, *First Roman Invasion*, 18. On the general location of *Victoria*, see Rivet and Smith, *PNRB*,

139-40. Ogilvie and Richmond, *Agricola*, 43, identified Strageath as Victoria, and were followed in this by Hind, 'Summers and Winters', 14-15. Rivet and Smith, *PNRB*, 499, prefer Inchtuthil, rejecting the possibility that the name commemorated a victory in battle, but Maxwell, *A Battle Lost*, 116-18, summarises reasonable objections on both points.

43   Hind, 'Summers and Winters', 14-15.

44   Watson, *CPNS*, 56; that these terms cannot be equated with Welsh *crwb*, a hump, has been shown by A. Breeze, 'Philology on Tacitus's Graupian Hill and Trucculan Harbour', *PSAS* 132 (2002), 305-311, at 305-06.

45   Watson, *CPNS*, 56; Jackson's comments in Feachem, 'Mons Craupius=Duncrub?', 120n, do not depend upon any particular meaning being assigned either to **Craupius* or *Crup*.

46   Rivet and Smith, *PNRB*, 370-71.

47   These nominative plural forms deduced with reference to R. Thurneysen, *A Grammar of Old Irish* (rev. and trans. D.A. Binchy and O. Bergin [Dublin, 1946], 181, 189.

48   K. Jackson, *Language and History in Early Britain* [henceforth *LHEB*] (Edinburgh, 1953), §22.1; also Sims-Williams, *CIB*, 23, 55. On comparable developments in Pictish, see Jackson, 'Pictish Language', 162. Jackson, in his analysis of the slim evidence, raised doubt as to whether 'i-affection' took place in Pictish based on the attested Pictish name *Alpin*. This form may be the result of Gaelic influence, since the 'i-affected' form of the name, *Elpin*, is attested in Pictish (as Jackson himself observed). Breeze, 'Philology on Tacitus's Graupian Hill', 305, notes that in the years after 1955 Professor Jackson seems to have wavered himself between the different possibilities.

49   That lenition took place in Pictish is established by Jackson, 'Pictish Language', 163-64.

50   On apocope in Pictish, see Jackson, 'Pictish Language', 166.

51   *Chron. Kings of Alba*, §44. The protagonists at the battle of *Druim Crup* were Dub (*Niger*), the king of Alba, and a man called *Caniculus* (Cainnech?); the named casualties of the fighting, in which Dub was victorious, are the two most important men in Atholl (the *mormaer* and the abbot of Dunkeld), suggesting the possibility that Caniculus was an Atholl-based rival to Dub's royal authority.

52   W.F. Skene, *Celtic Scotland: a history of ancient Alban*, Vol. I (History and Ethnology) (2nd edn, Edinburgh, 1886), 366. For Drumcroube, see J.M. Thomson (ed.), *The Register of the Great Seal of Scotland*, Vol. I (AD 1306–1424) (Edinburgh & London, 1984), no. 634 (dated 14 February 1380). I am grateful to Angus Watson and Simon Taylor for calling my attention to this reference.

53   Keppie, 'Mons Graupius', 83; followed by Hanson, *Agricola*, 130. On the dates of the marching-camps of Dunning and Abernethy, see *idem*, 84-85. The case is reviewed further, and with no greater optimism, by Maxwell, *A Battle Lost*, 101-04.

54   Smith, *First Roman Invasion*, 38-39. The philological argument based upon Watson's etymology must now, however, be abandoned.

55   AU 729.2. In modern Welsh this word is *mynydd*.

56   AU 728.4; AT 728.4.

57   The fact that the camp is not, therefore, oriented to face Duncrub is further evidence that the latter was not Mons Graupius.

58   T.M. Charles-Edwards, *Early Christian Ireland* (Cambridge, 2000), 13. Neither was Latin *mons* used exclusively for high mountains.

59   *Gask* itself (*gasg*) is simply descriptive of the ridge as a physical feature, Watson, *CPNS*, 500; no doubt locals knew it simply as 'the ridge', and *Druim Crup* ('Crup Ridge'), on this model, would be a name given by non-locals.

60   Maxwell, *A Battle Lost*, 120.

61   St Joseph, 'The camp at Durno', 282; see also Davies, *Welsh Military Institutions*, 53.

62   M.E.C. Stewart *et al.*, 'The excavation of a henge, stone circles and metal working area at Moncrieffe, Perthshire', *PSAS* 115 (1985), 125-50.

63   These twelfth-century assemblies are mentioned in the *Assise Regis Willelmi*, §iv, in *The Acts of the Parliaments of Scotland*, Vol. 1: 1124–1423 (London, 1844), 369-84, at 373. My thanks are owed to Alex Woolf for drawing my attention to this text.

64   Hanson, *Agricola*, 120-21. For a discussion of the evidence of a Flavian phase at Inveralmond, see H.C. Adamson and D.B. Gallagher, 'The Roman fort at Bertha, the 1973 excavation', *PSAS* 116 (1986), 195-204, at 202.

65   For a discussion of the rather different case surrounding the location of the Varian defeat of AD 9, see E.W. Sauer, 'A Matter of Personal Preference? The relevance of different territories and types of evidence for Roman history', in Sauer (ed.), *Archaeology and Ancient History*, 114-33, at 123-26.

66   Hanson, *Agricola*, 135; consider also Hoffman, 'Tacitus, Agricola and the Role of Literature', 160-61.
67   Hanson, *Agricola*, 136.

CHAPTER SIX: STRIKING TERROR

1   Tacitus, *Agricola*, §12.
2   Tacitus, *Agricola*, §27.
3   Tacitus, *Agricola*, §25.
4   Tacitus, *Agricola*, §25.
5   A fact of which I am reminded by Professor Ralston, personal communication.
6   Davies, *Welsh Military Institutions*, 84.
7   Goldsworthy, *The Roman Army at War*, 107-08; save for the matter of surveyors, this model seems more apt for Agricola than that given at 106-07, for the legate was anticipating battle.
8   Goldsworthy, *The Roman Army at War*, 143.
9   Goldsworthy, *The Roman Army at War*, 127.
10   A point rightly stressed by Goldsworthy, *The Roman Army at War*, 113.
11   For descriptions of this engagement, see R. Nicholson, *Edward III and the Scots: the formative years of a military career 1327–1335* (Oxford, 1965), 84-90; M. Penman, *David II, 1329–71* (East Linton, 2004), 47-48.
12   Cassius Dio, 'Historia Romana', lx.20, in H.B. Foster (ed.), *Dio's Roman History*, Vol. VII (Loeb Classical Library, London & New York, 1924); Caesar, *De Bello Gallico*, v.9.
13   Tacitus, *Annales*, xii.33.
14   Caesar, *De Bello Gallico*, v.9.
15   'Taliesin', *Arwyre gwyr katraeth gan dyd*, ll. 17-22. See also *E Gododin*, ll. 154, 268, 282-84, 1154; Davies, *Welsh Military Institutions*, 92. Readers will find the J.P. Clancy translation of *E Gododin* in Clancy, *Triumph Tree*, 47-78, both accessible and accurate.
16   J. Sinclair (ed.), *The Statistical Account of Scotland 1791–1799*, Vol. XI, 194. This being said, the depictions of the river north of Dunning on Adair's Strathearn maps of 1683 and *c*.1720 are not at all dissimilar to its modern course; cf. National Library of Scotland digital library.
17   J. Sinclair (ed.), *The Statistical Account of Scotland 1791–1799*, Vol. XI, 194.
18   Tacitus, *Agricola*, §18; *patrius nandi usus, quo simul seque et arma et equos regunt*.
19   Dio, *History*, lx.20.
20   Tacitus, *Annales*, xii.35.
21   Tacitus, *Agricola*, §29.
22   It is of course traditional to locate the Calidonii to the north of the Mounth, but recent work by Alex Woolf in particular, as well as by the present author, as yet unpublished in both cases, shows that it is more satisfactory to locate the Calidonii in the southern Pictish zone.
23   Alcock, *Kings and Warriors*, 156.
24   I am indebted to Alex Woolf, personal communiciation, for discussions of this question relating to ongoing work of his.
25   See for example Gluckman, *Politics, Law and Ritual*, 107-16.
26   Davies, *Welsh Military Institutions*, 64-66, 72-73.
27   Henig, *Heirs of King Verica*, 67.
28   Keppie, 'Mons Graupius', 85; Hanson, *Agricola*, 138.
29   Goldsworthy, *The Roman Army at War*, 130, discusses the lack of vigilance of the Helvetii against Caesar (*De Bello Gallico*, i.21-22).
30   Goldsworthy, *The Roman Army at War*, 51.
31   Diodorus Siculus, *Bibliotheca Historica*, v.31; Strabo, *Geographica*, iv.4; Caesar, *De Bello Gallico*, vi.16. Caesar does not mention human sacrifice in connection with divination, but as druidic sacrificial practice only, which must be regarded as extremely dubious propaganda intended to demonise the druids. For the name *vatis* (pl. *vates*), see Strabo, *Geographica*, iv.4.
32   Diodorus Siculus, *Bibliotheca Historica*, v.29; Strabo, *Geographica*, iv.4. The taking of heads by Roman soldiers, if most commonly auxiliaries rather than legionaries, is also attested; see Goldsworthy, *The Roman Army at War*, 271-76.
33   Athenaeus, *Deipnosophistae*, iv.36; Caesar, *De Bello Gallico*, vi.15.
34   Diodorus Siculus, *Bibliotheca Historica*, v.29-30; Strabo, *Geographica*, iv.4.

35   Tacitus, *Agricola*, §36; Davies, *Welsh Military Institutions*, 156-57.

36   Davies, *Welsh Military Institutions*, 28.

37   Diodorus Siculus, *Bibliotheca Historica*, v.30. The archaeological record suggests that such helmets had become obsolete in Gaul by this period (I. Ralston, personal communication). On a similar absence of helmets from early Wales, see Davies, *Welsh Military Institutions*, 147.

38   Vindolanda Writing Tablet 164, consulted at Vindolanda Tablets Online, http://vindolanda.csad. ox.ac.uk/

39   Davies, *Welsh Military Institutions*, 145.

40   Diodorus Siculus, *Bibliotheca Historica*, v.30; Strabo, *Geographica*, iv.4.

41   Tacitus, *Agricola*, §36.

42   *E Gododin*, ll. 94-95; see also Davies, *Welsh Military Institutions*, 143: 'these three items [shield, sword and spear] might vary in style and quality, but they were the standard arms of the military elite'.

43   Diodorus Siculus, *Bibliotheca Historica*, v.30.

44   Strabo, *Geographica*, iv.4.

45   On the arms carried by auxiliary infantry in this period, see Goldsworthy, *The Roman Army at War*, 20, 209-17. I am grateful to Fraser Hunter for particular advice.

46   M. Charles, 'Mons Graupius Revisited: Tacitus, Agricola and auxiliary infantry', *Athenaeum* 92 (2004), 127-38, at 136, has noticed both that Tacitus here describes the auxiliaries as if they were legionaries, and that his account follows literary models, but prefers to trust him. Tacitean error or stylisation at this point would tend to undermine but little Charles's argument that these auxiliaries fought as 'heavy' infantry at Mons Graupius, rather than as 'light' infantry.

47   Goldsworthy, *The Roman Army at War*, 45-46.

48   On the significance of experience, see Goldsworthy, *The Roman Army at War*, 25.

49   Tacitus, *Agricola*, §35.

50   Ogilvie and Richmond, *Agricola*, 115, 272.

51   Tacitus, *Agricola*, §35.

52   Diodorus Siculus, *Bibliotheca Historica*, v.29.

53   Caesar, *De Bello Gallico*, iv.33.

54   *E Gododin*, ll. 1145-46.

55   Caesar, *De Bello Gallico*, iv.33.

56   Dio, *History*, lx.20.

57   Diodorus Siculus, *Bibliotheca Historica*, v.30; on the sounding of horns in battle in medieval Wales, see Davies, *Welsh Military Institutions*, 182.

58   Tacitus, *Agricola*, §33.

59   *E Gododin*, A text, ll. 21-23, 39, 46-48, 103, 211, 418, 423, 735, 742-43, 753-54, 856-57, 864, 882-83, 952-53, 1016-17, 1214-16, 1244, 1249-50.

60   Goldsworthy, *The Roman Army at War*, 50.

61   *E Gododin*, ll. 77, 267, 668; 'Taliesin', *Arwyre gwyr katraeth gan dyd*, ll. 16, 25; see also Davies, *Welsh Military Institutions*, 182-83.

62   Davies, *Welsh Military Institutions*, 39.

63   Goldsworthy, *The Roman Army at War*, 131-32.

64   Tacitus, *Agricola*, §35. Ogilvie and Richmond, *Agricola*, 79, thought it unlikely that the British peoples can have supplied Rome with auxiliary cavalry, but the evidentiary record has changed sufficiently to allow us to take a different view; see Davies, *Welsh Military Institutions*, 159. The recruitment of local warriors as *auxilia* was common enough; see Goldsworthy, *The Roman Army at War*, 35.

65   Goldsworthy, *The Roman Army at War*, 21; see also C.M. Gilliver, 'Mons Graupius and the Role of Auxiliaries in Battle', *Greece and Rome*, 2nd series 43 (1996), 54-67, who argues the case with specific reference to Mons Graupius.

66   Gilliver, 'Mons Graupius and the Role of Auxiliaries', 58-59. Charles, 'Mons Graupius Revisited', *passim*, offers an aggressive counterbalance as regards the relative 'lightness' and 'heaviness' of legionary and auxiliary soldiers.

67   Tacitus, *Agricola*, §33. It seems possible that Tacitus can have modelled this oration upon an actual speech delivered by Agricola.

68   Tacitus, *Agricola*, §35.

69   Goldsworthy, *The Roman Army at War*, 145-46.

70   Tacitus, *Agricola*, §35. That Tacitus here implies no slur against the auxiliaries, even if modern commentators have read his words otherwise, is shown by Gilliver, 'Mons Graupius and the Role of

Auxiliaries', 60–62.

71   Tacitus, *Agricola*, §35.

72   Tacitus, *Agricola*, §35; Goldsworthy, *The Roman Army at War*, 138–40.

73   Tacitus, *Agricola*, §35.

74   On the matter of space, see Maxwell, *A Battle Lost*, 60; Goldsworthy, *The Roman Army at War*, 138–40. If every fourth cohort was not a double cohort, this estimate would have to be adjusted downwards fairly significantly.

75   Goldsworthy, *The Roman Army at War*, 261–62.

CHAPTER SEVEN: BRINGING MATTERS TO A DECISION

1   Goldsworthy, *The Roman Army at War*, 139.

2   Tacitus, *Agricola*, §35; Goldsworthy, *The Roman Army at War*, 123.

3   Goldsworthy, *The Roman Army at War*, 149–50. For a discussion of the different types of javelin that might have been involved, see Charles, 'Mons Graupius Revisited', 135.

4   Tacitus, *Agricola*, §36.

5   Tacitus, *Annales*, xii.35.

6   Goldsworthy, *The Roman Army at War*, 67, 187–88, makes the point that modern studies have shown that only a small proportion of fighting men in any unit tend to take the trouble to take aim before attacking with missile weapons, and that 'a target could be surprisingly easy to miss for the archer or slinger shooting without aiming'.

7   Goldsworthy, *The Roman Army at War*, 59–60, discusses such fighters in Gaul. There are various references to boys playing spear-throwing games in early Irish literature.

8   Tacitus, *Germania*, §29. This view is no doubt intended to flatter a people that had become valued allies.

9   Tacitus, *Agricola*, §36.

10   Goldsworthy, *The Roman Army at War*, 193.

11   Goldsworthy, *The Roman Army at War*, 178.

12   Goldsworthy, *The Roman Army at War*, 182, 257–58.

13   *E Gododin*, ll. 124, 444–45.

14   Tacitus, *Agricola*, §36.

15   Tacitus, *Annales*, xii.35.

16   'Taliesin', *Anwyre gwyr katraeth gan dyd*, ll. 17–18; *E Gododin*, l. 135.

17   Goldsworthy, *The Roman Army at War*, 197.

18   Tacitus, *Agricola*, §36.

19   Goldsworthy, *The Roman Army at War*, 253.

20   Tacitus, *Agricola*, §36.

21   Dio, *History*, lx.20.

22   Goldsworthy, *The Roman Army at War*, 194.

23   Keegan, *The Face of Battle*, 50–52.

24   Tacitus, *Agricola*, §37.

25   Goldsworthy, *The Roman Army at War*, 58.

26   Tacitus, *Agricola*, §36.

27   Tacitus, *Agricola*, §36.

28   Nicholson, *Edward III and the Scots*, 87–88.

29   Tacitus, *Agricola*, §37.

30   Tacitus, *Agricola*, §37.

31   Goldsworthy, *The Roman Army at War*, 154; Davies, *Welsh Military Institutions*, 32.

32   Goldsworthy, *The Roman Army at War*, 155–56.

33   Goldsworthy, *The Roman Army at War*, 203.

34   A point that Professor Ralston has raised with me in personal communication.

35   Tacitus, *Agricola*, §37. On the size of an *ala* of cavalrymen, see Goldsworthy, *The Roman Army at War*, 21–22.

36   Hanson, *Agricola*, 175.

37   Goldsworthy, *The Roman Army at War*, 230.

38   Goldsworthy, *The Roman Army at War*, 224, 227.

39   Goldsworthy, *The Roman Army at War*, 57.

40   Goldsworthy, *The Roman Army at War*, 138-39.

41   Tacitus, *Agricola*, §37.

42   Maxwell, *A Battle Lost*, 66.

43   *E Gododin*, ll. 24, 616.

44   Goldsworthy, *The Roman Army at War*, 262.

45   Nicholson, *Edward III and the Scots*, 89.

46   Tacitus, *Agricola*, §37.

47   Tacitus, *Agricola*, §37; *E Gododin*, ll. 224-25, 229, 233.

48   Goldsworthy, *The Roman Army at War*, 239.

49   Tacitus, *Agricola*, §37.

50   Goldsworthy, *The Roman Army at War*, 157.

51   Tacitus, *Agricola*, §§37-38.

52   Tacitus, *Agricola*, §37.

53   Tacitus, *Agricola*, §37.

54   Tacitus, *Agricola*, §38.

55   Davies, *Welsh Military Institutions*, 128-29, 133, 135.

56   Goldsworthy, *The Roman Army at War*, 47, 56-57.

CHAPTER EIGHT: DEVASTATION AND SILENCE

1   Goldsworthy, *The Roman Army at War*, 162, 167.

2   Maxwell, *A Battle Lost*, 67-68.

3   Goldsworthy, *The Roman Army at War*, 162, 167.

4   Tacitus, *Agricola*, §38.

5   Tacitus, *Agricola*, §38.

6   Tacitus, *Agricola*, §38.

7   Davies, *Welsh Military Institutions*, 91.

8   Tacitus, *Agricola*, §38.

9   Goldsworthy, *The Roman Army at War*, 51-52.

10   Tacitus, *Agricola*, §38.

11   Tacitus, *Agricola*, §38.

12   Tacitus, *Agricola*, §38.

13   For discussion see Rivet and Smith, *PNRB*, 272-73; see also Smith, *First Roman Invasion*, 40. T.F. O'Rahilly, *Early Irish History and Mythology* (Dublin, 1946), 528-29, was inclined to 'suggest tentatively' that a link be made between *Uoretia*, the contemporaneous name of the river Forth as suggested by early forms of this river-name in Gaelic and Welsh, and *Boresti*; see also Watson, *CPNS*, 52-54; Rivet and Smith, *PNRB*, 270.

14   Hanson, *Agricola*, 140.

15   Tacitus, *Agricola*, §38; Ogilvie and Richmond, *Agricola*, 66.

16   Tacitus, *Agricola*, §38.

17   Frere, 'Flavian Frontier', 91, believes that these forts were established in the previous year, and were among the *ultra castella* that came under attack.

18   Tacitus, *Agricola*, §38.

19   Tacitus, *Agricola*, §38.

20   Tacitus, *Agricola*, §38. For the argument that *Tru[t]ulensis Portus* is a corrupt reference to Richborough (*Rutupiae*) in Kent, and that 'the nearer shore of Britain' denotes the 'nearer shore' to Rome, i.e. the south shore of the island, see Rivet and Smith, *PNRB*, 478-80. For alternative explanations, see Hanson, *Agricola*, 141-42, and Breeze, 'Philology on Tacitus's Graupian Hill', 308-11.

CHAPTER NINE: THOROUGHLY TAMED

1   Tacitus, *Agricola*, §40.

2   Hanson, *Agricola*, 42; Maxwell, *A Battle Lost*, 115.

3   Tacitus, *Agricola*, §39-40.

4   Syme, *Tacitus* I, 23.

5   Syme, *Tacitus* I, 32-33 dates the 'decisive and evil turn' in Domitian's principate to 89. See also Dobson, 'Agricola's Life and Career', 11; Hanson, *Agricola*, 181.

6   The case is summarised by B.W. Jones, *The Emperor Domitian* (London & New York, 1992), 58.

7   Syme, *Tacitus* I, 65-70; Dorey, 'Agricola and Domitian', 69-70; Hanson, *Agricola*, 183-84.

8   The case is examined by Dorey, 'Agricola and Domitian', 66-71. For a similar suggestion that Trajan too was made out by his panegyrists to have been far more antagonistic towards Domitian than he had been in fact, see Syme, *Tacitus* I, 33-34.

9   Syme, *Tacitus* I, 23.

10   Tacitus, *Agricola*, §40.

11   Tacitus, *Dialogus de Oratoribus*, §§11-13. W. Peterson (ed.), *Tacitus: Dialogus, Agricola, Germania* (Loeb Classical Library, London & New York, 1932).

12   Syme, *Tacitus* I, 72.

13   Syme, *Tacitus* I, 69. Dorey, 'Agricola and Domitian', 70, argues that his 'retirement and early death were due to a breakdown in health occasioned by continuous overwork'. The possibility of a stress-related death certainly cannot be ruled out.

14   Tacitus, *Agricola*, §43; see also Hanson, *Agricola*, 182-83.

15   Tacitus, *Agricola*, §§41-42.

16   Hanson, *Agricola*, 149; the approach would seem to have much in common with that taken in Wales; cf. *idem*, 179.

17   Tacitus, *Historiae*, i.2.

18   Tacitus, *Agricola*, §30; *nulla iam ultra gens, nihil nisi fluctus ac saxa*.

19   Tacitus, *Agricola*, §30.

20   The evidence at successive stages of archaeological understanding is summarised by Ogilvie and Richmond, *Agricola*, 67-76; Frere, 'Flavian Frontier', 95-97; Hanson, *Agricola*, 146-66; and Breeze, 'Why did the Romans fail to conquer Scotland?', 9-10.

21   Breeze, 'Why did the Romans fail to conquer Scotland?', 6-11, shows how undaunting a prospect the conquest of northern Britain ought to have been. See also Hanson, *Agricola*, 151; but, for the suggestion that native aggression was a factor in the abandonment of some installations, see *idem*, 165-66.

22   Jones, *Domitian*, 133.

23   Keppie, 'Mons Graupius', 85; see also Burn, *Agricola and Roman Britain*, 157 ('Calgacus and his friends and the men who fell at Mons Craupius might have lost a battle, but they had won the war').

24   Maxwell, *A Battle Lost*, vii.

25   Goldsworthy, *The Roman Army at War*, 77, reminds us of this fact.

26   On the latter point, now recognised as a significant factor in the 'failure' of Rome to maintain the Agricolan conquests, see Hanson, *Agricola*, 152-53.

27   For discussion see J.E. Fraser, *The Battle of Dunnichen 685* (Stroud, 2002), 19-32.

28   See Hanson, *Agricola*, 168-69, for a discussion of this point.

29   Hanson, *Agricola*, 171.

30   Hanson, *Agricola*, 168-71 considers the evidence relating to settlement, economic and environmental factors.

31   P. Heather, 'State Formation in Europe in the First Millennium AD', in B.E. Crawford (ed.), *Scotland in Dark Age Europe* (St Andrews, 1994), 47-70.

32   Xiphilinus, epitome of Dio, *History*, lxxvii, in Foster (ed.), *Dio's Roman History*, Vol. IX.

33   See discussion in Heather, 'State Formation', 55-61. A comparable phenomenon, involving the formation of two 'confederations' in Ireland, has similarly now been posited by Charles-Edwards, *Early Christian Ireland*, 158-59.

CHAPTER TEN: FINAL THOUGHTS

1   Maxwell, *A Battle Lost*, vii.

2   Sauer, 'Matter of Personal Preference?', 126.

3   Ramsay MacMullen, *Christianizing the Roman Empire (AD 100–400)* (New Haven & London, 1984), 7.

4   Feachem, 'Mons Craupius=Duncrub?', 120; the wish is registered in the preamble to this article.

5   Keppie, 'Mons Graupius', 86.

6   Marren, *Grampian Battlefields*, 18-19, furnishes some examples of this enthusiasm.

Bibliography

ANCIENT AND MEDIEVAL SOURCES

'Aneirin', *E Gododin*. I. Williams (ed.), *Canu Aneirin* (Cardiff, 1938).

Annals of Tigernach. W. Stokes (ed.), *The Annals of Tigernach*, Vol. 1 (Felinfach, 1993).

Annals of Ulster. S. Mac Airt and G. Mac Niocaill (eds), *The Annals of Ulster (to A.D. 1131)* (Dublin, 1983).

Assise Regis Willelmi. The Acts of the Parliaments of Scotland, Vol. 1: 1124–1423 (London, 1844).

Athenaeus, *Deipnosophistae*. C.B. Gulick (ed.), *The Deipnosophists: Athenaeus*, Vol. II (London & New York, 1928).

Chronicle of the Kings of Alba, Paris, Bibliothèque Nationale, MS Latin 4126, 28v A–29v A, in Anderson, *Kings and Kingship*, 249–53.

Iulius Caesar, *De Bello Gallico*. H.J. Edwards (ed.), *Caesar: the Gallic War* (London & New York, 1917).

De Situ Albanie. Paris, Bibliothèque Nationale, MS Latin 4126, 26v A–27r B, in Anderson, *Kings and Kingship*, 240–43.

Cassius Dio, 'Historia Romana'. H.B. Foster (ed.), *Dio's Roman History*, Vols. VII and IX (London & New York, 1924).

Diodorus Siculus, *Bibliotheca Historica*. C.H. Oldfather (ed.), *Diodorus of Sicily*, Vol. III (London & Cambridge MA, 1939).

Míniugud Senchasa Fher nAlban. D.N. Dumville, 'Ireland and North Britain in the Earlier Middle Ages: contexts for *Míniugud Senchasa Fher nAlban*', in C. Ó Baoill and N.R. McGuire (eds), *Rannsachadh na Gàidhlig 2000* (Aberdeen, 2002), 185-211.

Plutarch, *De Defectu Oraculorum*. F.C. Babbitt (ed.), *Plutarch's Moralia*, Vol. V (London & Cambridge, 1936).

Strabo, *Geographica*. H.L. Jones (ed.), *The Geography of Strabo*, Vol. II (London & New York, 1923).

Register of the Great Seal of Scotland. J.M. Thomson (ed.), *The Register of the Great Seal of Scotland*, Vol. I, AD 1306–1424 (Edinburgh & London, 1984).

Tacitus, *Annales*. J. Jackson (ed.), *Tacitus: the Annals*, Vol. III (London & Cambridge MA, 1951).

Tacitus, *De Vita Agricolae*. R.M. Ogilvie and I. Richmond (eds), *Cornelii Taciti: De Vita Agricolae* (Oxford, 1967).

Tacitus, *Dialogus de Oratoribus*. W. Peterson (ed.), *Tacitus: Dialogus, Agricola, Germania* (London & New York, 1932).

Tacitus, *Germania*. W. Peterson (ed.), *Tacitus: Dialogus, Agricola, Germania* (London & New York, 1932).

Tacitus, *Historiae*. C.H. Moore (ed.), *Tacitus: the Histories*, Vol. I (London & New York, 1925).

'Taliesin', *Arwyre gwyr katraeth gan dyd*. I. Williams (ed.), *The Poems of Taliesin*. Dublin, 1968, poem II.

Vindolanda Tablet §164. Vindolanda Tablets Online, http://vindolanda.csad.ox.ac.uk/

SECONDARY STUDIES

Adamson, H.C. and D.B. Gallagher, 'The Roman fort at Bertha, the 1973 excavation', *Proceedings of the Society of Antiquaries of Scotland* 116 (1986), 195-204.

Alcock, L. *Kings and Warriors, Craftsmen and Priests in Northern Britain AD* 550–850 (Edinburgh, 2003).

Anderson, M.O. *Kings and Kingship in Early Scotland* (Edinburgh & London, 1973).

Armit, I. *Celtic Scotland* (London, 1997).

Armit, I. and I.B.M. Ralston, 'The Iron Age', in K.J. Edwards and I.B.M. Ralston (eds), *Scotland After the Ice Age: environment, archaeology and history,* 8000 *BC–AD* 1000 (Edinburgh, 2003), 169-93.

Barrow, G.W.S. 'The Tribes of North Britain Revisited', *Proceedings of the Society of Antiquaries of Scotland* 119 (1989), 161-63.

Birley, A.R. *The Fasti of Roman Britain* (Oxford, 1981).

Birley, A.R. *Tacitus:* Agricola *and* Germany (Oxford, 1999).

Breeze, A. 'Philology on Tacitus's Graupian Hill and Trucculan Harbour', *Proceedings of the Society of Antiquaries of Scotland* 132 (2002), 305-311.

Breeze, D.J. 'Why did the Romans fail to conquer Scotland?', *Proceedings of the Society of Antiquaries of Scotland* 118 (1988), 3-22.

Breeze, D.J. 'Agricola in the Highlands?', *Proceedings of the Society of Antiquaries of Scotland* 120 (1990), 55-60.

Breeze, D.J. *Roman Scotland: frontier country* (London, 1996).

Burn, A.R. *Agricola and Roman Britain* (London, 1953).

Charles, M. 'Mons Graupius Revisited: Tacitus, Agricola and auxiliary infantry', *Athenaeum* 92 (2004), 127-38.

Clancy, T.O. (ed.), *The Triumph Tree: Scotland's earliest poetry AD* 550–1350 (Edinburgh, 1998).

Collingwood, R.G. and R.P. Wright (eds), *The Roman Inscriptions of Britain,* Vol. 1 (Oxford, 1965).

Charles-Edwards, T.M. *Early Christian Ireland* (Cambridge, 2000).

Davies, S. *Welsh Military Institutions,* 633–1283 (Cardiff, 2004).

Dobson, B. 'Agricola's Life and Career', in *Agricola's Campaigns in Scotland: Scottish Archaeological Forum* 12 (1981), 1-13.

Dorey, T.A. 'Agricola and Domitian', *Greece and Rome,* 2nd series 7 (1960), 66-71.

Dunwell, A.J. and L.J.F. Keppie, 'The Roman Temporary Camp at Dunning, Perthshire: evidence from two recent excavations', *Britannia* 26 (1995), 51-62.

Feachem, R. 'Mons Craupius=Duncrub?', *Antiquity* 44 (1970), 120-24.

Fraser, J.E. *The Battle of Dunnichen* 685 (Stroud, 2002).

Frere, S.S. 'The Flavian Frontier in Scotland', in *Agricola's Campaigns in Scotland: Scottish Archaeological Forum* 12 (1981), 89-97.

Frere, S. *Britannia: a history of Roman Britain,* 3rd edn (London, 1987).

Gilliver, C.M. 'Mons Graupius and the Role of Auxiliaries in Battle', *Greece and Rome,* 2nd series 43 (1996), 54-67.

Gluckman, M. *Politics, Law and Ritual in Tribal Society* (Oxford, 1965).

Goldsworthy, A.K. *The Roman Army at War* 100 *BC–AD* 200 (Oxford, 1996).

Hanson, W.S. *Agricola and the Conquest of the North* (London, 1987).

Heather, P. 'State Formation in Europe in the First Millennium AD', in B.E. Crawford (ed.), *Scotland in Dark Age Europe* (St Andrews, 1994), 47-70.

Henig, M. 'Togidubnus and the Roman Liberation', *British Archaeology* 37 (September 1998).

Henig, M. *The Heirs of King Verica: culture & politics in Roman Britain* (Stroud, 2002).

Hind, J.G.F. 'Caledonia and its Occupation under the Flavians', *Proceedings of the Society of Antiquaries of Scotland* 113 (1983), 373-78.

Hind, J.G.F. 'Summers and Winters in Tacitus' Account of Agricola's Campaigns in Britain', *Northern History* 21 (1985), 1-18.

Hoffmann, B. 'Tacitus, Agricola and the Role of Literature in the Archaeology of the First Century AD', in Sauer (ed.), *Archaeology and Ancient History,* 151-65.

Jackson, K. *Language and History in Early Britain* (Edinburgh, 1953).

Jackson, K.H. 'The Pictish Language', in F.T. Wainright (ed.), *The Problem of the Picts* (Edinburgh, 1955), 129-66.

Jones, B.W. *The Emperor Titus* (London & Sydney, 1984).

Jones, B.W. *The Emperor Domitian* (London & New York, 1992).

Keegan, J. *The Face of Battle.* London, 1976.

Keppie, L. 'Mons Graupius: the search for a battlefield', in *Agricola's Campaigns in Scotland: Scottish Archaeological Forum* 12 (1981), 79-88.

Koch, J.T. 'The Stone of the *Weni-kones*', *The Bulletin of the Board of Celtic Studies* 29 (1982), 87-89.

Koch, J.T. *The Gododdin of Aneirin: text and context from Dark-Age North Britain* (Cardiff & Andover, 1997).

MacMullen, R. *Christianizing the Roman Empire (A.D.* 100–400) (New Haven & London, 1984).

Mann, J.C. and D.J. Breeze, 'Ptolemy, Tacitus and the Tribes of North Britain', *Proceedings of the Society of Antiquaries of Scotland* 117 (1987), 85-91.

Marren, P. *Grampian Battlefields: the historic battles of north east Scotland from AD84 to 1745* (Aberdeen, 1990).

Maxwell, G. 'The Evidence of the Temporary Camps', in *Agricola's Campaigns in Scotland: Scottish Archaeological Forum* 12 (1981), 25-54.

Maxwell, G. *A Battle Lost: Romans and Caledonians at Mons Graupius* (Edinburgh, 1990).

McCone, K. *Pagan Past and Christian Present in Early Irish Literature* (Maynooth, 1990).

Nicholson, R. *Edward III and the Scots: the formative years of a military career 1327–1335* (Oxford, 1965).

Ogilvie, R.M. and I. Richmond (eds), *Cornelii Taciti: De Vita Agricolae* (Oxford, 1967).

O'Rahilly, T.F. *Early Irish History and Mythology* (Dublin, 1946).

Penman, M. *David II, 1329–71* (East Linton, 2004).

Rivet, A.L.F. and C. Smith. *The Place-Names of Roman Britain* (London, 1981).

Sauer, E.W. (ed.), *Archaeology and Ancient History: breaking down the boundaries* (London & New York, 2004).

Sauer, E.W. 'A Matter of Personal Preference? The relevance of different territories and types of evidence for Roman history', in Sauer (ed.), *Archaeology and Ancient History*, 114-33.

Sims–Williams, P. *The Celtic Inscriptions of Britain: phonology and chronology, c. 400–1200* (Oxford & Boston, 2003).

Sinclair, J. (ed.), *The Statistical Account of Scotland 1791–1799*, Vol. XI.

Skene, W.F. *Celtic Scotland: a history of ancient Alban*, Vol. I (History and Ethnology). (2nd edn, Edinburgh, 1886).

Smith, I.G. *The First Roman Invasion of Scotland: a geographical review* (Edinburgh, 1987).

Stewart, M.E.C. *et al.*, 'The excavation of a henge, stone circles and metal working area at Moncrieffe, Perthshire', *Proceedings of the Society of Antiquaries of Scotland* 115 (1985), 125-50.

St Joseph, J.K. 'Air Reconnaissance in Britain, 1969–72', *The Journal of Roman Studies* 63 (1973), 214-46.

St Joseph, J.K. 'The camp at Durno, Aberdeenshire, and the site of Mons Graupius', *Britannia* 9 (1978), 271-87.

Syme, R. *Tacitus*, 2 vols (Oxford, 1958).

Thurneysen, R. *A Grammar of Old Irish*. Revised and translated by D.A. Binchy and O. Bergin (Dublin, 1946).

Watson, W.J. *The History of the Celtic Place-Names of Scotland* (Edinburgh & London, 1926).

List of Illustrations and Maps

ILLUSTRATIONS

1   Modern monument on the site of Trimontium. Author's collection.
2   Two peaks of Eildon Hill. Author's collection.
3   View across modern Perth from the Moncrieffe Hill hillfort. Author's collection.
4   Schiehallion, viewed from 'the Queen's View' on Loch Tummell. Author's collection.
5   View south down Strathtay from the King's Seat hillfort, Dunkeld. Author's collection.
6   The river Devon. Author's collection.
7   Dumyat Hill, viewed from Craigrie, Clackmannan. Author's collection.
8   Dumyat Hill, rising above Abbey Craig and the Wallace Monument. Author's collection.
9   The site of the Roman installation at Raedykes. Author's collection.
10 View of Stonehaven Bay from Raedykes. Author's collection.
11 Bennachie, viewed from the site of the Roman installation at Durno. Author's collection.
12 Upstanding remains of Roman ramparts at Ardoch. Author's collection.
13 Upstanding remains of Roman ramparts at Ardoch. Author's collection.
14 Upstanding remains of Roman ramparts at Ardoch. Author's collection.
15 The site of the Roman installation at Strageath. Author's collection.
16 View along the Roman road leading from Strageath and along the Gask Ridge. Author's collection.
17 The site of the Roman installation at Dunning. Author's collection.
18 Upstanding remains of Roman ramparts at Kincladie Wood, Dunning. Author's collection.
19 Upstanding remains of Roman ramparts at Kincladie Wood, Dunning. Author's collection.
20 Craig Rossie, viewed from the site of the Roman installation at Dunning. Author's collection.
21 The Cairnie Braes section of the Gask Ridge. Author's collection.
22 The Cairnie Braes above Dalreoch. Author's collection.
23 The Cairnie Braes above Forteviot. Author's collection.
24 The Cairnie Braes above Dalreoch. Author's collection.
25 The Cairnie Braes above Forteviot. Author's collection.
26 The Cairnie Braes above Dalreoch. Author's collection.
27 The Cairnie Braes above Forteviot. Author's collection.
28 View south up the Dunning burn from Baldinnies. Author's collection.
29 The river Earn at Forteviot Bridge. Author's collection.
30 The convex lower slopes of the Cairnie Braes. Author's collection.
31 The convex lower slopes of the Cairnie Braes at a distance. Author's collection.
32 View south from the Cairnie Braes towards Dunning. Author's collection.
33 View south from the Cairnie Braes towards Dunning. Author's collection.
34 View of the river Earn from the Cairnie Braes. Author's collection.
35 View of the river Earn from the Cairnie Braes. Author's collection.
36 View of the river Earn from the Cairnie Braes. Author's collection.

37   The Moncrieffe Hill hillfort. Author's collection.
38   The Moncrieffe Hill hillfort. Author's collection.
39   View westwards from the Moncrieffe Hill hillfort along the Gask Ridge. Author's collection.
40   Aberlemno battle scene. Author's collection.

MAPS

1   Caledonia in the time of Calgacos.
2   Strathearn and the Gask Ridge.
3   The Dunning Camp and the Cairnie Braes.
4   The Roman approach to Mons Graupius in context.
5   The Roman advance in context.
6   The British counter-strike in context.

Index

Aberdeenshire, 36, 71
Aberlemno battle scene, 91, 99
Abernethy, 73, 77, 115
Adam of Bremen, 134
Aedui, 44
Africa, 120
Agricola (De Vita Agricolae)
  composition by Tacitus of,
    11-14
  reliability of, 14-17, 127-28
  sources of, 14-15
  treatment of British peoples
    in, 44-45, 79, 121
  treatment of battle of
    Mons Graupius in, 12,
    69-70
Agricola, see Iulius Agricola
Alauna, see Ardoch
Alba, kingdom of, 77
Allan Water, river, 35, 59
Almond, river, 56
Ancalites, 34
Anglesey, 49, 83
Angus, 36, 71, 115, 121, 122, 125
Anuak, 40
Aquitania, 30
Ardoch (Alauna), 35, 59-60, 67,
    73, 77, 81
Argyll, 42, 124
Asia, 25, 26, 66, 120
Atholl, 34, 36, 60, 76, 122, 144
Atrebates, 45
Augustus, see under 'Iulius
    Caesar Octavianus'
Aulus Atticus, 102-03
Aulus Plautius, 20, 26, 52-53,
    82-83, 90, 98, 102
Aulus Vitellius, 26, 27, 28

auxiliaries, Roman, 27, 66, 83,
    87-88, 92, 102
Ayrshire, 35

Balgour, 95
Balliol, Edward, 82, 110
Banffshire, 71
Bankhead, 82, 89, 105-06
Bannockburn, 68, 127
Bassus, see Gaius Salvius
    Liberalis Nonius Bassus
Batavi, 92-93, 99-102, 113
Bennachie, 71-72, 77, 78, 129
Bernicia, 91, 124
Bertha, see Inveralmond
Boece, Hector, 67
Bolanus, see Vettius Bolanus
Boresti, 115-16
Boudica, 22-23, 24, 49, 64
Boudican uprising, 22-23, 24,
    28, 29, 47, 49, 56, 121
Breadalbane, 60, 76
Brigantes, 20, 28-29, 48, 50, 51,
    57, 62, 64
Britannia
  establishment of Roman
    province of, 20-21, 26
  support for Vitellius in, 26
Buchan, 34, 83

Caerleon, see Isca [Silurum?]
Cairnie Braes, 76-78, 80-82, 89,
    95, 99, 104-06
Cairnie Wood, 73, 76
Caledonia
  conquest of, 121-22, 123-25
  headmanship in, 38-41, 42-
    44, 83-84, 86, 105, 123

population estimates for, 84,
    112
  Roman invasion in AD 80
    of, 33, 35
  territorial extent of, 33-34,
    121
Caledonians, see Calidonii
Caledonii, see Calidonii
Calgacos
  appearance of, 37-38
  attitude towards Rome of,
    44-45
  fate of, 105, 107, 110, 123
  leadership of Calidonii by,
    37, 44, 59-60, 63-64, 68,
    77, 80, 84, 88, 94, 105, 107
  leadership qualities of, 38,
    41, 42, 43, 63, 80, 88, 98,
    105-06
  name of, 37
  social position of, 38-41
  treatment in *Agricola* of, 14,
    37, 44-45
Calidonii
  name of, 34-35, 63
  coalition of, 35, 37, 64-65,
    68-69, 79-80, 83, 125-26
  funerary inscription of a
    member of, 35
  military actions in AD 83
    of, 58-64, 70, 79, 83, 88
  military equipment of, 86-87
  reactions to battle of Mons
    Graupius of, 114-16, 122,
    123
Caligula, see Gaius Caesar
Camulodunum (modern
    Colchester), 22, 23, 35

Caniculus, 144

Caratacos, 21, 37, 43, 44-45, 49,
    82-83, 88, 94, 98, 100, 123

Cargill, 59

Cartimandua, 20, 28, 30

Cassiuellaunos, 43, 44-45

Catus Decianus, 23

Catuuellauni, 21, 43, 44-45, 57

centurions, 27, 29, 42, 48, 56-57,
    65, 100

Cerialis, see Petillius Cerialis

chariots, 89-90, 97-98, 103-04,
    105, 107

Chatti, 9

Chronicle of the Kings of Alba, 75

Círech, 36, 138

Clackmanann, 35

classis Britannica, 15, 53, 57-58,
    68, 80, 115, 116

Claudius Nero Germanicus
    ('Claudius'), 20, 45, 52

Claudius Ptolemaeus
    ('Ptolemy'), 33, 73-74

Clyde, firth of, 34

Clyde, river, 121, 124

Cocceius Nerva ('Nerva'),
    12, 26

Codex Aesinas, 11-12

Colchester, see Camulodunum

comitati, see household retinues

Commios, 45

Corbridge, see Coriosopitum

Coriosopitum (modern
    Corbridge), 53

Cornelius Tacitus
    composition of *Agricola* by,
        see *Agricola*
    consulate of, 11
    Dialogue on Orators of, 16,
        119-20
    hostility towards Domitian
        of, 12-13, 25, 44, 54-55,
        117-18
    legateship of, 11, 15, 28
    literary career of, 13, 15-16
    marriage to Iulia of, 25, 47
    origins, probably
        Narbonensian, of, 15
    patriotism of, 14
    praetorship of, 14
    relationship with Domitian
        of, 118
    quaestorship of, 54
    tribunate, possibly in
        Britannia, of, 14, 48, 54

Cowie Water, river, 71

Craigrie, Clackmannan, 35, 138

Craig Rossie, 75-76, 78, 81, 128

Culloden, 127

Cumbria, 29, 53

Dacia, 55

Dalginross, 67

Dalreoch bridge, 83

Danube, river, 52, 55, 122, 123

daryanogyon, 86

Decantae, 36-37, 84

Deganwy, 37

Dee, river, 37

Demetrios, Flavian sailor, 15

Deskford carnyx, 90

Deva (modern Chester), 49

Deveron, river, 37

Devon, county, 35

Devon, river, 35

Didius Gallus, 28

divination, 85-86

divinities, 35, 49, 85

Domitia, wife of Agricola, 25,
    48, 66

Domitian, see Flavius
    Domitianus

Domitius Decidus, father-in-
    law of Agricola, 25

Dorsum Crup, 75

druids, 49, 91

Drumalban, 34

Drummossie Muir, see under
    'Culloden'

Dub, king of Alba, 144

DVMNOGENOS, 35

Dumnonii, 35, 45, 53, 55, 56, 57,
    59-60, 63, 64, 73-74, 76-
    77, 80, 84, 122, 124

Duncrub, 72-77, 128-29

Duncrub Burn, 75

Dunkeld (*Dún Chaillden*), 34, 144

Dunning, 72-76, 78, 81-82, 93,
    97, 111, 128

Dunning Burn, 82

Dupplin Moor, 82, 110

Dupplin Moor, battle of, 82,
    104-05, 106, 107, 110

Durno, see Logie Durno

Earn, river, 59, 73, 76, 77, 78,
    82-83, 89, 92, 95, 97-102,
    105, 107, 111, 115

Eboracum (modern York),
    29, 48

Ecgfrith, 124

Elpin, 75

Exeter, see Isca Dumnoniorum

Fendoch, 67

fian-like bands, 41-42, 43, 59,
    84, 86, 88, 89, 91-92, 110

fianna, 41

Fife, 35-36, 56, 57, 64, 67

Flavian fortifications in
    Scotland, 56, 59, 64, 77,
    115, 116, 121-22, 123-24

Flavian survey of northern
    Britain, 33-34, 35, 36-37,
    53, 73-74, 83, 115, 121, 141

Flavius Domitianus
    ('Domitian')
    British policy of, 51-53, 54-
        55, 118, 120-22
    assassination of, 12-13, 123
    assumption of title
        Germanicus by, 9
    attitude towards alliances of,
        55-56
    attitude towards the familiars
        of Titus of, 52, 118
    campaign against the Chatti
        by, 9
    portrayal in *Agricola* of, 13, 25
    principate of, 19, 117
    reaction to battle of Mons
        Graupius of, 117
    threats to the principate of,
        55, 120
    visitation of Continental
        frontiers by, 53

Flavius Vespasianus ('Vespasian')
    British policy of, 47, 49-51,
        52
    capture of the principate by,
        26, 27
    character of, 48
    death of, 51
    favour towards Agricola of,
        26, 27, 30, 47, 51, 65, 118-19
    military experience in
        Britannia of, 26, 48, 51,
        57, 102
    portrayal in *Agricola* of, 13

Flodden, battle of, 127

Forteviot, 82, 83

Forteviot bridge, 83

Forth, river, 35, 50, 52, 53, 54,
    55, 57, 60, 72, 80, 120

Forth-Clyde isthmus, 33, 35,
    50-53, 56

Fortingall, 68

Forum Iulii (modern Fréjus),
    19, 26

Fothrif, 36

Fréjus, see Forum Iulii

Frontinus, see Iulius Frontinus
Fulda, 134

Gaius Caesar ('Caligula'), 13, 19
Gaius Salvius Liberalis Nonius
    Bassus, 51, 56
Gallia Narbonensis, 15, 19, 25,
    26, 30, 31
Galloway, 53
Gallus, see Didius Gallus
Gask Ridge, 73, 76-78, 80, 82,
    84, 92-93, 110, 115, 126,
    128-29
Gaul, 20, 24, 30, 34, 35, 37-38,
    39, 41, 44, 61, 65, 72, 86-
    87, 89, 91, 99, 103, 107,
    110, 146
Germania, 53, 65, 91, 92
Gododdin, see Uotodin
Gododdin elegies, 36, 42, 87, 90,
    91, 100, 110, 123
gosgordd, 39
Gowrie, 36, 77, 121
Graecinus, see Iulius Graecinus
Grampian mountains, 34, 36-
    37, 67, 71, 72, 83, 115,
    116, 121
Grampian region, 67
Gwen Ystrat, battle of, 82

Hadrian's Wall, 86, 124
Hersfeld, 134
horrea Classis, 73
household retinues, 39-40, 42-
    43, 59, 66, 86, 91-92
Humber, river, 20

Iberia, 61
Iceni, 21-23, 29, 56
Inchtuthil, 64, 122
Inveralmond ('Bertha'), 56, 59,
    73, 77
Iona, 75
Ireland, 41, 53, 76
Isca Dumnoniorum (modern
    Exeter), 48
Isca [Silurum?] (modern
    Caerleon), 48
Isla, river, 122
Iulia, daughter of Agricola, 25,
    47, 48
Iulia Procilla, mother of
    Agricola, 19, 20, 26, 66
Iulius Agricola
    appointment to the
        priesthood of, 31
    attitude towards Britannia

of, 47
birth of, 19
Brigantian war of, 50, 51
Caledonian campaign of 80
    of, 33, 35, 51, 55-56, 57,
    59, 60, 77
Caledonian war of, 37, 50-
    52, 57-64, 66, 77, 79-80,
    83, 88, 114-16, 120, 123-24
character of, 19, 23-25, 28,
    29, 30-31, 48, 49-50, 53,
    56, 60-61, 65, 89, 94-95,
    97, 99, 118, 120
chronology of British leg-
    ateship of, 9, 47, 52, 65
consulate of, 9, 11, 30
correspondences of, 15, 65,
    79-80, 95, 111, 113, 121
death of, 11, 120
elevation to patrician status
    of, 30
Gallic heritage of, 20
generalship skills of, 42, 47-
    48, 49, 58, 59-63, 69-70,
    80, 81, 85, 88-89, 92, 97,
    99-102, 106-08, 111, 113-14
grooming for proconsular
    legateship of, 29-30
legionary legateship in
    Britannia of, 26-30, 53, 62
making of northern
    alliances by, 55
marriage of, 25
Maternus in *Dialogus*
    possibly modelled on,
    119-20
mentorship of Tacitus by, 15,
    48, 118
Mons Graupius campaign
    of, 68-70, 76-77, 79-81
name of, 19
Ordouician war of, 49, 51,
    70, 83
ornamenta triumphalia of, 15,
    117, 123
political skills of, 25-26,
    119-20
praetorian legateship in
    Aquitania of, 30
praetorship of, 25-26
quaestorship in Asia of, 25, 66
relationship with Domitian
    of, 52, 54-56, 66, 93-95,
    117-20
relationship with Titus of,
    51-52, 118
reminiscences of, 15, 23, 24,

29, 44, 63, 79, 85, 94, 121
retirement of, 52, 117-20,
    122, 123
schooling of, 19-20, 24
south-western campaign in
    AD 82 of, 52-53
support of Vespasian by, 22,
    26-27, 29, 30, 48, 55
tribunate in Britannia of,
    20-24, 48-49, 56, 64
Tribunate of the People of, 25
use of native informants by,
    62, 69, 81, 116
use of scouts (*exploratores*)
    by, 62, 68-69, 81, 114-16
war diary possibly kept by, 15
Iulius Caesar ('Julius Caesar'),
    13, 19, 43, 44-45, 57,
    82, 90
Iulius Caesar Octavianus
    ('Augustus'), 13, 19, 119
Iulius Frontinus, 48-49, 50, 140
Iulius Graecinus, father of
    Agricola, 19, 20, 25, 31,
    66, 136

javelins, 87, 98-99, 102
Jerusalem, 51
Judaea, 26, 51
Julius Caesar, see under 'Iulius
    Caesar'

Keirwoodhead, 82, 89, 105-06
Kincardineshire, 68, 71
Kincladie Wood, 73, 81
King's Seat hillfort, Dunkeld, 34
Kinnaird Head, 34
Kintillo, 77
Kintore, 58, 72
Knock Hill, 143

Lanarkshire, 60
Lancashire, 29
Lauderdale, 53
legio II Adiutrix, 48, 52, 57
legio II Augusta, 48, 52, 57
legio IX Hispana, 22, 24, 28,
    29, 48, 52, 57, 62-64, 94,
    108, 109
legio XIV Gemina, 27
legio XX Valeria Victrix, 27-28,
    29, 47-48, 52, 53, 57
legions, character and
    organisation of, 27-28,
    43, 62, 91, 108
Lennox, the, 34, 83
Lincoln, see Lindum

Lindum (modern Lincoln), 22,
    29, 49
Lindum, probable name of
    Roman fort at Strageath,
    see Strageath
lluyd, 42
Logie Durno, 71–72, 77, 116
Lomond Hills, 67
Londinium (modern London),
    23
London, see Londinium
Lossie, river, 37
Lothian, 53

Maiatai, 126
Manau, 35
Mar, Earl of, 82, 104
marching-camps, see
    temporary camps
Marcomanni, 55
Marinus of Tyre, 33, 74
Masada, 114
Massilia (modern Marseilles),
    19, 24
'massive' metalwork, 37
Mauretania, 135
Mearns, the, 36, 115, 116
Menai Strait, 49, 83, 90
Menteith, 36, 121
Mersey, river, 20
Methven Moss, 110
military equipment,
    Caledonian, see
    Calidonii
military equipment, Roman
    auxiliary, 87–88, 98, 101,
    113
*Míniugud Senchasa Fher
    nAlban*, 42
Moesia, 52
Mona, see Anglesey
Moncrieffe Hill (*Monid Croib*),
    75–77, 80
Monid Carno, 75
Mons Graupius
    location of, 68–78, 81, 89,
        95, 98, 128–29
    name of, 72, 74–76, 128
Mons Graupius, battle of
    aftermath of, 109–11, 113–14
    Agricola's need for a
        decisive victory at, 56, 62,
        65, 79–80, 85, 111, 121
    auxiliaries at, 66, 81, 85,
        87–88, 90, 92–95, 97–105,
        107–11, 123
    Caledonian casualties at,

101, 104–05, 106–07, 108,
    111–12, 113
Caledonian host at, 39,
    42–43, 68–69, 76–77, 80,
    83–88, 94, 99, 107–09
Caledonian tactics at, 81–83,
    85, 89–92, 94, 97–108
coin issued in
    commemoration of,
    9, 117
date of, 9
legions at, 71, 81, 88, 93–94
length of, 108–09
Roman casualties at, 102,
    104, 108, 111, 113
Roman river crossing at,
    82–83, 92–93, 98–102, 107
Roman tactics at, 90, 92–95,
    97–108
Romans *expeditus* at, 68, 70,
    76, 80, 85, 93
size of Roman force at, 57,
    72, 81, 85, 92–95, 107
timing of, 69–70, 109, 115,
    117
Moray, 36, 71
Moray Firth, 33, 37
Mounth, the, see Grampian
    mountains

Nero Claudius Caesar ('Nero'),
    13, 19, 25, 26, 27, 119–20
Nerva, see Cocceius Nerva
Newstead (*Trimontium*), 53,
    64, 129
North Channel, 54
North Esk, river, 121
Nouantae, 53

Oathlaw, 68
Ochil Hills, 33
Ordouices, 21, 43, 49, 50, 51, 70
Ostorius Scapula, 21–22, 82–83,
    94, 98–100
Oswig, 124
Otho, see Salvius Otho
Ouse, river, 29

Pannonia, 20, 52
Pass of Grange, 143
Paulinus, see Suetonius
    Paulinus
Pennines, 29, 48, 56
penteulu, 43
Perth, 73, 76, 80, 110
Perthshire, 59, 61, 62, 64, 69,
    122, 125

Petillius Cerialis
    conquest of Brigantes by,
        29–30, 48, 50, 62
    defeat in Boudican uprising
        of, 22, 24
    links with Vespasian of, 22,
        26, 28
    mentorship of Agricola by,
        22, 26, 29–30, 48, 118
    military record of, 28–29
    proconsular legateship in
        Britannia of, 28–30, 49
Petronius Turpilianus, 23
Pictland, 36, 77, 83, 115
Picts, 37–38, 39–40, 42, 75–76,
    77, 86, 87, 90–91, 99
Plautius, see Aulus Plautius
Pliny the Younger, 140
Plutarch, 15
Prasutagos, 21–22
Procilla, see Iulia Procilla
Ptolemy, see Claudius
    Ptolemaeus

Quadi, 55

Raedykes, 71, 73, 77, 115
Ravenna *Cosmography*, 33, 141
Redesdale, 53
Renfrewshire, 35
Rhine, river, 9, 28, 65, 99
Richborough, 116
Rohallion, 34
Rome
    attitudes towards
        Caledonian war in,
        50–52, 54, 56, 63, 64–65,
        69–70, 79–80, 93, 118, 122
    attitudes towards tribal
        peoples in, 38, 44, 56
    acquisition of tribal allies by,
        44–45, 55–57, 79, 121–22
    military thinking of, 48, 58,
        59–61, 66, 70, 81, 109
    reaction to battle of Mons
        Graupius in, 123

St Albans, see Verulamium
Salvius Otho, 26, 27
Salvius Titianus, 25, 26
Schiehallion (*sìdh Chaillean*),
    34, 77
Scone, 77
Selgovae, 53
Sequani, 44
Severan campaigns in Scotland,
    72

Severn, river, 21
Silures, 21, 48-49
Slamanann, 35
Solway Firth, 53, 124
Spey, river, 37, 58, 116
Stirlingshire, 35
Stonehaven Bay, 71
Stormont, 68
Stracathro, 121
Strageath (*Lindum*?), 59-60, 73-74, 76, 77, 81, 83
Strathallan, 35, 67, 73, 77
Strathalmond, 67
Strathearn, 33, 35, 36, 56, 57, 67, 72, 74, 77, 81, 85, 121, 128
Strathmore, 68
Strathtay, 122
Suebi, 55
Suetonius Paulinus, 15, 20-23, 26, 29, 49, 56, 90

Tacitus, see Cornelius Tacitus
Taixali, 36-37, 84
Tay, firth of, 73
Tay, river, 33, 56, 57, 58, 59, 60, 61, 64, 67, 69, 73-74, 76, 77, 80, 110, 115, 121, 122
temporary camps, 58, 71-72, 73, 78, 81
teuluoedd, see household

retinues
Titus Flavius Vespasianus ('Titus')
    British policy of, 51-52
    death of, 33, 51-52, 55
    favour towards Agricola of, 30, 65
    military experience in Britannia of, 51
    participation in Vespasian's principate by, 30-31
Trajan, see Ulpius Traianus
Trimontium, see Newstead
Trinouantes, 22-23, 29, 44, 56, 57
Tungri, 92-93, 99-102, 113
Tweeddale, 53
Tyne, river, 53

Uacomagi, 36, 115, 121-22, 125
Uellocatos, 28
Uenicones, 36, 59-60, 76, 84, 121-22, 125
Uenutios, 28, 30, 88, 123
Uepogeni, 36, 45, 55, 57, 122
UEPOGENOS, 35
'Ueponii, 36
Ulpius Traianus ('Trajan'), 12, 25, 26
Uotadini, 53

Uotodin, 87, 90, 91, 110
Urbgen m. Cinmarch, 42
Usipi, 9, 65, 66

Vercingetorix, 129
Verulamium (modern St Albans), 23
Vespasian, see Flavius Vespasianus
Vettius Bolanus, 28
Victoria, 73-74, 76
Vindolanda, 86
Virgil, 119
Viroconium (modern Wroxeter), 27, 28, 29, 30, 48, 53
Vitellius, see Aulus Vitellius

Wales, 21-22, 27, 37, 39, 43, 48-49, 50, 53, 56, 59, 80, 82, 84, 86, 91, 101, 112
war-bands, see household retinues
Water of May, river, 82, 95
woad, 38
Wroxeter, see Viroconium

Yarrow, 35
York, see Eboracum
Ythan Wells, 72

TEMPUS REVEALING HISTORY

Scotland From Prehistory to the Present
FIONA WATSON
***The Scotsman* Bestseller**
£9.99
0 7524 2591 9

Flodden
NIALL BARR
'Tells the story brilliantly' *The Sunday Post*
£9.99
0 7524 2593 5

Forgotten Scottish Voices from the Great War
DEREK YOUNG
'A vivid picture of what it was like to be a Scottish soldier in the First World War'
Trevor Royle
£17.99
0 7524 3326 1

Scotland's Black Death
The Foul Death of the English
KAREN JILLINGS
'So incongruously enjoyable a read, and so attractively presented by the publishers'
The Scotsman
£14.99
0 7524 2314 2

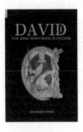

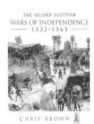
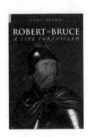

David I The King Who Made Scotland
RICHARD ORAM
'Enthralling... sets just the right tone as the launch-volume of an important new series of royal biographies' ***Magnus Magnusson***
£17.99
0 7524 2825 X

The Second Scottish War of Independence 1332–1363
CHRIS BROWN
'Explodes the myth of the invincible Bruces... lucid and highly readable' ***History Scotland***
£16.99
0 7524 2312 6

The Kings & Queens of Scotland
RICHARD ORAM
'A serious, readable work that sweeps across a vast historical landscape' ***The Daily Mail***
£20
0 7524 2971 X

Robert the Bruce: A Life Chronicled
CHRIS BROWN
'A masterpiece of research'
The Scots Magazine
£30
0 7524 2575 7

If you are interested in purchasing other books published by Tempus, or in case you have difficulty finding any Tempus books in your local bookshop, you can also place orders directly through our website

www.tempus-publishing.com